The Franciscan Heart *of* Thomas Merton

"How could I not be elated? Two of my favorite human beings running side by side through one fine book: Francis and Merton! Just the chapters on Duns Scotus, 'paradise consciousness,' or peace-making and prophecy would make the book well worth the read! What a treasure we have in young and insightful Daniel Horan!"

Richard Rohr, O.F.M.
Center for Action and Contemplation
Albuquerque, New Mexico

"Dan Horan's *The Franciscan Heart of Thomas Merton* is a fascinating study of both Thomas Merton and St. Francis of Assisi: how they and their spiritualities are alike, how they differ, how each one had a profound impact on the times in which he lived and on posterity, and, most interestingly, how deeply Merton was influenced by the life and spirituality of St. Francis. I was immersed again in two of the greatest influences on my own life and marveled at Horan's persuasive and comprehensive argument for why they are important to all of us today."

Murray Bodo, O.F.M.
Author of *Francis: the Journey and the Dream*

"Horan's book is a thorough and eloquent, yet personal and highly engaging, exploration of Merton's multilayered, multifaceted engagement with St. Francis and the Franciscan tradition."

Paul M. Pearson
Director of the Thomas Merton Center

"Combining scholarly insight with pastoral sensitivity, Daniel Horan shows in rich and fascinating detail why Francis of Assisi remained Thomas Merton's favorite saint and how the Franciscan intellectual and spiritual tradition continued to have a profound impact on Merton's thought even as a Cistercian—from Christology to ecology, from peacemaking to dialogue with other religious traditions. This is an accessible and absorbing exploration of a significant influence on Merton's life and thought, particularly welcome in this new 'Age of Francis.'"

Patrick F. O'Connell
Editor of *The Merton Seasonal*

"This new, uncovered information—that separates fact from fiction and profundity from caricature—confirms our suspicions of Francis's influence on Merton."

Monica Weis, S.S.J.
Author of *The Environmental Vision of Thomas Merton*

"This finely textured volume highlights Thomas Merton's intellectual and spiritual debt to the Franciscan tradition. Like the good householder of the Gospel, Daniel Horan draws forth old things and new and, in the process, beautifully reveals how the Poor Man of Assisi and the Trappist monk in Kentucky speak as one voice to our age."

Lawrence S. Cunningham
John A. O'Brien Professor of Theology (Emeritus)
University of Notre Dame

"Daniel Horan brings a fresh and welcome perspective to the life and legacy of the twentieth century's most celebrated monk. Schooled in the riches of the Franciscan tradition, the author shows how Merton the Trappist monk continued to be shaped by the Franciscan sources he had come to love in his young adulthood. In a voice at once deeply informed and warmly personal, Horan advances a most intriguing thesis: By not becoming a Franciscan friar, Merton became even more Franciscan in his spiritual orientations and outlook and remained so throughout his life."

Michael Downey
Editor of *The New Dictionary of Catholic Spirituality*

"In true Franciscan voice Daniel Horan offers us a glimpse of the rich and many ways Father Francis was the first and lasting teacher of his Cistercian son."

Kathleen Deignan, C.N.D.
Author of *Thomas Merton: A Books of Hours*

The Franciscan Heart of Thomas Merton

A *New Look* at the

Spiritual Inspiration

of His Life,

Thought,

and Writing

Daniel P. Horan, O.F.M.

ave maria press AMP notre dame, indiana

"The Canticle of the Creatures" is reprinted from *Francis of Assisi: Early Documents,* Volume 1, edited by Regis J. Armstrong, O.F.M. Cap., J. A. Wayne Hellmann, O.F.M. Conv., and William J. Short, O.F.M. Copyright ©1999 by Franciscan Institute of St. Bonaventure University, St. Bonaventure, NY. Used by permission of New City Press.

The poem "Duns Scotus" by Thomas Merton is reprinted from *The Collected Poems of Thomas Merton,* copyright ©1948 by New Directions Publishing Corp. Used by permission of New Directions Publishing Corp.

Scripture quotations are from the *New Revised Standard Version of the Bible,* copyright © 1993 and 1989 by the Division of Christian Education of the National Council of Churches of Christ in the USA. Used by permission. All rights reserved.

Founded in 1865, Ave Maria Press is a ministry of the United States Province of Holy Cross.

www.avemariapress.com

Paperback: ISBN-13 978-1-59471-422-1

E-book: ISBN-13 978-1-59471-423-8

Cover photograph of Thomas Merton by John Lyons. Used with permission of the Merton Legacy Trust and the Thomas Merton Center at Bellarmine University.

Cover and text design by Katherine Robinson.

Printed and bound in the United States of America.

Library of Congress Cataloging-in-Publication Data

Horan, Daniel P.

The Franciscan heart of Thomas Merton : a new look at the spiritual inspiration of his life, thought, and writing / Daniel P. Horan, O.F.M.

pages cm

Includes bibliographical references and index.

ISBN 978-1-59471-422-1

1. Merton, Thomas, 1915-1968. 2. Franciscans--Influence. I. Title.

BX4705.M542H67 2014

271'.12502--dc23

2014018913

To my parents,

Kevin and Ann Marie Horan

Long before

Thomas Merton

and

Francis of Assisi,

they were my first

teachers of faith.

Contents

ACKNOWLEDGMENTS

To write a book about either Francis of Assisi or Thomas Merton is a daunting task, for each figure has and remains incredibly influential and popular within contemporary Christian circles and so much has already been said about them. What's more, both of these icons of spiritual reflection, peacemaking, and interreligious dialogue find followers outside the boundaries of the Christian community and therefore have spoken and continue to speak to a vastly eclectic audience. To write a book about *both* Francis and Merton might be viewed, therefore, as foolhardy. Nevertheless, I felt that an important part of Merton's story remained untold, and this book is my attempt to tell that story.

Not only was Merton at one time interested in Francis of Assisi, the Franciscan Order, and the Franciscan intellectual tradition, but also these things continued to influence his life, thought, and writing until his death. To show just how and to what extent this is true from biographical, theological, spiritual, and socially oriented viewpoints is the aim of this book. And it couldn't have been written without the support, enthusiasm, and challenge of many friends and colleagues, as well as the opportunity to share some of my research that ultimately contributed to this book in the form of academic presentations, lectures, and published articles.

I am grateful for the opportunity to have delivered several lectures on subjects related to this book at the Washington, DC, New York City, and Chicago chapters of the Thomas Merton Society over the years, as well as to have presented academic papers at a number of the biennial conferences of the International Thomas Merton Society and the Thomas Merton Society of Great Britain and Ireland. A 2011 ITMS William Shannon Fellowship also permitted me to work on some research at

the Thomas Merton Center at Bellarmine University. I had
the honor of being invited to deliver the 2013 Annual Igna-
tius Brady Memorial Lecture at St. Bonaventure University,
the theme of which was related to my research for this book.
Additionally, portions of chapters 5 and 6 were first presented
at a religious-studies department faculty colloquium at Siena
College in the spring of 2011 during my time teaching there.
This material later appeared in another form as "Thomas Merton the 'Dunce': Identity, Incarnation, and the Not-So-Subtle
Influence of John Duns Scotus" (*Cistercian Studies Quarterly* 47
[2012]). Likewise, an early version of the material in chapter
10 first appeared in my article "'Those Going among the Saracens and Other Nonbelievers': Thomas Merton and Franciscan
Interreligious Dialogue" (*Merton Annual* 21 [2008]).

I wish to express my sincere gratitude to a number of individuals with whom I have discussed many of these themes
and shared drafts of this project, and without whom I could
not have completed such a book. In the Merton world, I am
thankful to Paul Pearson, Mark Meade, Anne McCormick,
Peggy Fox, Mary Somerville, Patrick O'Connell, Chris Pramuk,
Christine Bochen, Bill Apel, Michael Brennan, Raymond Raf-
ferty, Brenda Fitch Fairaday, David Belcastro, Gray Matthews,
Kathleen Deignan, and so many others. Special thanks go to
Monica Weis, S.S.J., who graciously read and commented on
an early version of chapter 7; Patrick O'Connell, whose keen
editorial eye caught some easily overlooked discrepancies in
the manuscript; and Paul Pearson, who offered some insightful feedback about several passages. At St. Bonaventure University, Paul Spaeth, the director of the Friedsam Memorial
Library (and successor to Father Irenaeus Herscher!); Sister
Margaret Carney, O.S.F., the university president; and Julianne
Wallace, a campus minister and dear friend, have all supported
me and this project in various and invaluable ways. Thanks
goes to David Golemboski, for his continued support, conversation, and friendship, which itself began when we first

met at a Merton conference in England many years ago. This litany of thanks wouldn't be complete without an expression of gratitude to Jessica Coblentz, one of my closest friends and colleagues, who was gracious enough to read nearly all of this book in its earliest stages and offer insightful comments and questions.

I owe special thanks to Patrick McGowan. In addition to being a longtime supporter of my work and writing, Patrick was the editor who saw this project through from the very beginning until its completion. He went above and beyond the call of duty when, after leaving Ave Maria Press after many years to work for another publisher, he continued working on this project in his spare time with the blessing of the publishers—this on top of moving to a new city and while anticipating the birth of his first child. Patrick is an editorial hero! Thanks also to so many others at Ave Maria Press for their support and skillful work, especially Robert Hamma and Amanda Skofstad.

Finally, this book is dedicated to my parents, Kevin and Ann Marie Horan. I am grateful for their love and support, for their many sacrifices, and for their example of the importance of faith in everybody's lives that made my brothers and me who we are today.

On "Merton's Heart"

Thomas Merton's mind and soul might have been monastic by virtue of his embrace of Cistercian life and prayer, but his heart was undoubtedly Franciscan. It is not at first apparent, and it has long been overlooked, but among the myriad influences that combine to shape and inform the life, thought, and writing of Thomas Merton stands the Franciscan intellectual and spiritual tradition.

It is widely known that Merton first sought to enter the Order of Friars Minor (the Franciscan friars) after discerning a vocation to religious life. Many also know that he was at first accepted into the Franciscan novitiate and shortly thereafter encouraged to withdraw his application under rather mysterious circumstances having to do with his earlier withholding of personal information during the interview process. What is not so widely recognized—in popular perceptions and scholarly studies alike—is the fact that the initial enthusiasm Merton held for St. Francis of Assisi and the way of life the medieval saint inaugurated stayed with him long after his hopes of becoming a friar were dashed.

The theologian Michael Downey—one of the few scholars who has previously noted the Franciscan influence in Merton's thought—has said that Merton's mentor and friend at Columbia University, Dan Walsh, had recognized early on in Merton a "Franciscan spirit," something of an intuition that naturally emanated from the young convert's personality and outlook.[1] It was at Walsh's recommendation that Merton selected the Franciscans from among the manifold options available to one considering religious life in the late 1930s. But it is usually at this point, Merton's "first-round try" at religious life and subsequent disappointment at being denied access to the Franciscan community, that the well-known story of Merton's Franciscan experience ends.

It is true to say that Merton never became a Franciscan, if by "Franciscan" one means "Franciscan friar" or a member of the Order of Friars Minor. However, it is untrue to say that Merton never became a Franciscan if we understand, in the proper way, "Franciscan" to include anyone professed in one of the *three* Franciscan orders that exist. For although the saga is often told about Merton's unrealized dreams of wearing the brown habit of the friars, what is seldom told is the continuation of Merton's Franciscan story, which includes the future monk's formal entrance into the Third Order of St. Francis— popularly known as the "secular Franciscans"—during his time teaching at St. Bonaventure College (now University).[2] But this is just the beginning of the commonly overlooked thread of influence in the life, thought, and writing of Merton. Beyond the devotional and spiritual life that is usually shaped by one's commitment to the Franciscan community of the Third Order, Merton engaged in deep and passionate study of the Franciscan intellectual tradition during the same time.

Beginning under the tutelage of Walsh, Merton's exposure to and love of the Franciscan intellectual tradition led him to explore the works of St. Bonaventure and Blessed John Duns Scotus. While teaching English and literature at St. Bonaventure College, Merton was privileged to study a whole array of the foundational works of the Franciscan intellectual tradition. His journals, notes, and correspondence from that time on campus reveal a telling enthusiasm for this study. The time during which Merton studied these texts and figures was additionally fortuitous because he "sat at the feet" of one of the twentieth century's greatest Franciscan scholars. Father Philotheus Boehner, O.F.M., under whose guidance Merton read Bonaventure, Scotus, and William of Ockham, was on campus to help found the now world-famous Franciscan Institute, which today remains the preeminent center for studying the Franciscan tradition in the English-speaking world. Scholars come from all parts of the world to research, teach, and study at the institute. That Merton studied with Boehner is no small deal or incidental fact. Nearly fifteen years after he first studied the sources with St. Boehner at St. Bonaventure, Merton the monk and author recalled his impressions of Boehner and shared the impact his relationship with the friar had on him in a letter written to the then president of St. Bonaventure University, Father Thomas Plassmann, O.F.M.

> Fr. Philotheus was, I think, one of those for whom no death is "sudden." His unassuming simplicity covered what was a real and deep holiness, I am sure. Like a true Franciscan, he was one who dared to be perfectly himself with our Lord. He helped me to make a crucial decision in my life, and I shall certainly not fail him, if he needs my prayers. I hope that in the meanwhile he will continue to help me now that he is close to God and in a position to gain many graces for us on earth who knew him.
>
> The loss of "Philo" will make itself felt at St. Bonaventure and in scholarly circles everywhere. The Franciscan Institute rested on him as on a cornerstone. But no man is irreplaceable. I hope he will find a successor filled with his own ardent love for St. Bonaventure and Duns Scotus—a love which I am thankful he communicated to me. I cannot say that he made me love Ockham because he never made me understand him.
>
> One thing none of us will forget about "Philo" was his truly Franciscan ardor and insight into the creatures of God. He was a true scientist, for whom natural beings

were only a step on the ladder by which a soul rises to the contemplation of God. And he certainly had an eye for the smallest of God's creatures.[3]

These remarks to Plassmann on the occasion of Boehner's death reveal a profound sense of heartfelt appreciation for the pastoral presence, intellectual formation, and personal attention Merton received from the deceased friar.

As Merton grappled with some of scholasticism's most challenging theological and philosophical treatises, he would have gained a well-grounded knowledge of and appreciation for the Franciscan intellectual tradition. Merton would later write that although he was exposed to it (as all religious students would have been in the early twentieth century), Thomism—the neoscholastic reading of Thomas Aquinas's work that was the standard theological source and model of method at the time—really didn't appeal to him. Unlike so many of his religious peers who would likewise have been steeped in the ways of Thomistic theology, Merton also benefitted from the best possible education in the Franciscan intellectual tradition of his time, thanks to the fact that he happened to study this material at the right time, at the right place, and with the right person. In fact, given the pre–Vatican II state of seminary education in the 1930s and 1940s, which was almost exclusively reliant on the Thomistic theological manuals of the time, had Merton actually entered the Order of Friars Minor when he wanted, he would likely have had *far less* exposure to the cutting-edge Franciscan intellectual scholarship than what he had received. One could say that his not becoming a Franciscan *friar* actually provided the very condition for Merton to ultimately become *more* Franciscan in his outlook! Such a case lends much credence to the saying that "the Spirit works in mysterious ways." It certainly did in Merton's life.

The fervor with which Merton continued to show his interest about the Franciscan tradition is tremendous, even if from time to time he was expressive about the pain he still felt about the impossibility of becoming a friar. Merton is often critical of the friars collectively in his correspondence and journals during his years teaching at St. Bonaventure but never of the tradition or of individual friars. It is commonplace for Merton to mention Francis of Assisi in his writing, to draw on the saint and his way of life as a model and goal for his own struggle to follow Christ. It is fair to say that Merton took his profession as a secular Franciscan very seriously and understood himself— spiritually at least—in terms of Franciscan life long after he made his commitment to the Third Order.

One might think that the decision to give monastic life a try would squelch Merton's earlier enthusiasm. One might logically assume that his study of the monastic theological and historical tradition as a Trappist novice and beyond would supersede his once obsessive embrace of all things "Franciscan." One might certainly anticipate a decline in the mention of Francis, Bonaventure, Scotus, and other Franciscan icons as time went on in the religious formation of this young monk. But this did not happen.

Even after his entrance into and formal profession of monastic life, Merton's life, thought, and writings continued to be shaped and informed by the Franciscan sources he had come to love. He continued to read the writings of the great Franciscan intellectuals. He continued to pray to and admire Francis of Assisi. He continued to acknowledge the Franciscan feasts that were not present on the Trappist liturgical calendar. He continued to write about the Franciscan theological and spiritual tradition in both overt and more implicit ways. He never stopped *being* a Franciscan, or at the very least, he never stopped being a *Franciscan-hearted person*. This is most notably captured in a 1966 letter Merton wrote to the young Buffalo, New York, journalist Anthony Bannon: "[I] will always feel that I am still in some secret way a son of St. Francis. There is no saint in the Church whom I admire more than St. Francis."[4]

This book aims to shed light on part of the story of Thomas Merton that has been all but entirely overlooked. I will show how Merton's heart became and remained Franciscan from his earliest days at Columbia University, to his entering the Roman Catholic Church, until his dying day on December 10, 1958, in Bangkok, Thailand. There are historical considerations to explore, such as the significance of studying the tradition with Boehner in 1940. There are theological and spiritual considerations to explore as well, such as how the Franciscan theological outlook continually appears in both Merton's published and his private work. This is no small task. The influence runs very deep, and to give it the attention it deserves requires a great deal of effort, the product of which is, I hope, this book.

Source and Location of Merton's Heart

Before I go on to explain the structure and give an overview of the content of this book, I want to add one more note about "Merton's heart." The title of this book is descriptive in that it conveys the deep-seated character of Merton's Franciscan foundations and outlook, but it is also borrowed from the name of an actual place. Overlooking the beautiful and remote campus of my alma mater, St. Bonaventure University in southwestern New York State, stands a clearing on a hillside within the Allegheny Mountains. While the hillside is otherwise covered in lush trees of the deciduous forest of the area, there is a legendary heart-shaped meadow that has affectionately become known as "Merton's Heart" over the years. The meadow was cleared for oil drilling in the early 1920s but had no longer been used for that purpose by the late 1930s when Merton arrived on campus. He was known to take walks along the hills surrounding campus, and it was from this connection that the site earned its name, long after Merton left St. Bonaventure.

A campus landmark pointed out to all visitors on tour even to this day, "Merton's Heart" is just one way the late

Trappist's memory continues to be linked to the Franciscan intellectual world. It is my hope that this book will also serve as a point of reference for those interested in learning more about Merton and what shaped his life, thought, and writing as much as the meadow named "Merton's Heart" continues to serve as a point of reference for the continued association of Merton with St. Bonaventure.

This book is not simply an academic study of the sources for a creative thinker's work. It is, I hope, a way for women and men of all backgrounds to glimpse into the life, mind, and, yes, the *heart* of a man who has inspired so many people over the decades. The Franciscan tradition has remained one of the most influential sources of spiritual guidance of the last eight hundred years, and its effect on Merton and the people he encountered was considerable.

Both Merton and the broader Franciscan tradition have shaped my own intellectual and spiritual outlook as well. I have been especially interested in the intersection of these two worlds: that of the most popular spiritual writer of the twentieth century and that of the medieval Italian saint and the movement he inspired. In taking a look at the particularly Franciscan dimensions of Merton's life, thought, and work, I hope that readers might in turn be inspired, informed, and challenged to see God, the world, and ourselves anew. To help contextualize this intersection between Francis and Merton, and to illustrate a few of the ways that this connection continues to be relevant for us today, this book takes a deliberately informal stride. Rather than offer a straightforward, and likely more boring, historical presentation of the themes and the development of Merton's thought as it was shaped by the Franciscan tradition, I will weave together stories and experiences from my own spiritual and intellectual journey as these two great traditions—the Franciscan movement and the life, thought, and writings of Thomas Merton—have touched my own Franciscan heart.

There is doubtless a deep sense in which people today are searching for the transcendent and hunger for a robust spirituality. In an age marked by constant contact with, and subsequent distraction by, information and communication technologies, the focus of our time is on the immediate and fleeting. Little popular attention is given to the eternal or deep questions of our existence. In their own times and in their own ways, Francis and Merton both struggled to discover the God who lovingly brought each into existence and continued to personally relate to all parts of creation. Our time is different from theirs, and each generation has its own challenges to faith and human flourishing. But the Christian insight of these two spiritual giants offers us a beacon of light and safety in what can often seem to be chaotic darkness. To be clear, it is not that our world is any more precarious or any less connected to God than in either Merton's or Francis's times. Rather, the distractions that vie for our attention, energy, and commitment can at times veil the truth of God's love and immanence in the world.

Merton, certainly more than Francis, was able to experience something akin to our contemporary social and spiritual landscape. His experience of the 1960s in the last decade of his life helped broaden and even redirect his attention from the contemplative and spiritual focus of his monastic vocation to the need the world continually has to hear both the good news and the challenge of Christianity. As a result, Merton began to consider how being a monk might speak to the world. From his place in the monastery he was, as my friend David Golemboski once put it, able to "pitch in" to the project of responding to the signs of the times by "dropping out" of the mainstream culture.[5] He was able to witness the reality of his day from the margins of society and contrast what he witnessed with what he knew to be God's plan for humanity and the rest of creation. He was able to *follow his heart*, inspired by the prophetic witness of Francis of Assisi and the broader Christian tradition to speak truth to power, cry out against injustice, and remind women and men to recall their divine calling as reflections of God's image and likeness.

What Francis was for Merton, Merton can become for us.

Both continually challenge me to be a better Christian, a better human person. I can say that there have been no greater spiritual influences in my life—apart, of course, from scripture and God in Jesus Christ. Merton doesn't simply serve as a conduit of latent Franciscan spirituality and theology but instead models for me a particular way to approach, appropriate, and live out the saint from Assisi's wisdom and guidance. Merton was also deeply informed and shaped by other Christian and non-Christian spiritual, intellectual, and cultural giants throughout his life. Yet his ability to form a mosaic of Christian inspiration, what some contemporary sociologists call a spiritual *bricolage*,[6] can serve as an example for us today. He was extraordinarily attentive and generous in his reading and correspondence with all sorts of people. Over time, Merton realized that the Holy Spirit speaks to the hearts of women and men in manifold ways, and not simply by means of stereotypically "Christian" forms. His openness to discerning the Spirit in all things anticipated the Second Vatican Council's profound declaration that there is in other religions and in other aspects of the modern world truth that all Christians could discover.

> Other religions found everywhere try to counter the restlessness of the human heart, each in its own manner, by proposing "ways," comprising teachings, rules of life, and sacred rites. The Catholic Church rejects nothing that is true and holy in these religions. She regards with sincere reverence those ways of conduct and life, those precepts and teachings which, though differing in many aspects from the ones she holds and sets forth, nonetheless often reflect a ray of that Truth which enlightens all [women and men].[7]

As we will see, especially in chapter 9, part of what Merton gleaned from the lived example of Francis of Assisi were tools and ways of approaching the world that allowed him to be more open, more generous, and more fully human in relationship with others. Merton's ecumenical and interfaith experiences were ahead of his time, yet anticipatory in the way they presciently presaged our universal Christian call toward fuller communion with all women and men.

In our time, Merton's model of Christian living has provided a helpful clue in my own understanding of what it means to follow the holy Gospel of Jesus Christ by following in the footprints of Francis of Assisi. Imperfect as my ongoing and lifelong attempt to do this is, I am encouraged by Merton's own struggles, successes, and journey. May you likewise find inspiration, challenge, and guidance in our deeper exploration of this part of Merton's life, thought, and writings.

Mapping the Way to Merton's Heart

This book is organized into four major parts. The first part offers a brief overview of the lives and contexts of Francis of Assisi and Thomas Merton in chapters 1 and 2 respectively. For those who are already fairly familiar with either or both of these figures, it might be more interesting to move directly to part two.

Part two presents a new look at and closer examination of the events in Merton's early life around the time of his conversion to Catholicism and during his initial discernment of a vocation to religious life and the priesthood. This period in Merton's life has been largely misunderstood or reduced to caricature. Few are familiar with the many factors that come together to help illuminate our understanding for what really took place from the time Merton approached the Franciscan friars with a desire to enter the community until he finally entered religious life at the Trappist Abbey of Gethsemani nearly two years later. Chapter 3 offers the most comprehensive examination of what happened in New York City and at St. Bonaventure University that led to his eventual withdrawal from Franciscan life. Chapter 4 introduces readers to three of the most significant figures and mentors in Merton's life during this time, each of whom was a Franciscan friar working at St. Bonaventure and all of whom helped guide Merton to what would become the realization of his true monastic vocation. Additionally, during this time, Merton studied and engaged the Franciscan theological, philosophical, and spiritual traditions in a way that indelibly shaped his life, thought, and writing.

Part three is a section dedicated to three of the areas of faith and spirituality in which Merton was most influenced by the Franciscan tradition. In chapter 5, we look anew at what is likely Merton's most famous insight, namely, the "true self." While this concept has inspired and positively challenged women and men for years ever since the publication of *Seeds of Contemplation*, few people are familiar with its explicitly Franciscan roots. Originally, Merton planned this book to be about the thought of the medieval Franciscan John Duns Scotus. While that never panned out in the way initially slated, the influence of Scotus remains the most central aspect of this text. In chapter 6, we look at how Merton's views on the Incarnation were shaped by the Franciscan tradition. Again, the mark of Scotus is found along with the Christocentric worldview of Bonaventure. In chapter 7, the most typically "Franciscan theme" of creation comes to the fore. Merton was especially drawn to the natural world and reflected on creation in ways that mirror several aspects of the Franciscan tradition, particularly its emphasis on humanity's kinship with the rest of the created order and God's presence in and through creation.

Part four focuses on the ways in which the Franciscan tradition helped shape Merton's views of the world. In chapter 8, we look at the theme of prophecy and how St. Francis and Bonaventure both informed Merton's self-understanding of the Christian vocation to be a prophet and how this was reflected in Merton's own life. In chapter 9, we see how St. Francis served as the paradigmatic model of interreligious dialogue for Merton. Merton's own approach to other faith traditions, something for which he is remembered for today, mirrored the example St. Francis and the tradition that bears his name. In chapter 10, we explore how the Franciscan tradition helped inform Merton's sense of Christian peacemaking and nonviolence. Rather than a vocation or calling for a select few, both St. Francis and Merton recognized this as a central tenet of Christian living for all people.

After a short conclusion, this book closes with an appendix containing a lengthy prayer written by Merton in his journal from 1941.

PART I

Two Kindred Hearts

CHAPTER 1

The Medieval Mendicant: Francis of Assisi

Everybody knows something about Francis of Assisi, or at least everybody *thinks* they know something about him. The popular stories of this medieval saint are fascinating and, at times, unbelievable. In some instances what is told of the *poverello* (little poor man) from Assisi, as he's sometimes called, borders on the absurd.

"He loved animals," people like to say when first asked what they know about Francis. Or, "He loved poverty," which is something I hear a lot from members of other religious communities that understand what makes the Franciscans "different" from their respective religious orders has something to do with this attitude in the world. And both of these responses and the intuitions about who Francis was and what he was about are true—sort of.

Francis of Assisi, we could say, did love animals but not in the same way that we might think of the love for a pet or the way children love a petting zoo. Slowly and over time, he came to have an incredibly capacious understanding of the inherent dignity and value of all of creation. His increasingly mystical consciousness of our interrelatedness with creation and the ethical implications contained therein reached its zenith with Francis's most famous writing: "The Canticle of the Creatures."[1] But, like his life more broadly, the canticle is often misunderstood or turned into an easily sung caricature. The richness and profundity of this poetic prayer is not generally appreciated for its complexity but seen in a romantic light and with rose-colored glasses. As we'll see later in this book, the way that Francis's view of creation is really presented has tremendous implications. His way of viewing the world has, in part, inspired millions of women and men to shift their understanding of what it means to be a part of and care for the rest of the created order. It certainly influenced Thomas Merton.

As for the issue of poverty, it is true that Francis desired that he and his brothers should live *sine proprio* (without anything of one's own). But he didn't value poverty for its own sake, nor did he hold what most people think of when they hear poverty as a good. Like many modern models of holiness, such as Dorothy Day and Catherine de Heuck Doherty, Francis saw the latent injustices that are perpetuated by economic systems. He detested abject poverty and was moved to action by the dehumanizing effects that this type of poverty and social marginalization has on the poor and voiceless of society. It was, in large part, this ongoing experience and awareness that allowed him to understand better what Jesus' life of itinerancy and evangelical poverty meant for all Christians. Francis would strive to follow in the footprints of Jesus Christ, who said, "Foxes have holes, and birds of the air have nests; but the Son of Man has nowhere to lay his head" (Lk 9:58). Yes, Francis loved poverty but in a way very different than we might initially think and in such a manner that a statement so simple could never adequately portray.

Love of animals and poverty are just two examples of the myriad aspects of Francis's life that need to be examined more closely. To take such simplified characteristics as the whole picture is to reduce the uniqueness, originality, and inspirational life that has inspired and continues to inspire millions of women and men, Christians and non-Christians, and believers and unbelievers for centuries. To stop at the level of love of animals or poverty, or any other similar descriptor, is to mistake the life of someone who indelibly inspired and shaped the life, thought, and writing of Thomas Merton for a plaster man in a garden birdbath. Such a pallid depiction of Francis lacks the color and life of one of *Time* magazine's ten most important personalities of the last millennium.[2]

In this chapter we'll take an all-too-short look at the life of Francis of Assisi. For those for whom knowledge of Francis's life is old hat, feel free to skip ahead. But for many, the general contours of the *poverello*'s life have been passed over and replaced by caricature and fiction. To understand *what* about this man and the tradition that bears his name centuries later was so influential for Thomas Merton, we need to have some basic understanding of *who* he was.

Neither a Sinner nor a Saint

Toward the end of his life, Francis is remembered to have told the brothers that were caring for him in his illness, "The Lord has shown me what was mine to do, may He show you what is yours to do." The process of coming to discern what God desired for Francis's life, what we might in other terms call his "vocation," begins in a way similar to every other person's journey in life. In so many ways, Francis of Assisi was just like you and me. He entered this world neither a sinner nor a saint but a person created in the image and likeness (*imago Dei*) of a loving God. Like all of us, he sinned and broke relationships, thought of himself at times before thinking of others, and almost surely made decisions throughout his life that he would later regret. Yet, also like all of us, there was something inherently good in Francis that was expressed in his love for family and friends, his chivalrous desire to make his hometown proud, and the generally good-natured reputation he held among his peers. Just as Francis was neither a sinner nor a saint, he was at the same time *both* a sinner and a saint. And for this reason he has much to teach us, for his story can also reflect much of our own experiences of life and faith back to us.

We are the beneficiaries of living during a time in which historical scholarship about the life and times of Francis of Assisi are presented in unprecedentedly clear and accurate ways. Two of the most acclaimed recent studies of Francis's life are Augustine Thompson's *Francis of Assisi: A New Biography* and André Vauchez's *Francis of Assisi: The Life and Afterlife of a Medieval Saint.*[3] These historians are the latest and most respected presenters of a life that reflects neither the depraved sinner-turned-saint nor the romantic figure in the birdbath. Their depictions of Francis help reveal a complex man whose story is as nuanced and complicated as any other.

Vauchez, for example, situates Francis closely to his hometown of Assisi, noting that Francesco di Bernardone (Francis's full given name), unlike many other well-known saints (Thomas *Aquinas* or Bernard of *Clairvaux*, for example), was born (likely at the end of 1181 or early 1182), raised, and ultimately died (1226) in the city associated with his name. He made trips throughout his life, some major expeditions and pilgrimages, such as his encounter with the sultan in Egypt in 1219, but the majority of Francis's short life was centered in or near Assisi, Italy. Most scholars tend to agree that although Francis's family did not come from the noble classes of his day, the shifting mercantile economy had allowed his father, Pietro di Bernardone, to become very wealthy. In addition to a cloth-selling business, procurement for which led to Pietro's frequent trips out of town and abroad, including on the day when Francis was born, he also had quite significant real-estate holdings.[4] Even though a wealthy merchant class was emerging in late twelfth-century Umbria, to which the di Bernardone family belonged, there was in Francis's time still a strong sense of feudalism, and the privileges of nobility were always present. As a young man and probably at the encouragement of his father, Francis aspired to join these ranks as a knight or perhaps through marriage to eventually secure the social status that only noble rank provided.

This is an important detail to keep in mind about the young Francis, for it reflects the tendency he had to be influenced and shaped by the external pressures and expectations of his day. These pressures were constantly present in the views of his parents, his society, and the still-present feudal culture of the age. A contemporary, if somewhat anachronistic, parallel might be the pressure many college students feel today to go into fields of business, law, medicine, or some other professional areas of employment. On the one hand, many young adults will assert that such a course of study and work is the product of their own desire and sincere intent. This is no doubt true, but on the other hand, there are also a lot of other pressures—both latent and explicit—that contribute to pursuing such paths in life. What Mom and Dad want (especially if they are footing the college bills!), as well as culture (does the culture you were raised in value one type of work over another?), and what society teaches about power, wealth, class, and so on, all come together in the exploration each person makes to carve out a life at a formative time in his or her life. Such was the case with Francis. The familial pressures, societal expectations, and personal aspirations in Francis's life eventually led to his becoming the knight he had desired to be. However, prior to Francis's military career, brief as it turned out to be, the young man would have been already working in his father's business for some time. Thompson explains:

> About the year 1195, as he was approaching the age of fourteen or so, Francis began to work as an apprentice in his father's business. He learned to sell cloth, keep financial records, and control inventory. It is likely that he even

traveled to France with his father to make purchases of
cloth. Gifted with a keen mind and an engaging and expansive personality, he quickly proved himself an able sales-
man. He made contacts and friends easily.[5]

His people skills, generosity, and sharp mind made him a
decent enough businessman. That would likely have been his
fate if it had not been for an intercity battle that called Francis
out of his quotidian work in textiles and into a chance to finally
live out his military aspirations and dreams of knighthood.

Franciscan historian Dominic Monti explains that during
Francis's young-adult years, Assisi and the surrounding areas
were shifting in political and cultural ways that bore a tumultuous hue. Monti describes the scene in the last decade of the
twelfth century as Francis was coming of age:

> Emperor Henry VI died suddenly in 1197, and with no
> clear successor in sight, the political situation in central
> Italy was thrown into chaos. The nascent communes seized
> the power vacuum to further their own advantage; the
> newly elected Pope Innocent III (1198–1216), seeking to
> strengthen his own hand in the region, supported these
> local attempts at greater autonomy. In Assisi, the common-
> ers, scenting a whiff of freedom, revolted against the hated
> imperial presence. Forming a militia—of which Francis
> was undoubtedly a part—in 1198 they stormed the cita-
> del that dominated the town, razing it to the ground. In
> its place, the citizens again organized a communal gov-
> ernment, using the stones from the dismantled Rocca to
> construct a wall enclosing the city. This action unleashed
> pent-up class tensions within Assisi: Since the aristocratic
> families, based in their rural castles, still pledged loyalty to
> the imperial cause, the commoners vented their anger by
> ransacking the townhouses of the nobility. Many of the dis-
> placed knights took refuge in Assisi's bitter rival, Perugia,
> across the valley. Smaller towns in the area took sides in
> the emerging conflict, as each of the two cities made raids
> into the territory of the other.[6]

As tensions between his hometown, sponsored by the commoners and the newly rising merchant class, and Perugia, the new refuge of the aristocratic Assisians, increased, Francis found himself among the ranks of Assisi's militia of young men.

Given Francis's relative wealth and ability to acquire a horse and armor, he was made a knight in the Assisi militia and went out to battle with his fellow impromptu soldiers. What resulted was a veritable disaster for the Assisi fighters. What they had anticipated would be a successful battle in Assisi's favor turned out to be a terrifically bloody loss. Thompson explains what happened next:

> Francis and his companions in arms were imprisoned at Perugia for a year or more. As was fitting for one outfitted with a horse, and so obviously from a rich background, Francis ended up imprisoned not with the ordinary soldiers, but with the aristocratic knights. Early biographers say that Francis did his best to keep spirit[s] up, reconciling disputes among the prisoners and even befriending a bitter knight whom the other prisoners had been avoiding. Whether this flattering picture is historical is hard to say. But prison was hard on Francis, physically and mentally. By the time of his release, probably in late 1203, his health was severely damaged. The once extroverted and cheerful young man had turned in on himself. Perhaps he was ransomed home by his family precisely because of his declining health.[7]

It is Francis's return home, weak and defeated, that generally marks the beginning of the young man's change in life. Like many who experience and survive the traumas of war, Francis returned to his parent's home in Assisi a different man. In his book *The Saint and the Sultan: The Crusades, Islam, and Francis of Assisi's Mission of Peace*, Paul Moses spends a great deal of time reporting on what the sources tell us about how the impact of battle, becoming a prisoner of war, and the illnesses Francis endured might have contributed to his lifelong renunciation of violence and his continual efforts to promote the peacemaking to which he was committed.[8] Moses makes the insightful, if bold, claim that "if we are going to understand Francis's transition from warrior to peacemaker, we must consider the uncomfortable notion that Francis killed men on the battlefield. No one can say for sure if Francis slew the enemy, but it is likely he did. His eventual decision to begin a life of penance hints that he believed he had sinned seriously on the battlefield."[9] Drawing on the professional expertise of contemporary military psychologists, Moses makes the suggestion that Francis might have returned home suffering from something akin to what we would today call posttraumatic stress disorder (PTSD). Regardless of what happened on the battlefield and in prison, Francis was never the same again. More introspective, more concerned about serious questions of meaning in his life, the happy-go-lucky youth known to generously spend his time and wealth on others had been left on the battlefield.

The Gospel Discernment Begins

Francis shifted from the ordinary life of a medieval Assisi young adult working in his father's business and aspiring to be a successful knight to a life centered on the Gospel lived in a very particular way, but this process did not happen overnight. Francis made this observation himself as he prepared for death. He doesn't talk about his experiences on the battlefield against Perugia, nor does he explicitly identify the time spent ill in prison, but instead he begins his reflection shortly after his return home from that experience. Francis attributes one of the most significant moments of his "conversion" to the encounter he had with lepers outside the walls of Assisi. Lepers in Francis's day were absolutely marginalized. Forced out of the ordinary boundaries of society, both literally and figuratively, and forbidden by civil and ecclesiastical ordinance to have any contact with inhabitants of the city, these people were banished to a place of nothingness where they could be practically ignored. Today we might find a contemporary analogy in the homeless men and women that populate the shadows of major cities in the United States. Effectively banished in order to be "out of sight, out of mind," the lepers of Francis's day were viewed as unclean, repulsive, and ultimately unhuman. Like his contemporaries, Francis would not generally have to encounter, let alone *interact with*, lepers except on the rarest of occasions, or unless he intentionally chose to do so. By his own admittance, however, Francis was disgusted by the presence and even the thought of lepers. Thomas of Celano, his first biographer, wrote, "For [Francis] used to say that the sight of lepers was so bitter to him that in the days of his vanity when he saw their houses even two miles away, he would cover his nose with his hands."[10] Francis himself wrote as much in his final testament:

> The Lord gave me, Brother Francis, thus to begin doing penance in this way: for when I was in sin, it seemed too bitter for me to see lepers. And the Lord Himself led me among them and I showed mercy to them. And when I left them, what had seemed bitter to me was turned into sweetness of soul and body. And afterwards I delayed a little and left the world.[11]

That Francis believed God had given him the grace to encounter, embrace, and start to love women and men who suffered from leprosy was a significant and symbolic turning point for the young man.

However, unlike the way his "conversion" is often depicted, this embrace of the leper did not result in a sort of "St. Paul on the road to Damascus" moment of immediate change. Francis makes it clear that he "delayed a little" before he left the only world he had previously known to begin living in the world in a new way.

I believe that this experience of Francis, frequently discarded in popular portrayals of the would-be saint's life, is instrumental for helping us understand what lifelong Christian conversion looks like. It can help us see how, even from the beginning, Francis's life serves as a model for us, just as it did for Thomas Merton in so many ways. Francis's transformation was, in fact, unique as ultimately are all of our life journeys. One thing we could say about this process of following the Gospel more closely in Francis's experience of "delaying a little" is that his experience of conversion—turning away from one way of living and toward another—was certainly more rapid than most people's experiences. It was certainly more rapid than Merton's. It was absolutely more rapid than my own lifelong struggle to do likewise. Francis only took a few years to begin this Gospel life, whereas it usually takes our whole lives for most of us to get started.

As we have already seen at the beginning of this chapter, evangelical poverty was indeed the *telos* or continual goal of Francis's experience of conversion, even if he didn't quite understand it at the start. The contemporary liberation theologian Gustavo Gutiérrez has written a lot about what moving more toward living a life of evangelical poverty in solidarity with the marginalized of our world could look like. He believes that we can recognize a general, three-stage process of conversion toward this way of Gospel life in classic historical figures such as Francis of Assisi. But this outline also applies in our own attempts to live more authentically our baptismal vocation to follow in the footprints of Jesus Christ. Gutiérrez says that this takes place in the following ways, moving from one to another:

1. Engagement with specific actions
2. Changes in style of life
3. A break with one's social class

This dynamic process occurs over time, and Gutiérrez draws on the preeminent model of self-emptying, the *kenosis* of God in the Incarnation, as the starting point for reflecting on what it means to move toward evangelical poverty and solidarity. He explains:

> Poverty is an act of love and liberation. It has a redemptive value. If the ultimate cause of human exploitation and alienation is selfishness, the deepest reason for voluntary poverty is love of neighbor. Christian poverty has meaning only as a commitment of solidarity with the poor, with those who suffer misery and injustice. The commitment is to witness to the evil which has resulted from sin and is a breach of communion. It is not a question of idealizing poverty, but rather of taking it on as it is—an evil—to protest against it and to struggle to abolish it. As Ricouer says, you cannot really be with the poor unless you are struggling against poverty. Because of this solidarity—which one must manifest itself in specific action, a style of life, a break with one's social class—one can also help the poor and exploited to become aware of their exploitation and seek liberation from it.[12]

As Gutiérrez notes well, solidarity is a comprehensive and integrated stance in the world. Unlike service work or charity (as popularly conceived), solidarity requires "specific action, a style of life, a break with one's social class." It is perhaps unreasonable to expect most Christians to so radically adopt a position of solidarity and a life of evangelical poverty in short order, but it is not beyond their capacity to begin to reimagine what a morally just and particularly Christian life might look like and then work in ways to make that commitment an ever-more concrete reality. These features of solidarity highlighted by Gutiérrez resound in the life experience of Francis of Assisi.

As a young adult, having suffered the trauma of war and after returning home a different person, Francis slowly came to live a life of solidarity with the poor and marginalized, much in line with the progressive sequence described by Gutiérrez. At first Francis engaged in concrete, specific actions. Thomas of Celano recounts that Francis was at first "changed in mind but not in body" and apparently took his time appropriating the will of God in place of his own, yet he desired to do so even in the earliest stages of his ongoing conversion.[13] It was then through the selling of his father's cloth for money to be used in restoring the church of San Damiano that he began to engage in specific actions. He sought to live at the church, without accumulating wealth associated with income, and sold all he could to give to the poor. It was in this transition of lifestyle that Francis exhibited the second characteristic of solidarity Gutiérrez notes. Finally, that famous scene depicting Francis's renouncement before the bishop of his father and the stability, status, and inheritance associated with him marks the definite break with the saint's social class. No longer was Francis somewhere in the realm of the merchant class and *majores* of Assisi, but instead he had intentionally moved to the place of the *minores*, or lesser ones, who were often outcast or dismissed.

In essence, whether intentional or not, Francis's movement from a place of power, wealth, and security to a social location of vulnerability and minority reflected the kenotic character of God becoming human in the Incarnation. It was a self-emptying that made possible the condition for solidarity, as opposed to service from another social, economic, and cultural place. In solidarity and in a life of evangelical poverty, one does not fall prey to the self-gratifying condescension that is rewarded in the "giving" of service to another from a remote location. Instead, solidarity depends on the poverty of Gospel life— modeled by Christ and echoed in Francis—that finds its source in the divestment of one's selfishness and self-centeredness expressed in the disassociation with others. Ilia Delio offers a reflection on this experience of conversion and Gospel living according to the Franciscan tradition when she writes,

> True poverty creates community because it converts self-sufficiency into creative interdependency where the mystery of life unfolds for us. Only those who can see and feel for another can love another without trying to possess the other. Poverty is that free and open space within the human heart that enables us to listen to the other, to respect the other and to trust the other without feeling that something vital will be taken from us. . . . Conversion to poverty and humility is the nucleus of Christian evolution because it is the movement to authentic love; a movement from isolated "oneness" toward mutual relatedness, from individualism toward community, where Christ is revealed in the union of opposites in the web of life.[14]

As Delio notes, the movement toward this poverty lived by Francis and described by Gutiérrez is the constitutive dimension of solidarity called for in authentic Gospel life. To put it another way, Francis, in a reflection on the Eucharist, expresses the core of this kenotic sense of solidarity that embraces evangelical poverty wholeheartedly. The *poverello* writes, "Brothers, look at the humility of God, and pour out your hearts before Him! Humble yourselves that you may be exalted by Him! Hold back nothing of yourselves for yourselves, that He who gives Himself totally to you may receive you totally!"[15]

The culmination of this experience of change in Francis's young life took place when he renounced his social status and, taking perhaps too literally the words of Jesus, "Whoever comes to me and does not hate father and mother, wife and children, brothers and sisters, yes, and even life itself, cannot be my disciple" (Lk 14:26), ultimately broke ties with his family and any stability, protection, and privileges those relationships would provide. He was on his own for the first time in his life. Although the bishop of Assisi is remembered to symbolically wrap his mantle around the now naked Francis after his public renunciation scene, the Church did not provide anything of substance or material support for this rogue penitent. Evangelical poverty was not easy, renunciation of his family and earlier life must have been difficult, but what was ahead for Francis would change the course of history forever.

Following the Holy Gospel

Francis was, in the beginning, a lone ranger. He originally set out intending to live the Gospel more closely on his own. As Franciscan scholar Regis Armstrong has said, starting a new religious order was not Francis's intention at all. Unlike some other founders of religious communities, Francis did not seek to create a new community but only sought to live out his own personal, baptismal vocation to follow Christ.[16] St. Bonaventure, the biographer of Francis who became the "official" biographer of the order some decades after Francis's death, tells the story in his *Major Legend of Saint Francis* of how Francis, while at Mass, heard the Gospel proclaimed about Jesus' commissioning of the disciples out into the world. It is this simple vision that became the earliest skeleton of the life of the friars minor. Bonaventure tells us that

> one day while he was devoutly hearing a Mass of the Apostles, the Gospel was read in which Christ sends out his disciples to preach and gives them the Gospel form of life, that they may not keep gold or silver or money in their belts, nor have a wallet for their journey, nor may they have two tunics, nor shoes, nor staff. Hearing, understanding, and committing this to memory, this friend of apostolic poverty was then overwhelmed with an indescribable joy. "This is what I want," he said, "this is what I desire with all my heart!" Immediately, he took off the shoes from his feet, put down his staff, denounced his wallet and money, and, satisfied with one tunic, threw away his leather belt and put on a piece of rope for a belt. He directed all his heart's desire to carry out what he had heard and to conform in every way to the rule of right living given to the apostles.[17]

It wasn't long before others were inspired by his actions and the charismatic spirit that naturally flowed from this inspiring, if odd, young man. For whatever reason, some men of varying personal backgrounds, including somewhat well-to-do men from Assisi as well as a priest and others, began to follow Francis, desiring to live their Christian faith the way he did, after his example, and near him.

It's not unreasonable to imagine that there were consistent "growing pains" from the appearance of the first follower of Francis until the would-be saint's death nearly eighteen years later. The earliest followers, such as Bernard of Quinatavalle, Peter Catania, and Brother Giles, who showed up on the scene around 1208, were both a blessing and a challenge to Francis. The challenge was made clear in Francis's need to reevaluate what he understood to be God's call in his life. As he would say in his final testament, "And after the Lord gave me some brothers, no one showed me what I had to do, but the Most High Himself revealed to me that I should live according to the pattern of the Holy Gospel."[18] This was, perhaps, how he understood the presence of these men. For Francis, the presence of the brothers who with him would form the friars minor—the "lesser brothers"—was a gift from God.

About a year after the first men came to live alongside and imitate Francis, it became clear that a more concrete plan of life, a *forma vitae*, was needed. The early sources tell us that Francis traveled to Rome in 1209 to present a *propositum vitae* (proposal of life) to Pope Innocent III for approval. Little is known about what this *propositum vitae* actually contained by way of plans, regulations, structure, and the like. But scholars do believe that it must have dealt primarily with three issues: work, money and alms, and dwellings.[19] These themes all stem from the early life shared among these brothers. Francis makes it clear in what would become the "Rule of 1221" (technically known as the *Regula non bullata*, because it was the proposed way of life that did not eventually receive the papal approval) and in the "Rule of 1223" (*Regula bullata*) that the brothers are to work.[20] Returning to the caricature of Francis discussed at the opening of this chapter, this is where his love of poverty, in terms of living *sine proprio*, comes into full view. His vision of following Christ consisted in being not beggars on the street or homeless men living lives identical to that of the lepers but men who took the value and dignity of labor seriously and who would accept *only what was needed* to sustain the community with the most basic of necessities. Francis despised money, which had emerged in force as the barter economy of Francis's youth shifted to a money-based system. It quickly became a dehumanizing system, one in which the value of a person could now be calculated in coins and debts. Karl Marx would, centuries later, recognize this system as one that alienated workers from their work and craftspeople from their products. Francis, even amid the nascent stages of this new way of living, saw the unjust writing on the wall and insisted that he and his brothers, in accord with authentic Gospel life, renounce that economy.

The brothers worked in the trades or professions they knew when they decided to join Francis and his community. Carpenters continued woodworking, priests continued sacramental ministry, and teachers continued teaching. But in place of the monetary remuneration they would ordinarily receive, the lesser brothers, the friars minor, would accept food, clothing, or temporary shelter in exchange for their services, products, or labor. Francis forbade his brothers from even touching money.[21] This would have surely caught the attention of others in the towns. The goal of this life was a simplicity that freed Christians from the burdens associated with property, wealth, and the protection received from and obsession with those things. It was also a radical statement about one's complete trust in and dependence on God. In addition to the ethical reasons Francis had for refusing to participate in a money economy, there were spiritual reasons that he felt required him and his brothers not to amass funds to maintain the security and comfort that the poor, marginalized, and powerless in his day could not have. Not only did the lepers and others Francis encountered experience, by no intentional act of their own, this radical dependence on God and others for survival, but Francis would also frequently point to Jesus Christ and his own day-to-day living. "So do not worry about tomorrow, for tomorrow will bring worries of its own. Today's trouble is enough for today" (Mt 6:34).

There is a tendency to romanticize the early years of Francis's community of brothers, suggesting that it was as idyllic as the depiction of the early Christians in the Acts of the Apostles. The famous verses from Acts read,

> All who believed were together and had all things in common; they would sell their possessions and goods and distribute the proceeds to all, as any had need. Day by day, as they spent much time together in the temple, they broke bread at home and ate their food with glad and generous hearts, praising God and having the goodwill of all the people. And day by day the Lord added to their number those who were being saved. (Acts 2:44–47)

It is difficult to know just how close to the truth this really came in regard to the early Church. In the case of the early followers of Francis, however, there was certainly contention, strife, and difficulties among the brothers with what was, at times, an unrealistic and downright hard way of life that Francis sought to live. The early sources are mixed in their recollection of the first years. To be sure, the young community was praised for the austerity and harmony that had emerged in their lives, but there are also accounts of Francis's overbearing evangelical perfectionism and idiosyncratic outbursts.[22] Nevertheless, the community continued to grow—rapidly so—during the less than twenty years of Francis's remaining life.

In 1210, the nobleman Favarone of Offreduccio and his family returned to their hometown of Assisi from the aristocratic exile of the previous decades. Favarone's daughter was named Clare. She would be the first woman to follow

Francis's way of life and would, in a very real sense, become the foundress of a religious community popularly known as the Franciscan Second Order, or the Poor Clares. As Lawrence Cunningham has keenly noted, following the historical work of Clarian scholars such as Marco Bertoli, Ingrid Peterson, and Margaret Carney, Clare deserves to be considered in her own right and "not merely as a star-struck adolescent who became infatuated with the example of Francis."[23] In this way we might more accurately talk about Clare, not *simply* as the first woman to follow Francis's inspired way of Christian living, but as something of a cofounder of the Franciscan movement. Clare, as it is well documented, was already an unusually spiritual and pious young woman when she encountered Francis for the first time at the Assisi Cathedral, during which time he was preaching. At this point, Francis would have already been well-known in Assisi and in the surrounding areas, with a coterie of brothers living in community, praying, and working together. It seems that one of Clare's relatives, Rufino, who had been one of the early followers of Francis, was the one to introduce the *poverello* to this young noblewoman who, if not quite "star-struck," was captivated by this odd yet charismatic man. We know that they met covertly, albeit with a few witnesses for the sake of propriety, over the course of many months. These encounters are recalled decades later by those early followers and witnesses as incredibly spiritual and energizing events. Vauchez explains that these several secret encounters "demonstrated to Francis and Clare that there was indeed a real affinity between them; the young girl aspired to share the way of life of the brothers."[24] Francis saw the spirit of the young woman alive with the zeal of the Gospel and encouraged her to embrace this way of life, centered as it was on evangelical poverty and following in the footprints of Christ.

On the night of Palm Sunday, March 28, 1212, with the assistance of the bishop of Assisi and some close confidants, Clare made plans to leave her home and met Francis and his brothers at the small church of St. Mary of the Angels, known as the Portiuncula. Here she committed herself to this penitential way of life after the model of Francis and demonstrated this commitment in the traditional religious gesture of cutting off her hair. Shortly thereafter, Francis placed her with the Benedictines nearby, where she was later joined by her sisters Agnes and Beatrice, who were also inspired to live this new way of Christian life. The movement inaugurated by Francis's experience of conversion and sincere desire to follow the Gospel now included not just men but women, too. As with Francis's community of friars minor, Clare's small community of cloistered women grew and expanded in rapid succession.

The impetus to follow the Gospel that drove Francis to live the way he did, and that in surprisingly short order inspired others to follow him, led to a number of innovative forms of ministry and ways of being in the world. While Clare and her religious sisters were still subject to the confines of the monastic cloister, Francis and his religious brothers moved beyond the walls of a monastery, rectory, or cathedral house—the typical locations of male religious life up to that time. Francis saw Jesus' personal model and his instructions in the Gospel as an example for an itinerant lifestyle that involved popular preaching, daily work, communal prayer, and encounter with women and men of all backgrounds and in all locations. It was both freeing and risky. As we've already seen, without the financial stability of a monastery, with its endowment and economically successful lands, the brothers were subject to the uncertain reward of their own labor and the generosity of others. Additionally, without the housing that comes with other forms of religious life, whether in the cloistered walls of a monastery or in the rural shelter of a parish house, the brothers were necessarily and always vulnerable to the vagrancies of Francis's way of life. While the life was not easy, it was, from Francis's vantage point, a good life marked by a freedom from the confines of unjust systems and the self-centeredness that seemed to the *poverello* to stand in opposition to authentic Gospel living.

Toward the "Transitus" of Francis

Now that we have an appreciation for Francis's original intention to live out his own baptismal vocation and his uncertainty in the face of a growing community of friars, it should come as no surprise that in late September 1220 Francis announced at the general chapter (a meeting of friars from all the provinces) of Saint Michael that he was planning to step down as the head of the order. This occurred not long after Francis returned to Italy from a historic trip to the Middle East where, accompanied by another friar, Francis famously crossed the crusaders' battle line and met with the Muslim sultan Malik al-Kamil (1218–1238) during the height of the Fifth Crusade (1213–1221). We'll take a much closer look at this particular encounter between Francis and the sultan later in the book, because it would have a longstanding influence on the interreligious and peacemaking efforts of Thomas Merton many centuries later. But for now suffice it to say this was a life-changing experience for the *poverello*.

Upon his return from Egypt, Francis encountered a religious order in turmoil. What was becoming the soon-to-be institutionalized Order of Friars Minor was at the threshold of its previously conceived limits. Never having considered that this community of friars would grow to be in the thousands in such a short time, Francis had always maintained a rather ad hoc attitude toward problem solving. If an issue of concern arose, he or one of his regional delegates (a minister provincial or custodian) would address the matter. However, that was no longer possible, nor sensible, given the size and unwieldy responsibilities that such an organization presented to its leader. Around the same time that Francis announced his desire to step down from formal leadership of the order, Pope Honorious III issued a papal bull titled *Cum Secundum* (1220), which imposed certain regulatory aspects to the Franciscan movement that made the friars adhere to a more institutionalized form of life. The most significant change this Roman imposition mandated was the requirement of a year of probation, what we today call a "novitiate" year, in which men who aspired to be friars would live in community, share communal responsibilities, pray together, learn the general way of life, and minister alongside vowed members of the community in order to (a) "test out" this way of life and (b) allow the broader community of friars to "test them out," too.

Previously, Francis had simply welcomed anybody who showed up expressing interest in becoming a friar. Generally, this wouldn't have been so problematic when the group was small and Francis along with the other brothers got to know everyone who came to the order. As time moved on, however, and the order grew to more than ten thousand, this was no longer the case. All sorts of random people, including the unbalanced and others who were simply not a good fit, were entering the community and professing religious vows. The pope and other Church leaders were no longer going to allow this to continue. In *Cum Secundum*, Pope Honorious III explains his reasoning:

> Practically every religious order has wisely ordained that those who propose to undertake a life of regular observance should first test it and be tested in it for a certain length of time so that they will not later have reason to regret their decision, which cannot be excused under pretext of levity. Therefore, by authority of these present letters, we forbid you to admit to profession in your Order anyone who has not first completed a year of probation.[25]

One might mark the shift in the history of the Franciscan way of life from a nascent movement that more or less resembled the earliest expression of Francis's own Gospel life to an officially sanctioned institution at around September 1220 with this papal intervention and Francis's resignation from leadership. Francis's biographers have suggested that this resignation reflects a moment in Francis's own personal spiritual journey when he desired to return to the way of life that appeared now to be lost. If the whole order wasn't going to live that primitive form of evangelical life, then at least he was going to try his hardest to do so himself.

In addition to his personal efforts to return to the way of life he knew at the beginning, he also spent a great deal of time after his resignation working on what we now call the "Earlier Rule" (1221) or, officially, the *Regula non bullata*. Scholars debate about when exactly this text was composed and over what length of time it was developed and expanded, but nearly all agree that Francis had a direct hand in the formulization of this particular document. It is a hodgepodge of a text, reflecting a variety of writing styles absent of any uniform method of composition. In addition to practical instructions, prohibitions, and guidelines for the Franciscan way of life, it includes prayers and other seeming oddities generally unbecoming for an official document of this sort. For this reason, two years after this rule is assumed to have been completed, another rule was finished and approved by the pope (the *Regula bullata* of 1223). This latter text is more concise, uniform, and juridical, bearing the methodological fingerprints of the Roman Curia. If Pope Honorious III's *Cum Secundum* represented the beginning of the institutionalization of the Franciscan movement, the *Regula bullata* marked its concretization. Thompson explains:

> The Later Rule [*Regula bullata*] reveals how much the brotherhood had changed from the early days at Rivo Torto, and not merely by increase in numbers. Above all, it serves to rationalize the internal governance of the brotherhood. The role of superiors and chapters (chapter 8), disciplinary procedures (chapters 7 and 10), and choir obligations (chapter 3) are spelled out and clarified.[26]

Though the early Franciscan movement was made to look more like other officially sanctioned orders in the Church, it still bore a great deal of its original charismatic and unique qualities. Preaching, evangelical poverty, itinerancy, fraternity, and the like were still highly valued and central to the text. However, what was becoming clear was that the community Francis was credited with inaugurating was no longer his. It belonged to the Church and to the collective community itself.

At around this time Francis's health was already in serious decline. The austere and penitential life that Francis rigorously demanded of himself, and always to a lesser degree from his fellow friars, had taken its toll. His remaining years were marked by both a cycle of frustration with himself for not quite living up to the model of *minoritas*—the lesser brotherhood and humility he sought to provide for his confreres—and a profound series of mystical religious experiences. Nearly all of what Francis is best known for—the Christmas scene in Greccio, the reception of the stigmata, and the composition of "The Canticle of the Creatures"—took place during these last three years or so of his life. In concluding this section of the chapter on Francis's life, it might be best to briefly look at each of these significant episodes.

Christmas at Greccio

In December of 1223, shortly after Francis's way of life had been "set in stone" with the official papal approval of his *Regula*, the would-be saint made his way to the Italian town of Greccio. He stayed in a little hermitage used by the friars near the town from December 1223 through early spring 1224. The early legends tell the story of that Christmas of 1223 when Francis, moved by his love of Christ and overwhelmed by the humility of a God who would enter our world as a defenseless infant, desired to celebrate Christmas Mass in conditions as close as possible to the poor circumstances at Bethlehem that the infant Jesus first encountered. He asked his friend John to prepare a place, and a stable was prepared. Lawrence Cunningham has remarked that "what was unique about Francis's notion was the use of live animals in an authentic setting of a stable."[27] What might seem unbecoming to the modern imagination—the smells and manure that accompany live stable animals, for example—was partly the reason Francis wished to have the celebration of the Mass in such a location. This is how God first humbly appeared. Why shouldn't we celebrate the appearance of Christ in the Eucharist under similar conditions?

As we will see later, the humility of God and the centrality of the Incarnation played an important role in Francis's own spirituality and subsequently shaped the Christological thought of Thomas Merton. The radical experience of that Christmas in Greccio, replete with animals, cold and uncomfortable weather, and circumstances presumably less than fitting for a nobleman, let alone God, is often lost today in the Christmas crèches that are set up in our homes and churches. Nevertheless, these forms of remembrance, whose origin is frequently attributed to Francis and that celebration in Greccio, should allow us to recall what Francis desired to re-create in that Italian stable: the humility and love of God.

The Reception of the Stigmata

This is one of the most famous and controversial episodes in the life of Francis of Assisi. What *exactly* happened in early fall 1224 when the ailing *poverello*[28] made his way to the remote caves and hermitages used by the friars on Mount La Verna to "refresh his soul by prayer, mortification, and solitude," is unclear.[29] The earliest sources tend to treat this episode variously, and popular legends and imaginations have embellished, changed, or convoluted the experience of Francis. What is generally said about his time in penitential solitude and prayer is that, inspired by his reading of the gospel accounts of Christ's passion, Francis spent his time in daily prayer meditating on the passion of the Lord. "Each day on the mountain

Francis identified himself more and more with the mysteries he was contemplating."[30] He became engrossed in prayer, and on one morning he had a vision that was both frightening and consoling. Bonaventure explains, in part of a whole chapter dedicated to the stigmata in his *Major Life of St. Francis,* that Francis saw a crucified man hovering over him in the shape of a seraph.

> While Francis was praying on the mountainside, he saw a seraph having six wings, fiery as well as brilliant, descend from the grandeur of heaven. And when in swift flight, it had arrived at a spot in the air near the man of God, there appeared between the wings the likeness of a man crucified, with his hands and feet extended in the form of a cross and fastened to a cross . . . seeing this, he was overwhelmed and his heart was flooded with a mixture of joy and sorrow.[31]

Bonaventure then tells us what supposedly happened after this vision. "As the vision was disappearing, it left in his heart a marvelous fire and imprinted in his flesh a likeness of signs no less marvelous. For immediately the marks of nails began to appear in his hands and feet just as he had seen a little before in the figure of the man crucified."[32] Francis's experience, we are told, was not just an intense identification with Christ's passion in terms of spiritual or mental reflection but a physical reality that resulted in bearing marks resembling the crucifixion wounds of Christ. The early sources suggest that Francis did not share the details of this experience or show the wounds to many people in life, but some claim that after his death the other brothers rapidly spread the word of this allegedly heavenly sign. Cunningham reminds us that three popes (Gregory IX, Alexander IV, and Nicholas III) each affirmed the historicity of the stigmata.[33]

Often people are distracted by the miraculous and unusual nature of an experience such as the stigmata, suggesting that what is really important to take away from this part of Francis's

story is the living confirmation of his sanctity, even before his
official canonization. While that might be a worthwhile point
to consider, I suggest that what is really at stake here is the
model of Christian living this particular episode presents to
us. It is not about putting Francis on a pedestal in order to laud
him as so exceptional that we cannot possibly relate but instead
about seeing in his example what it means to so deeply reflect
on scripture and the love of God that his *whole life*, mentally
and physically, was transformed by the experience of prayer,
solitude, and reflection. Whether the historicity of Francis's
stigmata can ever be verified in an apodictic way or not is
really of little importance, but the continued value of his pointing us toward a lifestyle that might bring us to a place where
such an overwhelming mystical experience of the Divine can
change our whole lives forever is key.

The Composition of "The Canticle of the Creatures"

If the fact that Francis is popularly remembered for "loving
animals" finds its most serious kernel of truth in a particular
writing of his, it is likely "The Canticle of the Creatures" that
deserves the credit. It is also undoubtedly the most famous of
his writings. Here is the entirety of the text:

> Most High, all-powerful, good Lord,
> Yours are the praises, the glory, and the honor, and all
>   blessing,
> To You alone, Most High, do they belong,
> and no human is worthy to mention Your name.
>
>   Praised be You, my Lord, with all Your creatures,
> especially Sir Brother Sun,
> Who is the day and through whom You give us light.
> And he is beautiful and radiant with great splendor;
> and bears a likeness of You, Most High One.

Praised be You, my Lord, through Sister Moon and the
    stars,
in heaven You formed them clear and precious and
    beautiful.

Praised be You, my Lord, through Brother Wind,
and through the air, cloudy and serene, and every kind of
    weather,
through whom You give sustenance to Your creatures.

Praised be You, my Lord, through Sister Water,
who is very useful and humble and precious and chaste.

Praised be You, my Lord, through Brother Fire,
through whom You light the night,
and he is beautiful and playful and robust and strong.

Praised be You, my Lord, through our Sister Mother
    Earth,
who sustains and governs us,
and who produces various fruit with colored flowers and
    herbs.

Praised be You, my Lord, through those who give
        pardon for Your love,
and bear infirmity and tribulation.

Blessed are those who endure in peace
for by You, Most High, shall they be crowned.

Praised be You, my Lord, through our Sister Bodily
    Death,
from whom no one living can escape.

Woe to those who die in mortal sin.
Blessed are those whom death will find in Your most holy
    will,
for the second death shall do them no harm.

Praise and bless my Lord and give Him thanks
and serve Him with great humility.[34]

There are lots of subtle and important features of this canticle that, while not at first apparent, help us to understand the
spirituality and worldview of the *poverello*. First, "The Canticle
of the Creatures" was not written in one sitting. It, like so many
of Francis's writings, developed over a period of time. Traditionally scholars have asserted that the text was composed
in three parts, a claim that is bolstered by some of the early
Franciscan sources. The first part about the natural elements
was written after his experience on Mount La Verna, after his
reception of the stigmata, and after his health had so deterio-
rated that his eyes had gone all but completely blind. Francis,
we are told, found it painful to be exposed to bright light,
making the opening line of his prayer all the more startling:
"Praised be You, my Lord, with all Your creatures, especially
Sir Brother Sun." The sun at this time would have been the
source of great physical pain, but Francis's recognition of the
inherent dignity and value of creation, as well as his realization
that the rest of the created order continues to praise God by
being what they were created to be—despite what negative
experiences he might have of those elements—allowed the
dying man to keep his mind always on God.

The second part of the canticle is said to have been composed by Francis upon hearing that the mayor (the *podesta*)
and the bishop of Assisi had a falling out that led to disputes,
excommunication, and the pursuit of legal action. Francis
added the line about human persons, following the pattern
of the previous nine verses about the rest of the created order,
which highlights the ways that creation praises God through
right and just actions in accord with God's intention. The
sun praises God by providing light, the wind praises God by
blowing, and so forth. Human persons, Francis explains in
the added verses, praise God by pardoning, bearing infirmity
and tribulation, and enduring in peace. When people do not

do these things, even in the face of conflict, they are not being what God intended them to be.

The third part of "The Canticle of the Creatures" is said to have been composed by Francis very close to the *poverello*'s death. Here we have one of the more stunning images of Francis's capacious and fraternal worldview. Death, that which is said to be the source of human angst and existential fear, is greeted not as an enemy or something to be avoided but as a sister and, like all the other elements and human persons themselves, part of creation. Francis recognized, even on his own deathbed, that death did not have the last word and nor would it be the end. It was a means of transition—in Latin, a *transitus* or passage—from this life to eternal life. Death shouldn't be feared but embraced in God's time, for it is the condition for the possibility of heavenly reward for those who love God and live in God's love.

Francis's own *transitus* took place on October 3, 1226. Francis sent word to Clare and the Poor Sisters at San Damiano that his time in this world was quickly coming to an end and then prepared for his own embrace of Sister Bodily Death. Francis did two important and unique things as he approached death. The first is that he asked his brother friars to strip him naked and lay him on the bare earth. Cunningham sees this aspect of Francis's death to be an essential element worth recalling.

> We cannot overstate how profoundly that final act of nudity brings certain themes of his life to a fitting conclusion. . . . Francis, lying on the ground in his nakedness, recapitulated his own birth when he came into this world like Jesus and every child naked to the world. When Francis stripped himself naked before his own father Pietro, and the Bishop of Assisi, Guido, [this was] part of his second birth as a wanderer for Christ. Once, he walked through a town naked with a halter around his neck to show his humility. . . . To these themes we now have Francis, giving away everything including his poor clothes, to be embraced by Mother Earth

whom he had hymned so beautifully in his preaching and
in his poetry. His nakedness is also a gestural reminder that
it is from the clay of the earth we come and it is to the earth
we return: "Ashes to ashes; dust to dust."[35]

Francis's love of poverty and fraternal view of creation,
matched with his recognition of the centrality of God's humility in the Incarnation, are all celebrated in this final act of preparing for death. This is not the request or action of a man
afraid of his fate but someone who understood for a long time
how he would prepare for it, should he have the chance.

The second thing Francis did on his deathbed was ask that
the gathered friars read him the gospel passage proclaimed
each Holy Thursday from the Gospel according to John, which
begins, "Before the festival of the Passover, Jesus knew that his
hour had come to depart from this world and go to the Father.
Having loved his own who were in the world, he loved them
to the end" (Jn 13:1). This pericope is the story of the Last
Supper that features the servant-leader Jesus washing the feet
of his disciples and then instructing them to do likewise in
their ministry, as a model of what it truly means to follow in
his footprints. Francis wanted to remind his brothers, as he
himself recalled near the end, what it meant to be a Christian
and to "observe the Holy Gospel of Our Lord Jesus Christ," as
the *Regula* of the Order of Friars Minor begins.[36]

The death of Francis brought about great sorrow among
those who had been with him from the beginning and those
who had been so inspired by his example that they too followed Francis in following Christ. The pope did not spare any
time in advancing the cause for Francis's canonization, which
was made official on August 14, 1228, in the promulgation of
Gregory IX's bull *Mira Circa Nos*.[37] In a way somewhat curious,
Pope Gregory IX never mentions the Order of Friars Minor
or Francis's "founding" of a religious community. There are
many ways to interpret this omission amid the several pages of
laudatory praise of Francis's personal holiness, but maybe one

way—perhaps the least cynical way—is to see in the official text of Francis's canonization a reflection of what the saint from Assisi really wanted all along: to live his baptismal vocation by observing the Gospel and following in the footprints of Christ. In shifting the focus from the institution of the friar community to the sanctity of the individual man Francesco di Bernardone, a model is raised up for all of the baptized who come after him, a model of authentic Christian living reserved not for some special religious women and men but for all people and in all times.

CHAPTER 2

The Modern Monk: Thomas Merton

In the spirit of Joe Friday's "Just the facts, ma'am," from television's *Dragnet*, this section about Thomas Merton's life will focus primarily on what I think will best be described as the essential facts of his life. Particular attention will be given to his early life, a period to which we will likely not return. Much of the rest of this book will explore more deeply the later parts of Merton's life, work, and thought. I would characterize the beginning of Merton's personal history as significantly shaped by a difficult childhood, but to talk about difficult childhoods is to enter into the realm of subjectivity, opinion, and conjecture. What makes one person's early life more challenging than another's? What factors can be recognized as universal hardships? While his was certainly not the sort of plight that the abject poor experience every day in various parts of our world, Merton's early life and young adulthood bear the marks of loss, sadness, loneliness, displacement, and insecurity. All of these things combined in such a way as to affect the future monk, although it is difficult to identify what, precisely, shaped Merton's life in one form or another. Surely, as with all of us, known and unknown dimensions of these formative years would impact the thought and behavior of the adult Merton.

Before moving into some of the ways Francis and the Franciscan tradition shaped Merton's world, we need to have a basic overview and sense of who Merton was. For the Merton enthusiasts out there, feel no shame about beginning at chapter 3 if you wish to avoid a recap of his biography. Less time will be spent here on Merton's chronology than was spent on Francis's because many of the particular details of Merton's life will come into clearer relief when we look at various themes of his thought in subsequent chapters.

A Difficult Start

Born on January 31, 1915, in Prades, France, Thomas Merton was the firstborn child of Ruth Jenkins and Owen Merton. Both of Merton's parents were artists who met as students in Paris during the year 1911. From infancy, Merton's early life was something of a nomadic experience. A year after Merton's birth, because of the impact of World War I, the young Merton family moved from France to Ruth's native United States, where the Mertons stayed for a time with her parents—Martha and Sam Jenkins—in Douglaston, Long Island, in New York. There was, at times, some tension between Owen, a native of New Zealand, and Ruth's parents. Michael Mott, the official biographer of Thomas Merton, surmises that this had to do with Sam Jenkins's concerns about Owen's ability to adequately provide for his family. Owen Merton was a very independent person whose passion for painting did indeed appear to take priority in terms of time and travel. However, he was not irresponsible. Owen worked for a time as a landscaper and as a church organist—the former he rather enjoyed, while the latter was a short-lived experience—in order to help support his family during their time in the States. While Owen's artwork was publicly shown in US and British galleries throughout his career and was purchased on a more or less consistent basis, the avant-garde and freestyle life of an artist probably caused the more conventional American Sam Jenkins a predictable amount of paternal anxiety.[1]

The second Merton boy, John Paul, was born on November 2, 1918. Merton's only sibling, John Paul would live a short life. He grew up under the care of his maternal grandparents, the Jenkinses in Douglaston; went to New York public schools and a military academy near Gettysburg, Pennsylvania, for a short time; and would attend Cornell University in Ithaca, New York. Like his older brother, John Paul became interested in Catholicism in his young adulthood. He was baptized a Catholic in 1942. Two years earlier John Paul had visited Toronto where he enlisted in the Royal Canadian Air Force. It would be in this service, while fighting in World War II over the English Channel in late April 1943, that John Paul would die in combat.

With the death of John Paul in 1943, Merton had, at age twenty-eight, suffered the loss of *every* member of his immediate family. The first person to die was his mother, Ruth, after being diagnosed with stomach cancer in the summer of 1921. In October of 1921, just a month before John Paul was to turn three, Ruth died in a New York hospital. Perhaps one of the more tragic and consuming aspects of her death was that she never said goodbye, in person, to the then six-year-old Merton. Biographers differ in explaining the cause of this. Some have suggested that it might have been hospital policy to prohibit children from visiting; others, including Merton's own speculation in his book *The Seven Storey Mountain*, suggest that it was Ruth's own desire not to have her son see her in a state near death. We now know that Bellevue Hospital, where Ruth spent her last days, had a policy that prohibited children from visiting the general wards.[2] This meant that the only way in which Ruth could said goodbye to her firstborn, Tom, was in a letter that the little Merton took outside to read. He recalls the experience in *The Seven Storey Mountain*:

> Then one day Father gave me a note to read. I was very surprised. It was for me personally, and it was in my

mother's handwriting. I don't think she had ever written to me before—there had never been any occasion for it. Then I understood what was happening, although, as I remember, the language of the letter was confusing to me. Nevertheless, one thing was quite evident. My mother was informing me, by mail, that she was about to die. And would never see me again.

I took the note out under the maple tree in the back yard, and worked over it, until I had made it all out, and had gathered what it really meant. And a tremendous weight of sadness and depression settled on me. It was not the grief of a child, with pangs of sorrow and many tears. It had something of the heavy perplexity and gloom of adult grief, and was therefore all the more of a burden because it was, to that extent, unnatural. I suppose one reason for this was that I had more or less had to arrive at the truth by induction.[3]

Upon later reflection, the twenty-seven-year-old Merton and author of *The Seven Storey Mountain* recalled the lack of support in that experience. "Prayer? No, prayer did not even occur to me. How fantastic that will seem to a Catholic—that a six-year-old child should find out that his mother is dying, and not know enough to pray for her! It was not until I became a Catholic, twenty years later, that it finally occurred to me to pray for my mother."[4] Of his two parents, his mother had been the only one to openly, if not publicly, practice some faith tradition intermittently, having gone occasionally to a Quaker service. Although Merton's father was less overt in expressing any religiosity, Merton talks about his father as an incredibly spiritual person, a man of faith in his own quiet ways. Jim Forest explains that it wouldn't be until 1928 that Merton saw a sign of his father's personal piety in any expressible way.[5]

After his mother's death, his father—never particularly adept at the finer points (or even the more general ones) of traditional domestic life—became a single parent with two sons, ages six and three. Mott suggests that Owen was essentially a stranger to John Paul, having spent relatively little time with the boy before Owen's own death. Merton's father would, however, take his older son to and from the United States in the frenetic years following his mother's death. The first trip was to Bermuda after a brief summer jaunt to New England, where Owen painted. The young Tom Merton thus had a rather unconventional and unstable life. This not-so-usual childhood, described by several of his biographers as freer than that of most other children, might very well help explain Merton's later troublemaking and acting out in more structured environments of British boarding schools and tradition-laden university settings. Conversely, this might also have contributed, as some scholars suggest, to Merton's longstanding desire for a more structured life, one with more accountability and guidance; he would find this structure within the cloister and during the regular itinerary of monastic life.

After Bermuda, Owen brought the young Merton back to live with his grandparents in Douglaston, where John Paul was already enrolled in school. Not long after, Owen returned to take Merton with him to France, a period of time Merton would later recall with great fondness. In 1928, Owen informed Merton, now a young teenager, that the two of them would be moving to England. It was at this time that Merton enrolled at Oakham, an English public school.[6] Just one year later, in the summer of 1929, Merton received some terrible news. Eight years after his mother's death, Owen told his teenage son that doctors had found a brain tumor in Owen's head. Precautions were made by both Owen and Merton's maternal grandfather, Sam Jenkins, to provide for Merton's future. Owen arranged for a family friend, Dr. Thomas Bennett of London, to be Merton's legal guardian after Owen's death. Sam Jenkins provided Merton with stock in the Grosset and Dunlap Company, the publisher where Jenkins had long been employed, as well as some parcels of land in the United States. Such preemptive efforts became necessary less than a year later when, on January 18, 1931, Owen Merton died.

Merton was now, practically speaking, alone in England. He had his brother and his mother's parents in Long Island and Thomas Bennett, his legal guardian, in London, but the sadness and depression of being an orphan took its toll. In response, Merton, now a sixteen-year-old, focused his efforts on school, telling us in *The Seven Storey Mountain* that he particularly enjoyed languages and writing. The summer before his final year at Oakham, 1932, Merton's grandparents and brother came to England to spend some vacation time with him. The following fall Merton sat for the entrance exams at Cambridge University and, having learned of his acceptance in early 1933, went off to Italy for a preuniversity vacation, not unlike what some contemporary students do today before shipping off to college. He will later, in *The Seven Storey Mountain*, remember that trip to Italy as something of a secular "religious experience."

By Merton's own admission, the darkest time of his life was at the start of his university career; Merton describes his arrival at Clare College as being "swept into the dark, sinister atmosphere of Cambridge."[7] It's difficult to say how much of this perspective is Merton's retrospective consideration of his short time at Cambridge and how much of it felt genuinely bleak. It's also a challenge to discern to what extent Merton was an exceptionally rambunctious and irresponsible university student, as he would persistently consider himself *ex post facto*, and how much he was a "normal college guy" as we might put it today. Regardless, Merton found himself drinking, occasionally brawling, and going to bed with various women during his first and only year at Cambridge.

Two more familial tragedies beset Merton during this time. The first was the death of his aunt Maud Pearce, of whom he was quite fond. Additionally, Merton's relationship with his legal guardian, Thomas Bennett, had begun to fall apart.

Merton's acting out and irresponsibility had continually tried Bennett's generosity. In April of 1934, their relationship was essentially lost. They would never again meet in person, although they would, out of necessity, occasionally exchange correspondence. One such exchange occurred in the summer of 1934 when Merton was on vacation with his grandparents and brother. Bennett wrote to advise Merton to stay in the United States. His poor academic performance during his first year of university, compounded by his misbehavior, would almost certainly guarantee that he would lose his Cambridge scholarship.

Merton returned to England that fall to get his things in order and apply for a visa to stay and study in the United States. He left Europe for the last time on November 29, 1934.

New Life in New York

Michael Mott explains that whereas "Cambridge was a carefully planned disaster for Merton[,] Columbia, a near-accident, was almost entirely successful from the very beginning in January 1935."[8] Closer to what remained of Merton's family, an ocean away from the escapades that marked his time at Cambridge, and settling into a new academic program, Merton changed in disposition and outlook. During that first semester, during the winter of 1935, Merton met a professor who would become influential in his studies, a mentor in discernment, and a lifelong friend. Mark Van Doren was a professor of English literature whom Merton came to admire as a teacher and as a person. At Columbia, Merton would also make other lifelong friends: the future poet Robert Lax; the future publisher Robert Giroux; his soon-to-be baptismal sponsor, Ed Rice; and the philosophy professor and additional mentor, Dan Walsh, among others. He became involved in several activities during his undergraduate studies at Columbia, including writing for and editing several student publications and the yearbook.

Merton's peers recognized him for his writing skills, and he frequently contributed cartoons for publications.

During his time at Columbia, Merton would dabble in associating with the Communist Party, certainly not a surprising experiment for a college student in New York at that time. He quickly became disillusioned with the association, however, seeing it as yet another vacuous political establishment, and shortly thereafter left such groups. One long-lasting commitment he did cultivate during his undergraduate years was a commitment to pacifism. This was perhaps a carryover from similar commitments he made while in England. The influence of his parents' personal ethics was no doubt an important part of this decision as well.

After completing his undergraduate degree at Columbia, Merton stayed and matriculated in the master of arts program in English literature. It was during this period of his New York life, from 1938 until 1939, that the postgraduate Merton would experience the life-changing events that would set in motion a trajectory leading to the Abbey of Gethsemani and beyond.

It all began, as Merton would later narrate, with the random purchase of a somewhat esoteric book by the French philosopher Etienne Gilson. In February of 1937, Merton happened to walk past Scribner's bookshop in New York City, and Gilson's *Spirit of Medieval Philosophy* caught his eye. He purchased the book and, upon reading it on his ride home, became indignant that it was an "officially approved" book, authorized by the Roman Catholic hierarchy for publication. This was indicated by the inclusion of the Latin inscriptions *Nihil Obstat* ("without error") and *Imprimatur* ("let it be published"). Nevertheless, he eventually cooled down and decided to give the book a try. In the end, Merton became fascinated with the content of the book, and as it were, his eyes became opened to the possibility that religion was not all about simple-mindedness or simplistic formulae that one was conscripted to believe. Christianity was a deeply rich tradition with complex and captivating philosophical explorations of theological doctrines.

A year later, toward the end of summer 1938, Merton—as he explained it in *The Seven Storey Mountain*—felt an internal compulsion to go to Mass. He walked into Corpus Christi Church on West 121st Street, near the campus of Columbia University. Upon entering the church, Merton was positively struck by the sincere piety of the women, men, and children praying without self-conscious concern for their appearance. In subsequent weeks, he returned to Mass and eventually asked the parish priest for information about becoming a Catholic. After some private instruction and catechetical reading, Merton was baptized on November 16, 1938. His classmate, Ed Rice, was his sponsor and godfather, and his friends Robert Lax, Sy Freedgod, and Bob Gerdy (all, as it happened, Jewish men) attended the liturgy in support of their friend. That day Merton also went to confession and received Holy Communion for the first time.

As Merton finished his master's work (a thesis on William Blake),[9] he enrolled in a graduate class on Thomas Aquinas with professor Dan Walsh. At the same time, Merton was privately discerning a sense that he might be called to become a Catholic priest. Speaking with Walsh about the possibility, Walsh suggested that Merton had the natural disposition and intellect to be a Franciscan friar. When, for reasons that will become clear in the next chapter, this possibility didn't pan out, Merton left Columbia, where he had begun the earliest efforts to pursue a doctorate in English, to take a teaching post at St. Bonaventure College, a Franciscan school in western New York. It was at St. Bonaventure, guided by some insightful and supportive friar-mentors, that Merton came to realize that God might still be calling him to religious life, even if it wasn't to be as a Franciscan friar. In April 1941, Merton visited the Abbey of Our Lady of Gethsemani outside Louisville, Kentucky, for the first time. He went for an Easter retreat and inquired about the possibility of entering the Trappist Order. With the preliminary okay, Merton returned to St. Bonaventure to finish teaching until resigning his faculty position on December 8 and traveling to Kentucky. On December 10, 1941, Thomas Merton entered the Abbey of Gethsemani and was received as a postulant in the Order of Cistercians of the Strict Observance.

The Making of a Monk

The renowned Merton scholar William Shannon claimed that Merton's life could be divided into two large chapters: the first included everything before his entrance into the Abbey of Gethsemani in 1941, and the second contained everything after that point.[10] Mathematically speaking, that's not a bad divide. Merton was about a month short of his twenty-seventh birthday when he entered in 1941, and he would be a Trappist monk of that monastery for exactly twenty-seven years, to the day, when he died on December 10, 1968.

Merton's entrance into religious life, his reception first as a postulant and later as a novice, and then as a professed member of the community, marked a significant shift in his life. Merton, in his journals and retrospective reflections, often thinks of this period in such a way. However, Thomas Merton and the later Father M. Louis Merton, O.C.S.O., are still one and the same person. He was a changed person, no doubt, and one who changes over time, but nevertheless a man whose temperament, personality, experiences, weaknesses, and gifts also came with him into the monastery. Those who want there to be a more dramatic divide or radical shift in Merton's life here will be disappointed to know that such things didn't happen for him. Saintly hagiographies and popular Christian imaginations might suggest a starker divide for those who enter religious life, but this rarely happens. To this I can also personally attest. Many who knew me before and after I became a Franciscan friar are sometimes surprised to learn that "some things never change" and that I am very much the same Dan many have known for years. Others, those who have only known me as a friar, are also sometimes surprised to learn that I watch television, enjoy beer, and read an assortment of popular books (not just the Bible, for example). Such was the case with Merton in his early years as a monk, especially before anyone knew who *the* Thomas Merton, the soon-to-be bestselling author, was. Merton was also surprised to discover how his life would continue in a similar, if at times different, way along a literary path that he had long ago begun in England while a student at Oakham, a newly orphaned teenager drawn to reading and writing.

Merton likely thought that he was, heroically perhaps, foregoing his literary ambitions upon entering the monastery gates of Gethsemani. However, what William Shannon calls Merton's "gift of writing" was not just his talent or gift to use or abandon. As his superiors would quickly realize, it could also be a gift *to* the religious life Merton now sought to live. Shannon explains the personal conflict of values, ideals, and practicality that Merton faced as he grappled with what it meant to live a religious life, and why he felt it necessary to "make a clean break" and to "leave 'Merton the writer' behind" as he entered the Trappist Order.[11]

> The Roman Catholic Church, to which he had been converted, tended to accept an asceticism that believed that the harder it was to give something up, the better one would look in the eyes of God. In such an ascetic atmosphere, it is not difficult to see how Merton, with the passionate thoroughness he gave to everything he did, might well conclude that it was more meritorious for him to give up his writing talent out of love for God than to use it in the service of God.[12]

Noble though his desires were to live an authentic ascetic life of a good Trappist, Merton's own internal compulsion to write could not be stopped, even by his own forceful will. As a novice, he felt—in a rather scrupulous way—that any desire to write (for he probably saw this as some sign of personal weakness or desire to return to the "secular world") should be confessed to his novice master. Maybe the new monk hoped that his superiors would intervene and give him some guidance about what to do with such desires and impulses. What happened, however, was an expressed intent on the part of his religious superiors that he should pursue some of these writing projects about which he felt so conflicted.

During the early years in the monastery, from 1941 until his ordination to the priesthood in 1949, a period of time called "formation" in religious life, Merton was concurrently engaged in several writing projects. What became his most famous book, *The Seven Storey Mountain*, something best described as a young man's spiritual autobiography, was published in 1948 and instantly became a bestseller. Overnight Merton's life changed. Even before his ordination, the young Trappist was a national literary and spiritual figure. He continued to write, both his own reflections (such as the journal that would be published as the book *The Sign of Jonas*) and projects commissioned or requested by his community or the larger Trappist Order.

In 1949, the Abbey of Gethsemani began receiving seven to ten letters a day from readers of *The Seven Storey Mountain*, posing a particularly unusual circumstance for a community unused to such attention and for a monk who would otherwise expect to receive mail just a few times a year, as was their custom.[13] As one might readily imagine, Merton's experience of religious life was hardly normative, and its exceptional impact on his life and on the life of the monastery was to follow him until his death. This would prove to be both a blessing and a curse for Merton, exacerbating the daily struggle he continued to endure to balance his personal desire for fame, attention, and recognition with his equally sincere desire for solitude, prayer, and authenticity. How Merton dealt with these struggles changed throughout his life.

At times he was appointed to leadership positions in the community related to formation. At different times he acted as master of scholastics and novice master. These are roles in which a solemnly professed monk would have to instruct and guide young monks in their early stages of religious life. On the one hand, it is an instance of poetic justice that Merton was tapped to work in religious formation. The success of his autobiography had inspired hundreds of men to enter religious life in those years, and the now overflowing monastery was, in part, Merton's fault. From a less cynical perspective, Merton's intelligence and natural teaching ability made him a logical choice. On the other hand, Merton often wanted to be a "normal monk," one who could pray, work, and live a quiet monastic life of austerity and anonymity. Serving the community as a formation director would be something of a real manifestation of this desire. The downside, of course, was that it also took him away from his writing. There are, even in a Trappist monastery, only twenty-four hours in a day.

Without rehearsing all the nuances of Merton's twenty-seven years in the monastery, suffice it to say that several concerns were perennial struggles for the monk. Among the common themes were his desire for balance between the routine of Trappist life and the demands and joys of being a well-respected writer. Merton, perhaps feeling pulled by all the writing requests, projects, and other demands such a schedule required, also became increasingly restless over the years, frequently requesting from his abbot that some exemptions be made for him to pursue a more solitary life. Some small capitulations to these requests were made from time to time, including the eventual assignment of a brother monk to assist Merton as a secretary, the permission to live a more eremitical life, and the opportunity to receive visitors on a scale enjoyed by no other monk in the community.

"An Apostolate of Friendship," a Premature End, and a Legacy Left Behind

The last ten years of Merton's life turned out to be rather dramatic. Merton had, at this point, become something of a household name in the United States and elsewhere, and he was a frequently sought-after contributor to several Catholic and secular periodicals. His voice, his thought, and his perspectives contributed to ecclesiastical and popular discourse to such an extent that he achieved the status of an American public intellectual.

During the late 1950s through his death in 1968, Merton became increasingly interested in the concerns of the day, both those of an American focus and those of international importance. One way to describe this decade is to talk about the shift in focus from the life of interior reflection, prayer, and solitude toward a focus on the active contemplation of social engagement. Widely read and highly regarded by many religious and civil leaders, Merton corresponded with an assortment of people including Nobel laureates, American civil-rights leaders, literary stars, and even popes. In fact, William Shannon has argued that Merton's November 10, 1958, letter to the newly elected Pope John XXIII signifies an important liminal experience that could, at least symbolically, mark the start of this outward-looking, world-engaged period of Merton's life and ministry. Shannon describes this letter as "Merton's mission statement" in which the now middle-aged monk lays out his understanding of his religious and social vocation.[14] Merton wrote as follows:

> I hope that I can bring joy to the paternal heart of Your Holiness by sharing with you the aspirations of a contemplative monk who has always loved his vocation, especially the opportunity it offers for solitude and contemplation. Perhaps I have exaggerated this love in some of my books; but since my ordination nine years ago and through my

2. The Modern Monk

experience as master of scholastics and then of novices, I
have come to see more and more what abundant apostolic
opportunities the contemplative life offers, without even
going outside the monastic cloister.

It seems to me that, as a contemplative, I do not need
to lock myself into solitude and lose all contact with the rest
of the world; rather this poor world has a right to a place in
my solitude. It is not enough for me to think of the apostolic
value of prayer and penance; I also have to think in terms
of a contemporary grasp of the political, intellectual, artistic
and social movements in this world—by which I mean a
sympathy for the honest aspirations of so many intellectuals everywhere in the world and the terrible problems
they have to face. I have had the experience of seeing that
this kind of understanding and friendly sympathy, on the
part of a monk who really understands them, has produced
striking effects among artists, writers, publishers, poets,
etc., who have become my friends without my having to
leave the cloister. I have even been in correspondence with
the Russian writer who won the Nobel Prize in Literature,
Boris Pasternak. This was before the tragic change in his
situation. We got to understand one another very well. In
short, with the approval of my superiors, I have exercised
an apostolate—small and limited though it be—within a
circle of intellectuals from other parts of the world; and it
has been quite simply an apostolate of friendship.[15]

Merton's "apostolate of friendship" brought him mentally
out of the cloister and introduced the major players in fields
of peacemaking, civil rights, art, literature, and contemporary
thought to the solitude of monasticism.

In his last years, Merton would publish several significant
books that in greater or lesser ways addressed the concerns
of his age: civil rights and racism, the Vietnam War, pacifism,
ecological concerns, interreligious dialogue, and the like. As we
will see in subsequent chapters, the Franciscan tradition played
an important, if infrequently acknowledged, role in the formation of Merton's thoughts on these matters. In addition to the

now classic texts that Merton was able to publish during these years, other manuscripts, letters, and notes were only allowed to be published posthumously because of certain ecclesiastical authorities who were concerned about a monk's meddling in "secular affairs." These texts were usually centered on nonviolence, peacemaking, and concerns of social justice.

One of the more startling things about Merton's writing and correspondence during that last decade is the prescience with which his words prophetically speak to our own condition, many decades later. Merton's reflections on technology, war, violence, social justice, peace, and so on, continue to speak to the hearts of women and men today.

Interreligious dialogue had become a priority for Merton during those years. Inspired by the ancient wisdom of several Eastern religious traditions, Merton was particularly interested in dialoguing with women and men from those religious traditions, especially those monks and nuns from Buddhist and other communities. This explains his enthusiasm for and intent in accepting an invitation from the Aide á l'Implantation Monastique group, a Benedictine organization that sought to help implement monastic renewal around the world after the close of the Second Vatican Council.[16] The group was planning a conference in Bangkok, Thailand, in December 1968, and the great monastic historical theologian Jean LeClerq had recommended Merton to give a keynote address. Merton's abbot, Dom Flavian, a relatively new superior in the community, gave Merton permission to accept the invitation to Asia, as well as permission to pursue an earlier US trip to various monasteries and communities on the West Coast and in the Southwest of the country. Merton would visit a number of Asian countries on his trip that fall, engaging in conversation with numerous Christian and non-Christian monks and nuns. He would have three audiences with the Dalai Lama and see so much of the world he had previously only experienced within the walls of his monastery. Reflecting in his journal around this time,

Merton remarked with astonishment and gratitude that he was so lucky to have an abbot who seemed to finally "get him," a religious superior who was as enthusiastic about Merton's passions and commitments as he was himself. Unfortunately, his newfound freedom—freedom to write, travel, and speak—would be short-lived.

It was on the afternoon of December 10, 1968, that Thomas Merton took an afternoon shower after giving a morning conference lecture titled "Marxism and Monastic Perspectives." The final lines of his talk have become famous, especially the last sentence. "I will conclude on that note. I believe the plan is to have all the questions for this morning's lectures this evening at the panel. So I will disappear."[17] It is frequently told that Merton then, in a lighthearted and extemporaneous way, suggested that everyone "have a Coke or something."[18] These would be his last words.

Merton's death was, of course, unexpected. No one could have planned for such an exit for this life, at that place and at that time. Yet his legacy and influence live on. Shannon concludes his 1992 biography of Merton with a short chapter in which the great scholar of Merton's work reflects on the tremendous resources that Merton has left this world. His legacy continues not just in the dozens of books, poetry collections, published journals, and correspondence but also in the still unstudied and unpublished work that remains in the archives and repositories at places such as the Thomas Merton Center at Bellarmine University or the Merton Collection at St. Bonaventure University. This work exists in the myriad forms of recorded conferences, notes, correspondence, and other texts. Merton is the type of complex and paradoxical person that, just when you think you understand him, continues to surprise you. Despite the tremendous amount of secondary literature, biographies, and introductions to his thought, whole portions of Merton's life remain landscapes in need of cartography, mysteries in need of solving, and wisdom in need of uncovering. The role of St. Francis and the Franciscan tradition in Merton's life, thought, and writing is but one example of just this reality.

Two Kindred Hearts

While neither of these two all-too-incomplete surveys of the lives of Francis and Merton presented in this and the preceding chapter adequately reflects the complexities, nuances, and individuality of these two great men, I hope that we are able to appreciate better their formative experiences and general history. Placed side by side, there are also some curious, if superficial, similarities that further highlight their kindred relationship across time. One key similarity is the age at which both men experienced the beginning of lifelong conversion. Francis and Merton where both in their early twenties when they started their religious lives. They both had to deal with near-instant, extreme popularity and attention during their respective lifetimes, both experiencing this as a blessing and a curse. Both men died at relatively young ages: Francis in his early forties, Merton in his early fifties. As we shall see later on, the style of theological reflection; the recognition of God in the world; the openness to women and men of other faiths; the concern for social justice; the priority of nonviolence and peacemaking; and the view of God, the Incarnation, and human personhood were all similarly reflected in the lives, writings, and legacies of both Francis and Merton.

In what follows, it is my hope that we can see this truth in even greater detail as I also share my attraction to their lives and writings, and invite you to do the same.

Franciscan Foundations

CHAPTER 3

The Rise and Fall
of a Vocation

The discovery of Thomas Merton's writings was for me as random and coincidental as my earliest encounters with the Franciscan tradition. When I was in high school I worked as the staff sacristan at my home parish. A sacristan is the person who basically runs the ship behind the scenes, preparing the church for all the weekend masses, locking and unlocking the building, and generally assisting the priests with whatever is needed. Even as a young boy, I was pretty certain that God was calling me to ordained ministry in the Church. For those who have never experienced, or think that they have never experienced, a religious vocation, I can say that it's less of a "call"—as in a concrete message—and more of a persistent feeling or curiosity about what life might be like as a priest or religious.

In my youth, I had little idea about what a member of a religious community was, let alone what a "Franciscan friar" might be. My world was that of diocesan ministry in central New York, which was in large part due to my close proximity to that life as a sacristan. When I was sixteen and going into my senior year of high school, I was convinced that I should attend what is called a minor seminary. Basically, a minor seminary is a very small, private college where men interested in becoming priests would study philosophy and theology, earning a bachelor's degree. This plan was short-lived because my parents, wisely, thought that someone in his teens was not ready to begin formation for the priesthood in such a secluded way without first going to a "normal" college (my parents' term) and living independently for a while. At the time I thought my parents were being closed-minded. Now, I think the Holy Spirit was fully involved in their decision.

With the minor seminary option off the table, I decided to apply to several Catholic universities in the Northeast and mid-Atlantic region. My only condition for adjudicating which schools to consider was that the college offer a theology major, because that is what I thought an aspiring priest should study. With my family, I visited schools all over. The final school I was slated to visit was St. Bonaventure University (SBU) in western New York. Because of my busy schedule, SBU was the last campus on the list. In fact, I had already been accepted at all of my schools, including SBU, by the time we were able to visit the campus in March of my senior year. Anyone at least vaguely familiar with western New York weather in March can imagine how cold, snowy, and gray the campus was that Saturday afternoon of our campus visit. From an objective standpoint, it was the worst time to visit SBU. But despite the environmental odds stacked against the otherwise gorgeous campus, I fell in love with the place. So did my family.

I cannot really identify what it was about that place or about the experience that made me so certain that SBU was the only place for me. I didn't know that it was a Franciscan school; I didn't know that Thomas Merton had lived and taught there; and I didn't know that it would be the location that would help determine and shape my entire life. All I knew on that four-hour car ride home was that I was going to St. Bonaventure that fall.

For my high school graduation, I received two gifts that mark the beginning of my exposure to Merton. My great aunt and uncle, as well as the pastor of my home parish, knew that Merton had some connection to St. Bonaventure University. Aunt Betty and Uncle Ron gave me a copy of *The Intimate Merton: His Life from His Journals*, the then newly published one-volume collection of Merton's journal reflections. The pastor of my parish and my employer during high school, Father Donald Karlen, gave me his first-edition copy of *The Seven Storey Mountain*. I had no idea at the time how significant this introduction to Merton would be for me, nor did I realize until years later that it coincidentally occurred at around the same time I would first come to know the Franciscan tradition.

Wisdom and Holiness:
An Intellectual Path to Faith

Thomas Merton's own introduction to the Franciscan tradition was not unlike my first encounter with his thought and the world of St. Francis. Both of our experiences began with books and were encouraged by friends and mentors who saw something in each of us that we might otherwise have overlooked.

As we saw in the last chapter, Merton's embrace of Catholicism and later discernment of a vocation to religious life and the priesthood began with a random purchase of a book. Etienne Gilson's *Spirit of Medieval Philosophy* was, as best as we can tell, Merton's first explicit encounter with the Franciscan tradition. What Merton discovered in Gilson's book was a panoply of creative thinkers and persuasive ideas, surely a surprise for someone who readily confessed to viewing all things Catholic with "hatred and suspicion" up to that point.[1] Whereas he had previously dismissed all things Catholic precisely because he thought them to be illogical, superstitious, and altogether worthless, he now developed an admitted respect for "Catholic philosophy and for the Catholic faith." He was so moved

by the exposure to the thought of medieval intellectual giants
such as Thomas Aquinas, Bonaventure of Bagnoregio, and John
Duns Scotus, among others, that he later wrote in his autobiography, "When I had put this book down, and had ceased to
think explicitly about its arguments, its effect began to show
itself in my life. I began to have a desire to go to church—and
a desire more sincere and mature and more deep-seated than
I had ever had before."[2] Merton identifies this experience as
significant in a way that remained forever imprinted in his
memory. At one and the same time Merton's intellectual and
spiritual lives began to converge on a trajectory that would
lead him toward a lifelong experience of conversion and faith.

In a little-known and somewhat autobiographical essay
from 1950, written after *The Seven Storey Mountain* and not
widely circulated, Merton highlighted how he understood
his conversion—or the beginning of his *ongoing conversion*—to
originate from the intellectual consideration of the Christian
tradition.

> The fact that God could exist had meanwhile been
> impressed upon me by Gilson's *Spirit of Medieval Philoso-
> phy*. . . . The intellectual basis of my conversion was simply
> this: I found that God existed, and that He was the source
> of all reality; was, in fact, Reality, Truth, Life itself. He was
> pure actuality. On the other hand, I found that I had an
> intellect made to apprehend the highest and most perfect
> Truth in a supernatural intuition born of love, and that I
> had a free will that was capable of turning all the powers of
> my being either toward that Truth or away from it. Finally,
> since I could not attain this consummation by my own
> unaided natural powers, I would have to enter into the
> economy of means and helps called "graces" won for me
> by Christ. Therefore I was baptized and became a Christian
> at least in name.[3]

There is a very "Franciscan" dimension to this understanding
of the relationship between the intellectual life and Christian

conversion. For example, Charles Carpenter argues that Bonaventure's understanding of the purpose of theology is, in large part, to inform, shape, and guide believers who study theology—particularly the friars—toward holiness.[4] Gregory LaNave, while offering a different perspective than Carpenter, recognizes that the Franciscan tradition as presented in Bonaventure's scholastic work charts a path from the intellectual or scientific study of theology, through holiness, and toward wisdom (*sapientia*).[5] That Merton would have recognized in his intellectual exploration of the philosophical and theological themes of Gilson's work the unfolding of a journey toward ongoing conversion, holiness, and faith reflects yet another inherent predisposition that strengthens our appreciation for Merton's attraction to and respect for the Franciscan intellectual tradition. How he moved from the intellect of study to the heart that seeks holiness in religious life leads us to consider the influence of his mentor and friend Dan Walsh.

Dan Walsh and the Discernment of a Religious Vocation

A man from the working-class town of Scranton, Pennsylvania, Daniel Cyril Clark Walsh became one of the most influential people in Thomas Merton's very small and close circle of lifelong friends. Walsh was there at the beginning of Merton's discernment of a religious vocation, and as fate would have it, Walsh and Merton found themselves together in Kentucky at the end of Merton's religious journey and life. In 1960, Walsh was invited by the abbot of Gethsemani, then Dom James Fox, to help the monks organize and restructure their philosophy program for the young monks in formation. This would highlight the end of Walsh's earlier career as a professor of philosophy, which began in 1934 after completing his PhD at the University of Toronto. Walsh wrote a dissertation on the medieval Franciscan philosopher and theologian John Duns

Scotus.[6] He was a professor at Manhattanville College from 1934 until 1960 and concurrently taught occasional courses at Columbia University from 1936 until 1960, when he moved to Kentucky. It was in his capacity as a visiting professor at Columbia that Walsh encountered Merton after the would-be monk enrolled in the philosophy professor's graduate course on Thomas Aquinas in 1939.

Walsh's connections in the philosophical world proved to be significant for Merton's own future correspondence. For example, it was Walsh who introduced Merton to Jacques Maritain, the renowned philosopher of the medieval period. But it might have been Walsh's personal relationship to Etienne Gilson, under whom Walsh studied at the University of Toronto, that was the most interesting connection and mutual point of interest initially shared by the two at Columbia. It was just a little more than a year earlier that Merton had randomly and fortuitously picked up Gilson's *Spirit of Medieval Philosophy* and his whole outlook on philosophy, theology, and Catholicism began to change.

However, it wasn't simply Walsh's academic connections and background that caught the attention of the postgraduate Merton. Walsh was, as Merton would explain in *The Seven Storey Mountain* and elsewhere, an outstanding teacher and an admirable individual for personal as well as academic reasons. Merton wrote, "Dan Walsh turned out to be another one of those destined in a providential way to shape and direct my vocation. For it was he who pointed out my way to the place where I now am."[7] Walsh was instrumental not just in pointing Merton to the Trappist Order, a community with which the philosophy professor was greatly impressed, but also in the character and intellectual formation of the young man.

One of the things that deeply impressed Merton about Walsh was the way the professor seemed at ease with reading, engaging, and teaching a variety of thinkers across various "schools of thought." This capacious intellectual disposition was something that Merton believed Walsh picked up from his former teacher, Gilson. It is also something that Merton would become known for exhibiting during his years as a writer. Walsh's largely apolitical approach to philosophy and theology gave Merton a particular confidence in Walsh's opinion, particularly when it came to matters of faith and reason. In *The Seven Storey Mountain*, Merton recounted one of his earliest memories of Walsh after befriending the professor:

> I very quickly made friends with him, and told him all about my thesis and the ideas I was trying to work with, and he was very pleased. And one of the things he sensed at once was something that I was far from being able to realize: but it was that the bent of my mind was essentially "Augustinian." . . . Of course, to be called "Augustinian" by a Thomist might not in every case be a compliment. But coming from Dan Walsh, who was a true Catholic Philosopher, it was a compliment indeed.[8]

What Walsh realized early on in his mentorship with Merton is precisely something that Michael Mott summarized in his biography of Merton: "Walsh had already suggested the Franciscans. From what he knew of him, Merton would make a good Franciscan."[9] Trusting in the honesty and generosity of Walsh, Merton reflected on what it meant to be viewed as an "Augustinian in intellectual outlook," partly with regard to how St. Augustine was so closely associated with the Franciscan tradition in the Middle Ages.

> Therefore, to be called an "Augustinian" by Dan Walsh was a compliment, in spite of the traditional opposition between the Thomist and Augustinian schools, Augustinian being taken not as confined to the philosophers of that religious order, but as embracing all the intellectual descendants of St. Augustine. It is a great compliment to find oneself numbered as part of the same spiritual heritage as St. Anselm, St. Bernard, St. Bonaventure, Hugh and Richard of St. Victor, and Duns Scotus also.[10]

After remembering this comment from Walsh and reflecting on its meaning, Merton suggested to his readers that this really meant, in practical terms, that in the stereotypical way the two schools of the "Thomists" and the "Franciscan-Augustinians" are often characterized, Merton naturally gravitated toward the Franciscan primacy of love and the will more than the more traditionally Thomistic priority of the intellect.

It was clear that Merton, as well as his friends Robert Lax and Bob Gerdy, thought very highly of Walsh. In an effusive reflection published in *The Seven Storey Mountain* that would later embarrass Merton for the excessive attention that he gave to Walsh in this book,[11] Merton wrote,

> I pray to God that there may be raised up more like him [Walsh] in the Church and in our universities, because there is something stifling and intellectually deadening about textbooks that confine themselves to giving a superficial survey of the field of philosophy according to Thomist principles and then discard all the rest in a few controversial objections. Indeed, I think it a great shame and a danger of no small proportions, that Catholic philosophers should be trained in division against one another, and brought up to the bitterness and smallness of controversy: because this is bound to narrow their views and dry up the unction that should vivify all philosophy in their souls.[12]

Merton learned a lot about medieval philosophy and theology from Walsh and was very likely exposed, both in formal classroom settings and in informal conversations, to a great deal of John Duns Scotus's original ideas. That Walsh had written his dissertation on Scotus, occasionally gave academic papers on the Subtle Doctor's thought, and taught courses at Columbia on the medieval Franciscan seems to suggest that the ideas Merton was first exposed to in the important Gilson book were later expanded and explained by Gilson's own former student, Walsh. It will become clearer in later chapters that Walsh's influence in this regard was quite significant. Later, Scotus, an influential yet often unacknowledged medieval thinker, would play a major role in Merton's early theological and spiritual writing. Yet, at this time, Walsh's influence on Merton's relationship to the Franciscan world had more to do with a meeting that Walsh set up for Merton at the Province of the Most Holy Name of Jesus headquartered then—and today—at St. Francis of Assisi Church on West Thirty-First Street, not far from Penn Station and Madison Square Garden. It was Walsh who arranged for Merton's interview with Father Edmund Murphy, O.F.M., then the provincial secretary. It was Walsh who was responsible for leading Merton to the province of Franciscan friars that nearly seventy-five years later I myself would join.

The Franciscan-Friar Vocation Saga

What happened next is one of the best-known, yet frequently misunderstood, events in Merton's famous life. Or rather, it would be more appropriate to say that what followed was a *series* of misunderstood *events*. Merton's interview, initial acceptance, and ultimate withdrawal from the Franciscan order—all before ever setting foot in a Franciscan friary as an actual novice—took place over the course of several months, a fact all too often overlooked in the popular imagining of this period. What most people recall is the blur of Merton's own edited recollection of the desire to be a Franciscan friar and the seemingly abrupt end to that possibility after the confession of some now unknown information that Merton had not disclosed during the earlier meetings with the friars. Because of the emotional reflection that appears in *The Seven Storey Mountain*, it has long been presumed that Merton was "rejected" by the friars, prohibited, as it were, from entering the order. However, a closer look at Merton's own account and a consideration of what little additional information is available reveals a more complex event, one that suggests a gray scenario rather than a black-and-white decision.

So what happened? Why didn't Thomas Merton ever become "Thomas Merton, O.F.M."? The answer to these questions can be traced back to the beginning of Merton's discernment of religious life. From the start, Merton was unsure about what God was calling him to be. Michael Mott has pointed out that Merton's discernment was a process that can easily be described as difficult, confused at times, and generally unclear at each stage. This might have been largely because Merton did not know much about religious life, nor was he aware of the variety of communities that composed the wide-ranging styles, spiritualities, and charisms of Catholic religious orders. Merton was, of course, a recent convert to Catholicism at this time and one who once was, in something akin to the conversion experience of St. Paul, previously hostile to his now newly embraced faith.

There is no doubt that Dan Walsh played the most significant role at this time in Merton's life. How Merton eventually came to believe that he had a vocation to be a Franciscan is frequently attributed to Walsh throughout Merton's writings. On October 16, 1939, Merton wrote in his journal,

> When I first knew I must be a priest, I went to Father Ford, who put the idea in my head that I had never had: of being a secular priest. But it was not long after that, that I went to ask Dan Walsh about it, and he told me to go into an order, suggesting that, from what he knew of me personally, I should go to the Franciscans.[13]

The reason, as Merton put it in his journal, that he should follow Walsh's suggestion was that Walsh knew Merton better than Father Ford or anyone else in this regard. Mott believes that Merton was not at first settled on the Franciscans. He wasn't really settled on any particular order. The only thing that seemed to be constant from the beginning in this aspect of his vocational discernment was Merton's total lack of interest in becoming a diocesan or "secular" priest. So convinced was he that this was not to be his path that he wrote in his journal and later in *The Seven Storey Mountain* that he was pained to go to Corpus Christi Church to acquire the necessary paperwork to apply to religious life because the parish priests from New York kept insisting that he not join a religious community.

Mott notes that Merton even briefly considered becoming a Jesuit but that this feeling quickly passed. Walsh had originally listed the Society of Jesus along with several other possibilities when Merton first approached him about his vocation. At that time, Merton was quite opposed to the idea of becoming a Jesuit; in *The Seven Storey Mountain*, he writes that his primary opposition to the Jesuits originated in his perception of their rigorous life, which is the same reason he rejected Walsh's alternative suggestions that he might consider a monastic community. If only Merton knew where life was eventually going to take him!

The one community that Merton seemed drawn to without a lot of resistance was the Franciscan Order. Merton's journals from this time reveal his fascination with the saint from Assisi and the tradition that bears his name. On September 26, 1939, Merton wrote a very lengthy entry all about Francis and the spirit of this saint who so deeply challenged and inspired him. Despite his then only rudimentary familiarity with the Franciscan tradition, Merton's consideration and pondering about what Francis meant to him nevertheless bears a profundity reflective of a deep appreciation for the theological and spiritual distinctiveness of the Franciscan movement. Among the themes he considered from Francis's life and writings were the authenticity of following the Gospel in the spirit of evangelical poverty (what Franciscans call *sine proprio* or "to live without anything of one's own"), the contingency and dignity of *all* created things in this world, and the gratitude for all of God's gifts.

On October 4, 1939, the Feast of St. Francis of Assisi, Merton went to Mass at St. Francis of Assisi Church in Manhattan and wrote in his journal that there was nowhere else that he would rather be than with the friars singing the liturgy. He concluded that entry with a reaffirmation of what he intended to do next: "But anyway, soon I will have all the necessary documents together and will write Father Provincial."[14]

Within two weeks Merton had met with Father Edmund Murphy, O.F.M., at the friary on Thirty-First Street in Manhattan. In his October 16, 1939, journal entry, Merton again attributes his having met with Father Murphy to Dan Walsh (in this one journal passage, Merton credits Walsh no less than three times for the discovery of his Franciscan vocation). Father Murphy affirmed Merton's desire to apply to the order by writing to the provincial. Merton added, "I returned to Father Murphy, who told me strongly enough he was sure mine was a Franciscan vocation."[15] Walsh and Murphy weren't the only ones to so explicitly name this aspect of Merton's personality. When he approached his local pastor at St. Joseph's Church to get a letter of recommendation for his application to the friars, he was pleasantly surprised by this particular diocesan priest's response, especially in light of the way the priests at Corpus Christi had reacted to his desire to become a Franciscan. Merton wrote in his journal, "Then I went to Saint Joseph's rectory, because I live in Saint Joseph's parish, to get a letter. Father Cassery was fine and enthusiastic and kind, and, of a remark I let fall, said I seemed to have the Franciscan spirit which was a kindness I was floored by."[16]

The specific details of the discussions between Merton and the friars at Thirty-First Street remain unknown. Several pages of Merton's journal from this time were torn out, perhaps by the young Merton himself before leaving St. Bonaventure University for the Abbey of Gethsemani two years later. Likewise, the vocation office of Holy Name Province (the Franciscan community to which I belong and to which Merton sought entry) does not have records of these meetings. Unlike today, when all correspondence between aspiring friars and officials from the order are kept on file, the process in Merton's time was far less formal. What we do have are the recollections of Merton in what remains of those early journals, what he wrote in *The Seven Storey Mountain*, and what he expressed in letters to his friends at that time. For example, he wrote on February 16, 1940, to his Columbia University friend Robert Lax, who would later become a world-renowned poet and remain a life-long friend of Merton's, about his enthusiasm for becoming a Franciscan friar:

> The reason that seemed silly is because I am amazed I ever thought it was possible for me to be anything else but a friar. This has nothing to do with buildings, clothes, hats, sandals, types of salutations, breakfasts, etc. I didn't understand that clearly at first: but there is no reason why I should have either. Now, I do understand the whole thing clearly because it is continually being demonstrated to me everyday, tenthousand [sic] times every day.[17]

We also have, thanks to the exceptional research of Michael Mott, the product of interviews from the 1980s of several close companions of Merton from that time in his life. In light of all of this information, we know with some certainty that Merton and the friars did discuss a few things.

One thing that seems clear is that the friars were encouraging Merton to begin work at Columbia University on his doctorate in English literature. Due to the time in the calendar year when Merton approached the friars, he would have to wait some months before entering the novitiate with the following year's class. In the meantime, the Franciscans, who were then running two colleges in New York—St. Bonaventure in western New York and Siena College near Albany—saw Merton's potential as someone who might work in educational ministry by teaching at one of the schools. This was something Merton himself looked forward to doing.[18] Something else that appears to have been discussed (although Merton's own reflections on religious life neglect to mention this) was Merton's writing career. The friars apparently encouraged the

young aspirant to continue pursuing his writing. According
to Virginia (Jinny) Burton, a woman very close to Merton and
his circle of friends at the time, the friars had clearly given
Merton the "thumbs up" on his hopes of becoming a published
author. As Mott explains, "There are difficulties on the date
here, but it was clear to Jinny Burton and others that Merton's idea of his religious vocation included writing."[19] That
Merton would have been encouraged to continue his writing
reflects both a core aspect of the Franciscan Rule or way of life
and yet another expression of Merton's draw to this religious
community. According to St. Francis's rule, all of the friars are
to work, but—unlike most other religious communities with
dedicated missions and ministry—Francis never specified *what*
the friars were to do. He only proscribed two types of work.
First, the friars could not do any kind of work that was intrinsically sinful. Second, the friars were not to do anything that
interrupted their spirit of prayer and devotion. All else was
possible! Being a friar and a writer are not incompatible ways
of being in the world for the Franciscans. Decades later, when
Merton was already a Trappist, he would receive an ever-
increasing number of exemptions from the regular Trappist
way of life: he received and sent mail frequently; he was given
time, space, and resources to write; he was permitted many
visitors; he was eventually given his own hermitage; and so
on. Who he was did not always fit with the standard life of a
monk, but his superiors made allowances. According to the
Franciscan way of life, who he was and what he did fit quite
naturally, at least in principle. For this reason, Merton was
surely reconfirmed in his belief that Walsh's early recommendation, Cassery's further affirmation, and the stirrings of his
own heart were correct. He should be a friar.

As we already know, Merton never became a Franciscan
friar. To understand what we can about this well-known but
poorly detailed episode in Merton's life, we have to recall that
Merton was told that the earliest he could enter the Franciscan

novitiate was in August 1940. This left the young man with the better part of a year to fill. During the early part of 1940, Merton traveled around the East Coast and then to Cuba. When he returned to New York in May, he packed up his things and moved out of his Perry Street apartment. He had plans to spend the summer with his Columbia friends at the cottage in Olean near St. Bonaventure University, where they had spent the previous summer working on novels and living the life of college students on summer break. Unlike the relatively quiet summer a year earlier, the occupancy of the cottage during the summer of 1940 grew to include a number of friends and other friends of friends. It became crowded, and in late June, Merton decided to move onto the campus of St. Bonaventure. Spending the summer on campus had its clear advantages for someone about to enter the Franciscan novitiate. Merton was able to go to daily Mass, and he became close to the friars who lived there. He was able to talk with them about what he might expect when he moved in short order to Patterson, New Jersey, to begin the process of becoming a Franciscan.

During his time on the campus of St. Bonaventure that summer, Merton had lots of time to reflect, think, write, and pray. Immediately prior to leaving his friends at the cottage for St. Bonaventure, Merton had found himself on the defensive when it came to inquiries and critiques from his friends concerning his decision to enter the Franciscan Order. Some saw him as lazy, simply seeking security, or as Ad and Joan Reinhardt had bluntly put it, "He was simply looking for free meals for life."[20] Others recalled him sharing that he recognized the monastery as an opportune, quiet, and focused place within which to write. Still others accused Merton of only being interested in avoiding the draft.[21] In addition to his friends' incredulity about his seriousness or the authenticity of his motivations, Merton himself began to doubt that this was the right move. Was God *really* calling him to live as a Franciscan? Was he *really* the type of person to be a good friar and priest? Was his past *really* not a problem or an impediment for entering religious life? Of all the possible questions, doubts, and concerns Merton might have discerned and upon which he reflected that summer, this last question is what most scholars believe was the most overwhelming factor in the aspiring Franciscan's mind and heart. But what *was* this past that troubled his vocational discernment so much?

Typically, as the story is generally told, the issue of "Merton's past" is reduced to the experience at Cambridge University some years earlier when the young university student, admittedly immature and rambunctious, fathered a child. This episode in Merton's life, something for which he continued to feel guilty, occurred after both his mother and father had died. Tom Bennett, the friend of Merton's father and then guardian of the student, discreetly arranged for the matter to be resolved. This resolution was, quite simply, a legal and financial agreement that provided paternity support for the child and, in turn, gave "Tom Merton a chance to start again in America."[22] Undoubtedly, this experience and the enduring knowledge of it troubled Merton's heart and mind. Sacramentally, Merton's Baptism, entrance into full communion with the Roman Catholic Church, and regular participation in the sacrament of Penance accounted for the "sins of the past," as Mott describes them. Bennett's legal and financial handling of the paternal responsibilities in the United Kingdom essentially wiped the civil slate clean as well. However, this did not seem to quell Merton's doubts about his own fittingness for religious life, and to make matters worse, the fact that he had not disclosed this part of his history to the friars when applying to the novitiate further exacerbated his worry.

It is clear that his having fathered a child out of wedlock, the legal and financial "cover-up," and the guilt associated with both things became the locus of worry and concern. However, this was not the only thing that bothered Merton during the summer of 1940 as he waited to enter the Franciscan novitiate.

What he understood to be his general proclivity to certain sinful behaviors, thoughts, attitudes, and desires seemed to haunt him, both as ghosts from the past and as specters preemptively tempting him in the future. "I had suddenly been faced with the agonizing doubt, the unanswerable question," Merton wrote in *The Seven Storey Mountain*: "Do I really have that vocation?"[23] He continues,

> I suddenly remembered who I was, who I had been. I was astonished: since last September I seemed to have forgotten that I had ever sinned. And now I suddenly realized that none of the men to whom I had talked about my vocation, neither Dan Walsh nor Father Edmund, knew who I really was. They knew nothing of my past. They did not know how I lived before I entered the Church. They had simply accepted me because I was superficially presentable, I had a fairly open sort of face and seemed to be sincere and to have an ordinary amount of sense and good will. Surely that was not enough.[24]

At this crisis of discernment, just some six weeks before he was scheduled to enter the Franciscan novitiate, Merton packed up for New York in order to meet with Father Edmund and talk to the friar about what was troubling him.

The precise details of the conversation have been lost to history. Merton tells his readers in *The Seven Storey Mountain* that he made an appointment with Father Edmund at which he "told him about my past and all the troubles I had had."[25] The friar's response, according to Merton's recollection in his autobiography and in his journal, was one of kindness and friendliness. Father Edmund, after Merton had gone on for some time about what was troubling him, asked that he have some time to think and pray about what the young Merton had told him. Anxious to have an answer to his questions about the possibility or impossibility of his entering the novitiate in light of his past, Merton insisted that he meet again with

Father Edmund sooner rather than later, so an appointment was made for the next day.

When they met, Father Edmund suggested that Merton consider withdrawing his application, at least for a time. Merton's description of the reasons for the friars' recommendation that he withdraw his application for admission to the order is not entirely trustworthy. While the end result is starkly presented—Merton should write to the provincial minister and request a reconsideration of his previously approved application for entrance to the novitiate—the complexity of the converging factors that led to this unfulfilled aspiration to the Franciscan Order does not come across in *The Seven Storey Mountain*. Likewise, what the friars knew on their end was somewhat conjectural and shaded by Merton's own erratic, zealous, and worrisome demeanor. There was a lot of surmising and a lot of misunderstanding on both ends of the conversation about whether or not Merton *could* enter religious life and whether or not Merton *should* enter religious life.

Whether Merton "Could" Have Become a Franciscan Friar

With regard to the first consideration, whether Merton could become a friar, there was some sense that he ascertained from his discussion with Father Edmund that there might be legal impediments to this possibility. There were, to be specific, two types to consider. The first was Merton's fear of a canonical (Church law) impediment that would prevent him, due to his past, from becoming a friar. Almost two years later, while teaching at St. Bonaventure, another friar and confidant of Merton's—Father Philotheus Boehner—offered an immediate, clear, and distinct response to this question. No, there was no canonical impediment as far as Boehner could tell. As Merton later wrote in his journal on November 29, 1941, Father Edmund actually only mentioned in their discussion the possibility of a "legal impediment," not specifying whether it was civil or canonical. Nevertheless, it seems apparent from his recollections in *The Seven Storey Mountain* and his journals that Merton left his meeting with Father Edmund at least still somewhat convinced of a canonical impediment. With regard to the chance of a civil impediment, it is quite possible that Father Edmund, someone unskilled in the particular details of American law, raised that as a conceivable if unlikely concern. The issue here arises from whether or not the British settlement would be legally binding in the United States. Given that neither Merton nor Father Edmund were experts in international jurisprudence, it is not surprising that both would see this as a specter that haunted Merton's chances of being a fitting candidate for religious life. Ultimately, it appears that it would not have been a major concern had the friars or Merton himself consulted an attorney or did some additional investigation. This step was never taken, however, because the question of *could* Merton enter the Franciscan Order was overshadowed by the truly pressing question of *should* Merton become a friar.

Whether Merton "Should" Have Become a Franciscan Friar

There are several converging factors that come into play when one looks back at the desire Merton had to enter the Franciscan Order. The first is that Merton was already wavering in his sense of his own fittingness and surety that the Franciscan life was for him. On the one hand, he wrote in his journals and later conveyed in *The Seven Storey Mountain* that his aspirations were beyond his own sense of his sinfulness and limitations. He had the greatest admiration for St. Francis of Assisi, and there were times when it appears he could not do justice to living after the saint's example. On the other hand, there are also times when Merton expresses incredulity about or even some disdain for what he interprets as the friars' "easy life." This comes across

most clearly in *The Seven Storey Mountain* when Merton, on St.
Bonaventure's campus for the summer before he was scheduled to begin the novitiate, reflects on the young friars (called
at that time "clerics") who have arrived for summer school.
"Certainly these clerics as I saw them were leading a life that
could not by any stretch of the imagination be called hard."[26]
While he looks down upon what he determines is a "less than
challenging" religious life, Merton nevertheless admits that
the activities that he shared with them that summer brought
him great joy. "I don't think I had ever been so happy in my
life as I now was in that silent library, turning over the pages
of the first part of the *Summa Theologica*, and here and there
making notes on the goodness, the all-presence, the wisdom,
the power, the love of God." Additionally, he took advantage of
the location and recreational activities for which he otherwise
judged the young friars: "In the afternoons, I would walk in
the woods, or along the Alleghany River that flowed among
the trees, skirting the bottom of the wide pastures."[27]

As Merton oscillated between the fear of living up to the
tradition that bore the name of Francis of Assisi and internally
criticizing the ostensible ease with which the young friars in
formation lived their lives, he continued to doubt his own
call. This was something that was surely conveyed to Father
Edmund, something about which Merton writes in *The Seven
Storey Mountain*. He describes this uncertainty and sense of
unfittingness for the Franciscan Order as either God or the
devil asking him a question about his vocation.[28] He writes,
"One day I woke up to find out that the peace I had known
for six months or more had suddenly gone ... then everything
began to fall apart, especially my vocation to the monastery."[29]
His own doubt and lack of confidence about God's calling him
to the Franciscan life unsettled him, but it likely sent a signal
of concern to Father Edmund when they met that summer of
1940. How *sure* was this young man that he wanted to do this?
How *committed* would he be to the formation program?

The second factor that might have suggested that Merton probably should not enter the Franciscan novitiate was the unpredictable scrupulosity that he alludes to in *The Seven Storey Mountain* when recounting his confession-like revelation of not just the child from his Cambridge relationship but also probably "every difficulty he had had in New York, both before and after his conversion," as Mott puts it.[30] While it is unclear that Merton came across to Father Edmund as a religious fanatic or someone who truly struggled with scrupulous tendencies, Merton's own description of his encounter with a Capuchin friar shortly afterward, during which time he burst into tears, leads one to believe that Merton was extremely anxious, feeling guilty, and apparently inconsolable at the time. Regardless of the content of Merton's revelations to Father Edmund, it is certainly true that the young man conveyed some sense of emotional instability.

A third factor to consider was the overcrowded incoming class of novices. While this is perhaps the least compelling and most insignificant of the converging details that shaped the friars' decision to ask Merton to withdraw his application to the order, it is nevertheless something that Merton went out of his way to identify in *The Seven Storey Mountain*.[31] That there was already an abundance of young men applying to join the Franciscan community would understandably necessitate a more discerning approach toward vetting would-be candidates for the novitiate. Merton seemed to recognize this himself, considering his own circumstances sufficient to have shed enough complexity and doubt on the situation that Father Edmund and the other friars were left with little choice.

The final factor to be considered was that Merton had converted to Catholicism less than two years prior to his applying to the Franciscan Order. Common sense might suggest that a new convert to any particular tradition might be so filled with the fervor and zealotry that led to the conversion that he or she might not have settled into the this new phase of life sufficiently and comfortably enough to make such a major life decision so soon. Perhaps Father Edmund wasn't excluding the possibility of religious life for Merton forever, but the confusion and the heightened emotions allowed any opportunity for clarification to slip by. Decades later, Merton himself would offer this factor as the primary reason Father Edmund suggested he withdraw his application to the order. In a 1966 letter, Merton explains, "As you know, I first thought of being a Friar, but that did not work out because Fr. Edmund, down in the provincial's office in N.Y., thought I was still too new a convert and was not yet ready."[32] It seems reasonable to interpret the significance of Merton's recent conversion as a factor that alone might not have been a hindrance to his acceptance into the Franciscan Order but with the constellation of other considerations seemed to be the best decision at the time.

At this point in Merton's story it would seem logical to assume that, because he was not able to become a Franciscan friar and believed that would forever be the case, Merton would abandon this community, its spirituality, and the rest of the tradition that could not seem to accommodate him. However, this is not the case at all. While his formal quest to follow in the footprints of Francis of Assisi as a friar ended the day he left Father Edmund's office on Thirty-First Street in New York City after being encouraged to withdraw his application, the lifelong influence of the Franciscan tradition had really only just begun.

We get a foreshadowing clue in an otherwise odd remark Merton includes in *The Seven Storey Mountain*, when the young Merton tells the friar that he will take the advice to write to the provincial and withdraw his application. Merton explains, "I promised I would write at once, and that I would proclaim my undying loyalty to the Friars Minor in doing so."[33] Indeed, his commitment to a Franciscan worldview was soon to be concretized in the next year and a half. Not long after his meeting with Father Edmund, Merton wrote to his friend Robert Lax to relay the news in a very short letter:

> Dear Lax,
>   No Monastery. Maybe look for a job. I don't think Jinny & Lilly come up to Olean, Here it is nice. I'll come to Olean some time.
>
>   Lv,
>   Merton[34]

Merton did find a job, and he did go to Olean. The job was teaching English at St. Bonaventure, and it was during that time that Merton became a Franciscan in both a concrete way and many intangible ways. If Dan Walsh planted the new seeds of the Franciscan tradition in Merton's heart, then it was the friars at St. Bonaventure that nurtured them to birth.

CHAPTER 4

A Franciscan in Blue Jeans

By the time that Thomas Merton had come to the conclusion that becoming a Franciscan friar was not for him, the love of the Franciscan tradition had already settled into his heart. As we've already seen, and as Dan Walsh and others had told the young man directly, there was something about Merton's personality and outlook that aligned naturally with the Franciscan spiritual and intellectual tradition. While he wasn't going to Patterson, New Jersey, to join the sixty or so other soon-to-be novices, Merton's own months of prayerful and intellectual discernment were about to begin within a particularly Franciscan context.

Through coincidence or perhaps divine providence, a friar English professor at St. Bonaventure had been transferred during the summer of 1940 to teach at Holy Name College in Washington, DC. As it happened, Merton was in need of a job. He had a master's degree in English literature from Columbia, had experience teaching some courses during his graduate studies, and knew the friars at St. Bonaventure personally from his summers at the cottage in Olean and through the connections he formed by way of his friends in the area. Michael Mott explains that Merton had already known about Father

Valentine Long's transfer to Washington, DC, and therefore about the opening of a position in the English department at St. Bonaventure before he left for his fateful discussion with Father Edmund in New York. After the interview, Merton stayed in New York for a while and traveled with some friends before returning to Olean to meet with Father Thomas Plassmann, the president of the university and someone that Merton came to admire and even revere,[1] about the possibility of filling the open English position. He was offered the position and received a letter from the office of the president confirming his expected arrival to campus before the start of the fall semester. It simply reads as follows:

> September 7, 1940
> Mr. Thomas Merton
> 50 Rushmore Avenue
> Douglaston, Long Island
>
> Dear Friend:
> Our Freshmen will report here on September 13. Hence, you may come any time next week.
>
> With kind greetings,
> Sincerely yours,
> (Rev.) Thomas Plassmann, O.F.M.[2]

This particular period in Merton's life is difficult to describe succinctly. It is, without a doubt, one of the most emotionally and spiritually tumultuous episodes, although it would not be the only period of this sort he would encounter. What makes reconstructing the particular nuances of his experiences, thoughts, and encounters so difficult is the way in which Merton had, at the time and subsequently, redacted or reworked his own journals.[3] The accounts and reflections that appear in *The Seven Storey Mountain* and then again in various published and unpublished journal entries of the time vary significantly. Why this is the case is not really clear. What is more unsettling is that there are more than eighty pages torn out of Merton's original journal notebooks, which scholars believe were removed by Merton himself.[4] Merton acknowledges as much in a journal entry on December 4, 1940: "Last night I tore a handful of pages out of last year's journal."[5] We might imagine that these pages, which Mott believes included entries from February through October of 1940, contain more details about his discernment, spiritual and emotional struggles, the conversations with Father Edmund, and the like. It is quite possible that Merton was exceptionally frank about *what exactly* was disclosed in those discussions and was later embarrassed by what he said and then wrote, but the evidence to support any speculation of this sort is lost to history. However, Merton's journals, passages in his autobiography, and correspondence from this time still offer us an abundance of insight into the way that St. Francis of Assisi and the Franciscan tradition—from the historical intellectual resources he studied to the contemporary friars he befriended—shaped his thought, theology, and outlook.

To understand the year and a half that Merton lived and taught at St. Bonaventure University and to appreciate the lifelong significance of what began there in terms of a foundational Franciscan formation, we have to recognize that this time was for Merton a truly liminal experience. Near the end of his time at St. Bonaventure, before he entered the Abbey of Gethsemani, Merton wrote to Catherine de Hueck on November 10, 1941, stating that he never felt that St. Bonaventure was the place he was destined to stay. "Meanwhile, about being at St. Bonaventure: That's easy," Merton wrote. "I cannot even give myself half an argument that this is the place for me to stay. From the moment I first came here, I have always believed nothing about the place except that, for me, it was strictly temporary."[6] Michael Mott explains that Merton entered this phase of his life on the campus of St. Bonaventure with the intention of using that time as something like his own personal novitiate or "way of testing." Mott explains that "he may even have made a trial of himself as a Franciscan (though hardly the order) in a kind of 'ordeal by honesty.'"[7] He acquired a set of prayer books to pray the Divine Office, or the "Liturgy of the Hours" as it is called today, as would all professed Roman Catholic religious communities.

Merton writes in *The Seven Storey Mountain* that shortly after his conversation with Father Edmund in New York, he made a decision to live as much as a religious as he could outside religious life. This was in part what the acquisition of the four-volume set of prayer books meant for him.

> The four books represented a decision. They said that if I could not live in the monastery, I should try to live in the world as if I were a monk in a monastery. They said that I was going to get as close as possible to the life I was not allowed to lead. If I could not wear the religious habit, I would at least join a Third Order and would try my best to get a job teaching at some Catholic college where I could live under the same roof as the Blessed Sacrament.[8]

Merton sought to discipline himself in terms of prayer and study, both of which were shaped by the Franciscan milieu of his environment and his internal disposition. The whole experience at St. Bonaventure is summarized by Mott's description that, after not being able to enter the Franciscan Order to become a friar as such, "Merton was to find another way to membership among the 'tramps of God'—*in blue jeans, if not patched brown cloth.*"[9]

The Franciscan life in blue jeans reached its definitive climax when Merton formally entered the Franciscan Third Order, also known as the "secular Franciscans," on February 19, 1941. This order dated back to the earliest days of St. Francis of Assisi's early movement, when lay women and men—oftentimes wives, husbands, and those in various careers—were inspired to live their Christian lives in a way modeled after Francis's teachings and example. There is a formal rule or way of life that women and men in the Third Order promise to follow, and they prepare to make that commitment after years of study and mentorship in a way analogous to the formation of friars and sisters in formal religious life. In a letter to his former Columbia teacher and friend Mark Van Doren, in the spring of 1941, Merton relayed the news of his entrance into the Third Order and explained it succinctly in his own terms: "Some time ago I became a Franciscan Tertiary, which is an order for people in the world (Dante was one), and a good thing because it has a rule of prayer and relative penance, etc. that has made many since."[10]

Merton wrote in his journal on February 19, 1941, the day he was received into the Franciscan Third Order, that he "was thinking of entering the Order long ago—last fall. Things happened, or didn't happen and I am not in it until now."[11] While he notes there that he recalls wanting to enter the Third Order as recently as the previous fall, it seems that, according to *The Seven Storey Mountain* and Mott's biography, Merton was thinking about the possibility—or something like it—as early as the previous summer. Mott notes that, among the things Merton and Plassmann discussed during his interview for the English job at St. Bonaventure, they talked about "Merton's desire to become a member of the Third Order of Franciscans."[12]

Beyond acknowledging his entrance into the Third Order in his journals, in *The Seven Storey Mountain*, and to various friends, Merton doesn't say much more about the event's practical impact on his everyday life beyond an affirmation of his already expressed commitment to pray the official prayer of the Church and go to Mass daily. This decision was perhaps more symbolic than influential, expressing in an explicit way what he had already borne deep within his heart, namely, a love and admiration for St. Francis and the Franciscan tradition. It would be the personal relationships with Franciscan friars at St. Bonaventure that would mentor Merton in developing what he would call some years later in his journal his "Franciscan side, which continues to grow."[13]

Merton's Friendship with the Friars

Despite his disappointment about not being able to concretely explore a vocation to the Franciscan Order, Merton came to be quite close to several friars at St. Bonaventure, and these became lifelong friends. Three Franciscans in particular played a significant role in Merton's spiritual and intellectual formation at this time, aiding him toward what would become his true religious vocation as a Trappist monk.

The first friar of lasting importance in Merton's life is Irenaeus Herscher, O.F.M. Although Father Irenaeus was thirteen years Merton's senior, they had a number of similarities that helped foster their connection: both were born in France, both earned master's degrees at Columbia University, and both had a love of good writing. Born in the Alsace region of France on March 11, 1902, Father Irenaeus's baptismal name was Joseph. Having immigrated to the United States in 1913 along with the rest of his family, he studied in the public school system in New Jersey until, at the age of eighteen, he met with the provincial of Holy Name Province in New York to request entrance into the Franciscan Order. After his formation and studies for ordination to the priesthood, Irenaeus—the name he received in August 1924 when he became a novice—worked for a short period of time as an assistant "Master of Clerics," or formation director for friars in training for ordination (yet another similarity Merton and he would eventually share when, decades later, Merton himself became a formation director of the monks at Gethsemani). In 1934, Irenaeus earned a master's in library science from Columbia and moved to St. Bonaventure to become assistant librarian until 1937, when he became the head librarian, a position he would hold until 1970.

Merton recounts meeting Father Irenaeus for the first time in *The Seven Storey Mountain* when visiting the campus of St.

Bonaventure with his friends Robert Lax and Ed Rice in the summer of 1939. Lax, whose mother was taking some courses on the campus, introduced Merton and Rice to Father Irenaeus. Despite being corrected by Lax, Father Irenaeus called Merton "Mr. Myrtle."[14] According to his autobiography, Merton was very impressed by Father Irenaeus. He struck Merton as someone who had a memorable energy and joy about him. He lent Merton and his friends as many books from the St. Bonaventure library as they liked, a sign of the friar's generosity. Father Irenaeus's generosity would be demonstrated in other ways that touched Merton personally. Such was the case the following summer in 1940 when Merton moved onto the campus of St. Bonaventure prior to his entrance into the novitiate. Merton recalls in *The Seven Storey Mountain* that Father Irenaeus gave him a key to the philosophy seminar room in the library so that Merton could work there at his leisure, reading and studying the writings of Thomas Aquinas, St. Bonaventure, and others. During this time, there isn't much to confirm in what ways Father Irenaeus directly influenced Merton's own Franciscan outlook, but decades later in a 1966 letter to Anthony Bannon, Merton warmly recounted his longstanding friendship with Father Irenaeus and how, over many years, the friar assisted him with interlibrary loan books. "Of course last but not least was my old friend Fr. Irenaeus, who remains my link with Bona's, as we occasionally correspond about books and other such things. He still lends me books, I have one of them here now."[15]

During his time teaching on the campus of St. Bonaventure, Merton's friendship with Father Irenaeus continued to grow. William Shannon has noted that Father Irenaeus and Merton would go for walks on campus during that time, sharing their lives and talking about faith, literature, and St. Thérèse of Lisieux, for whom Father Irenaeus had a particular love and to whom Merton would later pray as he walked the campus during the evenings in solitude and discernment about a religious vocation.[16]

After Merton had entered the monastery, his relationship continued with Father Irenaeus through correspondence and included a personal visit by the friar to the Abbey of Gethsemani during the summer of 1964. Merton mentions it in his journal on August 16 only in passing: "And on Thursday Father Irenaeus of St. Bonaventure was here with a group of Franciscans and Capuchins. I had not seen him in twenty-three years."[17] Shortly thereafter, in a letter to Father Irenaeus dated August 24, 1964, Merton opens the note with a recollection of the Franciscan's visit: "Well, it certainly was a pleasure to see you again, as young as ever after all these years. I enjoyed your brief visit very much. Thanks for coming."[18] They continued to correspond periodically until Merton's death. Among the extant letters between them are several Christmas cards Merton sent the friar during the 1950s and 1960s, which reflects their lifelong warm friendship.

Another friar who played a significant role in Merton's life during his time at St. Bonaventure and beyond is Father Thomas Plassmann, O.F.M. Father Thomas was the president of St. Bonaventure who hired Merton. As mentioned already, Merton held Father Thomas in the highest regard, stating in his journal that he even revered the friar—a compliment the oftentimes cynical and wry young Merton rarely offered. When describing his encounter with Father Thomas during his interview for the English teaching position, Merton noted in *The Seven Storey Mountain* that "all the students and seminarians at St. Bonaventure held him in great awe for his learning and piety" and that even the local residents of the neighboring town respected him: "Back in Olean his reputation was even greater."[19]

Merton's respect for the stately yet approachable college president and Franciscan friar helps explain why he frequently went to him for advice. Father Thomas played a key role in one of the earliest concrete examples of Merton's emerging views on nonviolence that took place in March 1941 when he mailed a letter to the US Draft Board expressing his views of war and his reasons for being classified as a conscientious objector, the major reason being, "So as not to have to kill men made in the image of God."[20] After he completed the letter, he went to Father Thomas to get his approval.

Merton's relationship with Father Thomas was markedly different from his friendship with Father Irenaeus. For one thing, Father Thomas was much older than both Father Irenaeus and Merton. He was born in 1879 in Germany, came to the United States when he was fifteen years old, and then joined the Franciscan Order. From Merton's various references to Father Thomas, it seems reasonable to describe their relationship in warmly parental terms. This is confirmed in a previously unpublished letter Merton wrote to Father Irenaeus in 1959 after receiving a telegram from the Franciscan librarian informing him of Father Thomas's death. It also summarizes well the deep appreciation and kind feelings Merton had for the man who mentored him, gave him the job at St. Bonaventure, and served as something of a father figure during a difficult time of discernment.

Feb. 20, 1959

Dear Father Irenaeus:

We are just coming out of our annual retreat, at the beginning of which I received your telegram announcing the death of good Father Thomas. I have been able to remember him during my Masses and prayers during this time of special recollection. Thank you for letting me know the sad news.

Naturally Father Thomas was the kind of person that one does not forget. I shall always remember my indebtedness to him for his kindness and helpfulness. He was a really paternal man and a true priest of God, with great love for Christ our Lord, for souls and for his vocation. Generations of students will remember him with gratitude and affection and his memory will be undying at St. Bona's where he was such a force for good.

Remembering Father Thomas brings back to mind that some of the very happiest days of my life were spent there on the campus among all of you Friars, and with the students, under Father Thomas as president of the college. In praying for the repose of his good soul, I am conscious of renewing the bond that exists between me and your community, and the gratitude for that bond. My novices will continue also to pray for Fr. Thomas, who was recommended to the whole community by Father Abbot early in the retreat.

With every best wish,
Fraternally yours in Christ,
Fr. M. Louis[21]

Despite Merton's occasionally conflicting feelings about the Franciscan community at St. Bonaventure during his discernment struggles, it is clear from his later recollections—such as in this letter to Father Irenaeus—that the time in western New York was formative and significant.

The third friar who held a special place in the life of Merton was the most influential in terms of Merton's exposure to and knowledge of the Franciscan intellectual tradition. Philotheus Boehner, O.F.M., was a true polymath. Born in Germany on February 17, 1901, he entered the Franciscan Order in 1920 and earned a doctorate in biology from the University of Münster in 1933. During his advanced studies in biology, Father Philotheus was drawn to the study of philosophy. He translated several works of Etienne Gilson from the original French into his native German. This translation work and his love of philosophy led to a close friendship between Gilson and Father Philotheus. The two of them actually collaborated on a project titled *Die Geschichte der christlichen Philosophie* ("The

History of Christian Philosophy"), which was published in
1937. That Father Philotheus and Gilson were close friends is
yet another iteration of the providential web of relationships
that Merton experienced during his intellectual conversion. It
was Gilson's book that opened Merton's eyes and heart to the
possibility of becoming a Catholic; it was Dan Walsh—a student of Gilson—who shepherded the Columbia student during
that formative time; and it would be Father Philotheus who
became the theological and philosophical guide for Merton's
journey into the Franciscan intellectual world.

As early as September 1940, shortly after Merton arrived
on the campus of St. Bonaventure, he expressed his interest in
studying with Father Philotheus to Father Joseph Vann, O.F.M.,
a friar he had met in New York while still a student at Columbia. He updated his New York friend about the change in plans
from his going into the novitiate to teaching at St. Bonaventure
and added, "I hope that perhaps I will have time and ambi-
tion to do some work of my own around here. If so, I will take
advantage of Father Philotheus's presence here to try and find
out something about the aesthetic of St. Bonaventure, and also
of Scotus, and maybe some day I can use that towards a PhD
dissertation in English or philosophy or whatever department
at whatever university will consider such a topic."[22] Merton
did begin studying the work of several medieval Franciscan
thinkers under the tutelage of Father Philotheus. Among the
most important were Bonaventure, John Duns Scotus, and
William of Ockham. Merton's journal during this time is filled
with notes, excerpts, and reflections on what he was reading
with Father Philotheus. In *The Seven Storey Mountain*, Merton
writes that "here at St. Bonaventure's there was one priest
whom I had come to know well during this last year, a wise
and good philosopher, Father Philotheus. We had been going
over some texts of St. Bonaventure and Duns Scotus."[23] Additionally, in a letter to Mark Van Doren dated January 28, 1941,
Merton relays again that he has been studying with Father

Philotheus: "I have been reading St. Anselm's *Proslogion* and St. Bonaventure's *Itinerarium* with this Franciscan philosopher from Germany, and I am finding out all sorts of good things about scholastic philosophy, and, incidentally, learning to be critical of St. Thomas, which is a good thing for a Catholic to be, I find—and a rare one."[24] What he identifies in his letter to Van Doren as the beginning of an intellectual shift is one of the longstanding aspects of the influence Father Philotheus had on Merton's thought and writing. As we will see in the following chapters, what Merton first discovered under the skilled instruction of Father Philotheus, he carried with him his entire life.

One of the early signs of the immediate enthusiasm and captivation Merton had with the Franciscan intellectual tradition comes through most strongly in the writing of his that was never published. In fact, there are two significant collections of Merton's theological and philosophical musings that editors, censors, or he himself deemed to be too boring, too niche, and too uninteresting to the rest of the world. The first comes in the form of his original journals from the time he was at St. Bonaventure. While many of those texts have been transcribed, edited, and published—most completely in the paperback version of *Run to the Mountain*, the first volume of his journals—portions of his journal from this time consisting of notes and reflections on some of the medieval Franciscan texts he was reading with Father Philotheus were edited out of the published versions.[25] These included pages of notes on Bonaventure's *Itinerarium Mentis in Deum* and *Collationes de Septem Donis Spiritus Sancti*, among others.

Another sign of Merton's enthusiasm for his studies with Father Philotheus at this time comes across in the original manuscript for *The Seven Storey Mountain*, which was significantly edited by Merton, the Trappist censors, and Robert Giroux, who was his editor at Harcourt Brace. One of the earliest typescripts weighs in at around six hundred pages and was ultimately cut down closer to four hundred. Throughout the earlier version of *The Seven Storey Mountain*, Merton makes frequent reference to the thought of John Duns Scotus and Bonaventure, sometimes citing their original texts at length. The Boston College manuscript of *The Seven Storey Mountain* (one of three manuscript copies), the one that Merton sent to Father Terence Connolly, S.J., for an exhibit at the university in 1949, reveals precisely this tendency with pages and pages of reflections on Scotus's insight. So frequent were the references that Naomi Burton, Merton's literary agent, wrote to him in 1946 to request he take some of them out. In response, Merton wrote, "Also I'd like to keep as much as I can of the references to Duns Scotus because even Catholics don't know him, and they should."[26] In the end the lengthy passages were cut, but the commitment to keep them in further illustrates the significance and impact of what Merton had studied with Father Philotheus.

The relationship that Merton and Father Philotheus forged was not simply an intellectual or an academic one. After Merton had visited the Abbey of Gethsemani for a retreat in 1941 and began thinking about the possibility of a religious vocation again, he wasn't sure with whom to speak about it. On the one hand, he was convinced that becoming a religious or being ordained a priest was a closed possibility. Yet, on the other hand, he was still feeling drawn to religious life—this time to the Trappist monastery. During the last week of November 1941, Merton wrote a lot in his journal about this discernment process and possibility. He was deciding between joining Catherine de Heuck Doherty's Friendship House in Harlem and going to the Abbey of Gethsemani to see if they would accept him into the Trappist Order. On November 27, 1941, Merton concluded his lengthy entry with this line: "Now what will I do? Pray? Speak to one of the friars."[27] The next day, he wrote, "Eventually I calmed down, and prayed. Then the idea it would be a good notion to see Fr. Philotheus gradually

crystallized out."[28] That evening he prayed to St. Thérèse of
Lisieux, "the Little Flower," a saint to whom Father Irenaeus
had introduced Merton earlier that year, and then looked for
Father Philotheus at the friary. When Merton found the friar,
they spoke about the concerns the aspiring monk had, the most
pressing being, Did Merton have a canonical impediment that
inevitably prevented him from entering religious life? Father
Philotheus did not think so. "Instantly he says that, in his opinion, there is no canonical impediment in my case," Merton
explained. "And he advises the thing that was so obvious I
hadn't thought of it—go to Gethsemani as soon as the Christmas vacation begins, and tell the whole story to the Abbot."[29]

It seemed to be the Franciscans that initially prevented
Merton from achieving what he believed he was meant to do
in becoming a friar, but in the end it would be the Franciscans
at St. Bonaventure who encouraged, guided, and supported
Merton along his vocational journey of discernment to the
Trappist life. They also provided the condition, context, and
space for Merton to discover his true self, to find who he was
in God. Along the way, Merton was introduced to Franciscan
intellectual giants—Bonaventure, Scotus, William of Ockham,
and others—who would remain his companions and sources
of spiritual inspiration in the decades that followed.

PART III

Reflections on Faith

CHAPTER 5

The "True Self": Getting to the Heart of Merton's Most Famous Insight

In a journal entry written on September 3, 1941, after a Latin quotation of St. Francis's famous *Admonition XIX*, which reads, "What a person is before God, that he [or she] is and no more,"[1] Thomas Merton offers what might be the earliest glimpse of the seed that eventually grew into his most famous insight: *the true self*. Merton writes,

> What we are—our identity—is only truly known to God— not to ourselves, not to other men. The greatest terror of the particular judgment is that, the moment after our death we instantly appear before the face of God and learn our identity—truly; we finally see ourselves as we really are! The measure of our identity, of our being (the two are the same) is the amount of our love for God.[2]

At the core of Merton's understanding of the true self stands the conviction that our *real* identities—each unique, particular, unrepeatable, and individually loved into being by God—are found only in finding God, because God created us, knows us, and loves us for who and what we really are. So much of life, particularly in our modern, hyper-busy, and technologically saturated world, tends to pull us away from the path toward discovering our true self, from the journey into God. We are told in big and little ways every day that we must construct our identities, supplement ourselves with products and services, look a certain way, speak a certain way, and *be* a certain way. What results from following that path is what Merton will call the "false self," what he sometimes refers to as our "masks."

The idea that our spiritual journeys are connected to the quest to discover our true selves is not simply one idea among others for Merton. James Finley has argued that "Merton's *whole spirituality*, in one way or another, pivots on the question of ultimate human identity."[3] Put another way, "The spirituality of Thomas Merton centers upon the fact that the whole of the spiritual life finds its fulfillment in bringing our entire life into a transforming, loving communion with the ineffable God."[4] The life of faith and the journey of the spirit is motivated by and directed toward answering two questions for Merton: who am I, and who is God? Yet these are not separable searches. The answers cannot be discovered apart from each other. In order to discover *who I am*, I must come to recognize that the answer rests in finding God.

While many women and men have been aware of and inspired by Merton's writings on the true and false selves, few have an appreciation for the origin and foundations of his contributions to the modern sense of human identity in Christian terms. Finley has noted that the general ideas of the "true self" and "false self" are not unique creations credited to Merton. For millennia, women and men of faith and good will have sought to discover their authentic selves and God, recognizing that there are many snares and distractions along the way. However, Merton's "genius," Finley writes, rests not in his originality per se but "in drawing forth unrecognized and unappreciated, yet vitally important, elements from various traditions. He brings these elements together in new configurations more meaningful to contemporary [people]."[5]

This is indeed true. Merton was a spiritual genius, one whose intellectual breadth and depth in the Christian spiritual tradition was likely unmatched in his time. While Finley and others have observed correctly that Merton was indebted to "unrecognized and unappreciated" elements from various traditions, the role that the Franciscan intellectual tradition played in his thought and writing on the true self has been especially overlooked. It is no accident that the earliest iteration of Merton's reflection on authentic human identity in his 1941 journal entry follows after the quotation taken from St. Francis of Assisi. It is also no mere coincidence that during the time when he was working most directly on the idea of the true self he was also captivated by the thought of the medieval Franciscan John Duns Scotus. We can see this by looking more deeply into the background and foundation of Merton's "true self." A close look reveals that it was, in many ways, shaped and inspired by Scotus and the Franciscan tradition. As we will see in the next chapter on Merton's Christology, Scotus played an important role in other aspects of his thought, too. But first we will look at the Franciscan influence on Merton's understanding of the human person.

Thomas Merton's Interest in John Duns Scotus

Merton was so captivated by Scotus that in a 1946 letter to Mark Van Doren he expressed an interest in writing a book about the Subtle Doctor's thought. He wrote,

> Duns Scotus and St. Bonaventure are tremendous. A book on that Scotus is brewing, I can see that: it will take time, though, and God will have to give me a lot of special graces if [I] am going to do it well, because Scotus is something big. The thing is: while St. Thomas got off with Aristotle and tended to be intellectual and systematizing, Scotus knew how to take Aristotle and leave him alone and he

keeps the full tradition of St. Augustine and St. Anselm—
which keeps love in the first place all down the line—in its
purity. Also he is the one who most glorifies Christ, that is
gives to the Incarnate Word, the Man-God, the full limit of
everything that can be given Him.[6]

As we've seen already, this admiration for and interest in
Scotus began when Merton was a student of Dan Walsh at
Columbia University.[7] We know it was Walsh who introduced
him to what Michael Downey has called "a profoundly Fran-
ciscan-Scotistic intuition."[8] Downey's comment about the Scotistic quality of Merton's Franciscan intuition is significant
because most people associate the Franciscan intellectual tradition primarily with that of Bonaventure, a thinker who varies
in style and content from the Subtle Doctor.

Also early in his life, we recall the significance Scotus had
for Merton while he was working on *The Seven Storey Mountain*.[9] In his original manuscript he spent so much time on the
theological insights of Scotus that Naomi Burton insisted that
he take them out. Michael Mott describes this: "It seemed clear
Merton was under the spell of Duns Scotus, a name which
might mean something to one reader out of a hundred."[10]
Merton's enchantment with Scotus was strong, for when he
responded to Burton's request, he asked to keep as much of
Scotus in as possible. He also proposed to complete a doc-
toral dissertation on Gerard Manley Hopkins, a Scotist himself,
while at Columbia University. Some of Hopkins's own most
famous insights are inspired or derived from his dedicated
reading of the Subtle Doctor. For example, on July 19, 1872,
Hopkins wrote in his journal, "At this time I had first begun
to get hold of the copy of Scotus on the Sentences in the Bad-
dely library and was flush with a new stroke of enthusiasm. It
may come to nothing or it may be a mercy from God. But just
then when I took in any inscape of the sky or sea I thought of
Scotus."[11] Three years later, Hopkins wrote to Robert Bridges
and included this line about his current endeavors: "After all

I can, at all events a little, read Duns Scotus and I care for him more even than Aristotle and more *pace tua* than a dozen Hegels."[12] It seems fair to say that in addition to the theological and philosophical insight acquired directly from Scotus's work, Merton might have also gleaned some Scotist thoughts from the poetry of Hopkins that he so admired and who was so instrumental during the period of Merton's decision to enter the Catholic Church.[13]

Within a year of writing to Mark Van Doren about his interest in the possibility of authoring a book on Scotus, Merton composed a poem titled "Duns Scotus" that again illustrates the highest respect and fascination the twentieth-century monk had for the medieval Franciscan.

> Striking like lightning to the quick of the real world
> Scotus has mined all ranges to their deepest veins:
> But where, oh, on what blazing mountain of theology
> And in what Sinai's furnace
> Did God refine that gold?
>
> Who ruled those arguments in their triumphant order
> And armed them with their strict celestial light?
> See the lance-lightning, blade-glitter, banner-progress
> As love advances, company by company
> In sunlight teams his clean embattled reasons,
>
> Until the firmament, with high heavenly marvel
> Views in our crystal souls her blue embodiment,
> Unfurls a thousand flags above our heads—
> It is the music of Our Lady's army!
>
> For Scotus is her theologian,
> Nor has there ever been a braver chivalry than his precision.
> His thoughts are skies of cloudless peace
> Bright as the vesture of her grand aurora
> Filled with the rising Christ.

But we, a weak, suspicious generation,
Loving emotion, hating prayer,
We are not worthy of his wisdom.
Creeping like beasts between the mountain's feet
We look for laws in the Arabian dust.
We have no notion of his freedom

Whose acts despise the chains of choice and passion.
We have no love for his beatitude
Whose act renounces motion:
Whose love flies hope forever
as silver as felicity,
Working and quiet in the dancelight of an everlasting arrow.

Lady, the image of whose heaven
Sings in the might of Scotus' reasoning:
There is no line of his that has not blazed your glory in
the schools,
Though in the dark words, without romance,
Calling us to swear you our liege.

Language was far too puny for his great theology:
But, oh! His thought strode through those words
Bright as the conquering Christ
Between the clouds of His enemies:
And in the clearing storm, and Sinai's dying thunder
Scotus comes out, and shakes his golden locks
And singles like the African sun.[14]

From the time Walsh first introduced and encouraged Merton to explore the work of John Duns Scotus until his death, the Subtle Doctor was to have a lasting impression on the thought of Thomas Merton. The explicit references to Scotus in the journals and letters of Merton are too numerous to name here, but particularly early in his religious life such incidents were common.[15] As time went on, Merton was less overt in his naming of Scotus. Nevertheless, the original theological, philosophical, and spiritual insight found in the thought of the Subtle Doctor clearly left an indelible imprint of influence. In some ways, after the first decade in the monastery, the world of Scotus had thoroughly saturated Merton's own outlook.

One of the most fascinating dimensions of Merton's bestselling book *New Seeds of Contemplation* is the captivating concept of the "true self" that has been the object of much reflection and study.[16] Of the many contributions that Merton made to Catholic spirituality in the twentieth century, the true self is quite possibly his most famous, but where did it come from? Most of the research available in Merton studies dealing with the true self focuses on its application in contemporary spiritual, pastoral, psychological, and theological contexts, yet there exist few examinations into the sources and influences of preceding thinkers on Merton's reflections in this regard.

John Duns Scotus (d. 1308): His Life and Work

Little is known about the particular details of Scotus's life. Like so many medieval figures, records and chronicles that feature a single individual who was not a national ruler or pope are scarce. However, there are a few basic facts that most scholars agree upon that help establish a reasonably reliable chronology for the Subtle Doctor. Scotus was a Franciscan friar who was born sometime before March 17, 1266. This date is determined by dating backward from the known date of Scotus's ordination to the priesthood, recorded as March 17, 1291. The minimum age for ordination was twenty-five, so it is presumed that his birth was somewhere around late 1265 or early 1266.[17] It is largely believed that he was born in Duns, Scotland, just above the border of England.

We know that Scotus entered the Franciscan community as a young man (probably around the year 1279) and likely studied both in the Franciscan *studium*, which was the regional house of studies to train Franciscan friars in theology and ministry, and later at the University of Oxford beginning around 1288. Many believe that he might have also spent some time studying at the University of Paris somewhere between 1288 and 1300.[18] We know that Scotus was working on his *Ordinatio*, the revised lecture notes of his commentary on the Sentences of Peter Lombard, in 1300. This is one of the most significant texts we have from Scotus. It was also one of the texts that Merton read in the original Latin with Father Philotheus Boehner at St. Bonaventure and later on his own while a monk in training at the Abbey of Gethsemani. We also have manuscripts of various versions of his *Lectura*, the earlier version of his Sentence commentary. In July 1303, we know that Scotus had already moved from Oxford to Paris where he is recorded as a member of the Franciscan community there. Two years later, in 1305, he became a "master of theology" there. Three years after that, he died in Cologne, Germany, on November 8, 1308.

The last eight years of Scotus's life were both productive and controversial. He continued to revise his commentary on the Sentences, while also writing some smaller treatises including his *De Primo Principio* (On the First Principle),[19] which is perhaps his most famous work. Having been caught up in a political scuffle between King Philip the Fair of France and Pope Boniface VIII, Scotus was deported from France around late 1303 and early 1304. He returned to Paris in April 1204 when a new pope was elected and the king allowed the exiled friars to return. At the appointment of then minister general Gonsalves of Spain, Scotus began his regency as the Franciscan master in 1305 until, in 1307, the minister general sent Scotus to Cologne to oversee the teaching of theology at the school. He died there after one academic year at the young age of forty-two. The combination of Scotus's early death and his frequent movement resulted in the further complication of the Subtle Doctor's work and increased challenges, posed to the generations of Scotists that would follow in his footsteps. Scholar Mary Beth Ingham explains the situation well:

> To a great degree, the events of Scotus's life explain why his works have been so difficult to study and understand.

Scotus's travels during his years of study and teaching, along with his early death, leave scholars with an enormous quantity of textual material in various states of completion. This textual situation accounts for the variety of scholarly opinions on Scotus's positions on important questions, not the least of which are those dealing with the nature of freedom and the way in which God relates to the created order. The complex textual situation has also been responsible in part for the negative verdict brought against him by some historians of philosophy.[20]

Additionally, Scotus's thought is incredibly complicated, nuanced, and logical. He earned the nickname *Doctor Subtilis* (Subtle Doctor) during his lifetime for the difficulty and penetrating quality of his work. This helps explain why so few have ventured to explore his thought and work—it is, simply put, not easy. What little is known about him and his thought has often been reduced to caricature or stereotype, further clouding the popular understanding of his work. That said, he is still hailed as one of the most innovative and creative thinkers of the high Middle Ages. It is likely his genius, insight, and particularly positive theological and philosophical outlook that captured the attention and interest of Thomas Merton.

Scotus and Merton's "True Self"

Among his many original contributions to Christian theology and philosophy, John Duns Scotus held that what made something an individual or particular thing was intrinsic or coextensive with the very being of that particular thing. This notion will eventually come to be called *haecceitas* (literally "this-*ness*" in Latin). Scotus's doctrine of *haecceitas* stood in contrast to a number of previously conceived proposals for understanding the nature of individuals that were derived from either the Platonic world of forms or the Aristotelian explanation of identity rooted in the accidental—that is, exterior—qualities of a given object.[21] For Scotus, "the individual possesses a unity that is more perfect than the specific unity [of matter and form], for it excludes even the division into subjective parts . . . *haecceity* is not just a perfection added to the form and within the form, but a new mode of being that affects matter, form and the composite, i.e., the whole common nature [or universal]."[22] Put plainly, what makes something a particular person or thing is not an external characteristic or quality that is combined with or added onto a generic "humanity" or other substance to make you, me, or this or that tree. It seemed to Scotus that the views that relied upon this type of framework were beneath the obvious dignity of God's creative work. Instead, he insisted, individuation is rooted in the very substance of a thing or person and not simply in its accidents (shape, color, number, etc.).[23]

Allan Wolter explains the significance of Scotus's development of this notion of *haecceitas*:

> [Scotus] makes an important claim, that where rational beings are concerned it is the person rather than the nature that God primarily desired to create. His remark is in answer to an objection that individuals do not pertain to the order of the universe, for order is based on priority and posteriority, and individuals are all on par with one another. Not only do individuals pertain to the order of God's universe, Scotus retorts, but, in communicating "his goodness as something befitting his beauty, in each species" he delights in producing a multiplicity of individuals. "And in those beings which are the highest and most important, it is the individual that is primarily intended by God" (Ordinatio II, d. 3, n. 251).[24]

This principle has dramatic implications for our lived experience of community, society, and faith. Scotus argues for the primacy of God's creative intent in the creation of every single person. Therefore, we cannot limit the reading of Genesis 1:31 to suggest that humanity in general was created "very good" but that each and every person was created *very good*. Wolter goes on to explain that this notion of *haecceitas*, when applied to the human person, "would seem to invest each with a unique value as one singularly wanted and loved by God, quite apart from any trait that person shares with others or any contribution he or she might make to society."[25] In other words, it is not what we do, what we have, or how we act that makes us loved by God and worthy of love from others. Rather, it is *who we are*—individually created, willed, and loved into being by God—that is the source of our dignity and value.

One can see already the appeal of such a metaphysical position for Thomas Merton. The concept of that which makes each of us who we are being absolutely intrinsic and unique carries with it certain theological and moral implications that align well with the twentieth-century monk's outlook. That George Kilcourse has suggested "it is plausible that *Seeds of Contemplation* had evolved as a semblance of the desired Scotus book" Merton intended to write suggests that it is a good starting point to examine this influence.[26] Although there were some revisions and additions to the text when it was later published as *New Seeds of Contemplation*, those sections that most concern us in our study of Scotistic theological influences also appeared in the original *Seeds*. Perhaps the most overt instance of Merton's appropriation of Scotus's principle of individuation, or *haecceitas*, comes to us in chapter 5 of *New Seeds*, titled "Things in Their Identity."[27] Not surprisingly, this is also the chapter in which Merton first introduces his concept of the true self.

The chapter begins with a hymnic reflection on the nature of a tree's relationship to the Creator in and through its simple existence as a particular tree, being itself and striving after nothing else. Merton writes, "A tree gives glory to God by being a tree. For in being what God means it to be it is obeying Him. It 'consents,' so to speak, to His creative love . . . a tree imitates God by being a tree. The more a tree is like itself, the more it is like Him."[28] While Merton's use of a tree in this

case is an allegorical prelude to his reflection on humanity and
the struggle each person has to embrace the true self, his use
of a nonsentient aspect of creation mirrors Scotus's own use
of a stone to initially illustrate his own principle of individuation.[29] This also reflects the spiritual foundation for Scotus's
own theology and work, that is, the thought and writings of
St. Francis of Assisi.

That Merton talks so clearly about nonhuman aspects of
creation giving glory to God by *being what they were created to
be* parallels what Francis writes in his famous "The Canticle of
the Creatures." In that text, Francis presents a Christian vision
of the created order that recognizes the rich interrelationship of
all creation, which originates with God's loving and free creation of the universe. The sun, moon, water, fire, and so on all
praise God—Francis writes—by providing light, life, heart, and
whatever each particular element is meant to do by virtue of its
created nature. It is only humans, he notes, that do not live up
to what it means to give praise to God naturally, because we so
often choose to be someone or something other than our *true
selves*, as Merton would put it. We cannot, Francis seems to say,
give praise to God when we are living as the false self. To talk
as Merton does about a tree giving "glory to God by being a
tree" further bears a kinship to the Franciscan heart that beats
within and so often gives life to Merton's spiritual corpus.

From this point onward in *New Seeds*, Merton's own articulation of the principle of individuation, what he calls the true
self, comes in the form of an easily accessible paraphrasing
and contextualization of Scotus's *haecceitas*. Merton does a
tremendous job, as Finley has noted, of digesting what might
otherwise be very difficult theological and philosophical writing from the Middle Ages and presenting the rich wisdom to
modern readers in an understandable way. Following his tree
allegory, Merton writes,

> No two created beings are exactly alike. And their individ-
> uality is no imperfection. On the contrary, the perfection

of each created thing is not merely in its conformity to an
abstract type but in its own individual identity with itself.
This particular tree will give glory to God by spreading
out its roots in the earth and raising its branches into the
air and the light in a way that no other tree before or after
it ever did or will do.[30]

Merton then goes on to repudiate what might best be described
as some vague form of Neoplatonic individuation. His concern
with the commonly held prioritization of the universal over the
particular, the general over the individual, seems to prompt
his strong reaction to these types of individuation theories.
An example of this response is found above when Merton
rejects a thing's identity as "conformity to an abstract type,"
instead opting for an individual's perfection simply in itself.
This sort of process—the naming of Platonic forms or ideas as
inadequate for understanding a thing's individuation and then
advocating an approach rooted in *haecceity*—occurs several
times in this chapter. It, like the use of nonsentient dimensions
of creation to highlight the universality of *haecceitas*, bolsters
one's conviction that Merton's method, and not simply his
outlook, is indeed heavily influenced by Scotus.

Continuing the critique of other theories of individuation,
Merton asks the question, "Do you imagine that the individual
created things in the world are imperfect attempts at repro-
ducing an ideal type which the Creator never quite succeeded
in actualizing on earth?"[31] This is Merton's way of pointing
out the problems with theological systems rooted in certain
features of ancient Greek philosophies. Theories of individuation that contain latent Aristotelian or Platonic undertones do
not adequately represent his theological outlook, and, Merton
asserts, such views seem to suggest some imperfection with
God. Likewise, Scotus similarly addresses these concerns in
his *Lectura* when responding to the question, "Is a material
substance individual through some positive entity restricting
the nature to be just this individual substance?"[32] A creature's

identity, its inherent dignity or holiness, cannot be an accidental attribute. This is made most explicit in Merton's discussion of human individuation. Merton writes, "For us [human beings], holiness is more than humanity."[33] It is more than the substance humanity modified by the form of our particular accidental attributes. Instead, Merton points out, first using the example of nonhuman creation and then humanity, "Their *inscape* is their *sanctity*. It is the *imprint* of His wisdom and His reality in them."[34] Those even remotely familiar with the work of Gerard Manley Hopkins will recognize his neologism "inscape," found prominently in Merton's writing on the *haecceity* of human persons. As we saw earlier, Hopkins himself associated his recognition of the inscapes of the created universe with Scotus in his journal. Robert McPartland, writing on the Scotist influence on the poetry of Hopkins and Merton, observes,

> Merton's attention to landscapes and objects reflects Hopkins's "admiration for particular things," for as Hopkins writes in his journal: "All the world is full of inscape." Rather than viewing the world pragmatically, in a utilitarian sense, or as a scientist, who seeks physical processes, or like a philosopher who seeks universals, Merton and Hopkins see the thing as unique, individual, so that each object is like a little world.[35]

That "little world" that is really the true self of each human person is another way of describing *haecceitas*.

Merton's identification of each person's inscape as identical with that person's individual call to holiness is a description of a principle of individuation that is a constitutive element of a thing's very *being* or existence. We can recall Merton's early journal entry in 1941 when he likewise recognized the inherent link of each person's identity with his or her very being: "The measure of our identity, of our being (the two are the same) is the amount of our love for God."[36] Whereas the commonly held position suggests an external, accidental quality or character that individuates, Merton is adopting the sense of Scotus's internal and intrinsic principle. Scotus holds that a thing's *haecceity* is *really* identical with its *being*, while also being *formally distinct*. In other words, it is inseparable from a thing's very being but can be considered apart conceptually.

Merton does not simply adopt Scotus's *haecceitas* but instead uses it as the foundation for the development of his understanding of vocation. Unlike trees, mountains, blades of grass, or animals, human beings are not simply left to be individuals in some passive sense. God delights in all of creation simply as it is, because most of creation exists as God has intended it. Human beings, however, by virtue of rationality and free will, have some say in how to live in the world. While human dignity is a foundational element of God's freely loving each particular thing into existence, human behavior and self-understanding is largely subjective. We have been given that gift as part of creation in God's image and likeness. Merton explains that this principle of individuation is the source of *who we really are* but that most often men and women do not realize this. He explains, "God leaves us free to be whatever we like. We can be ourselves or not, as we please. We are at liberty to be real, or to be unreal. We may be true or false, the choice is ours."[37] Human beings have the challenge of being cocreators with God and ultimately discovering the meaning of our existence and our true identity in God alone. Merton puts it this way: "We are free beings and sons [and daughters] of God. This means to say that we should not passively exist, but actively participate in His creative freedom, in our own lives, and in the lives of others, by choosing the truth."[38]

This freedom is also something about which Merton writes in the original, unpublished version of *The Seven Storey Mountain*. It is in a section late in the manuscript, while he is talking about Scotus's theology of freedom and love, that he writes about humanity's "true nature" in a way anticipating his concept of the true self expressed in *New Seeds*:

Our happiness consists in the recovery of our true nature: the nature according to which we are made in the image of God, and in the fulfillment of our purified natural capacities by supernatural grace and glory. Our happiness consists in being like God, being identified with Him, in Christ.

One of the things rooted in our nature which constitutes us in God's image, is our innate liberty. God is infinitely free, because He is infinitely powerful and beyond any other determination except that of His own love; and love is, of its essence, free.

The freedom that is in our nature is our ability to love something, someone besides ourselves, and for the sake, not of ourselves, but of the one we love. There is in the human will an innate tendency, an inborn capacity for disinterested love. This power to love another for his own sake is one of the things that makes us like God, because this power is the one thing in us that is free from all determination. It is a power which transcends and escapes the inevitability of self-love.[39]

The more concretized concept of the true self emerges from a reflection of Merton's on the identification of sanctity with one's true identity or *haecceitas*. He writes, "For me to be a saint means to be myself. Therefore the problem of sanctity and salvation is in fact the problem of finding out who I am and of discovering my true self."[40] This sanctity, this inscape, this *haecceitas*, and this true self are all references to that which makes us who we truly are as opposed to that which we construct or imagine ourselves to be. The context within which we focus on the false self (or "selves") is what Merton suggests is original sin. "To say I was born in sin is to say I came into the world with a false self. I was born in a mask. I came into existence under a sign of contradiction, being someone that I was never intended to be and therefore a denial of what I am supposed to be."[41] The false self is "false" insofar as it is anything apart from that identity, that inscape, or that *haecceitas* that God created. It's a ruse or, as Merton will say later in *New Seeds*, an "illusory self" and an "unreality."[42] Nevertheless, as Merton says in his original version of *The Seven Storey Mountain*, "the essential constitution of our nature is never destroyed."[43] Despite our focus on our false selves, our true self remains.

The way to overcome this false self is to seek the true self, which is only found in God. Merton summarizes the true self's location: "The secret of my identity is hidden in the love and mercy of God. But whatever is in God is really identical with Him, for His infinite simplicity admits no division and no distinction. Therefore I cannot hope to find myself anywhere except in him."[44] Beyond the notion of an intrinsic, coextensive principle of individuation inspired by the thought of Scotus, Merton's thought echoes Scotus's arguments for a univocal concept of being, a philosophical concept that grounds all knowledge of and language about God.[45] This is seen further in the end of Merton's chapter on identity in *New Seeds* when he writes, "For although I can know something of God's existence and nature by my own reason, there is no human and rational way in which I can arrive at that contact, that possession of Him, which will be the discovery of Who he really is and of Who I am in Him. . . . The only One Who can teach me to find God is God, Himself, Alone."[46]

Traces of the notion of *haecceitas* and its related doctrines (such as the univocal concept of being) can be found throughout Merton's written corpus. At times the careful reader of Merton's writings cannot help but sense the specter of Scotus at work behind the theological scenes. Such is the case with Merton's later work *Conjectures of a Guilty Bystander*. It has been generally assumed by some scholars that what Merton is primarily alluding to in his reflections following the now famous "Fourth and Walnut" experience is the mystical insight of Meister Eckhart.[47] Elsewhere in his writing, particularly in his discussions about Islam and Christian mysticism, this connection is at times made more directly. While the influence of Eckhart and others—such as Merton's concurrent reading of Eastern spiritual authors, both Christian and Zen, and his earlier Thomistic intellectual formation[48]—in this respect might have indeed been instrumental, I offer a supplementary reading based on both Merton's earlier work in *New Seeds* and the penchant for Scotist theological leanings evident throughout his writings. Consider the following: "Then it was as if I suddenly saw the secret beauty of their hearts, the depths of their hearts where neither sin nor desire nor self-knowledge can reach, the core of their reality, the person that each one is in God's eyes. If only they could all see themselves as they really *are*. If only we could see each other that way all the time."[49]

If we recall the meditation on identity and individuation in *New Seeds*, we can see here a vestige of *haecceity* present in this experience. There is a sense in which Merton is drawing from his earlier work on the "true self." The use of phrases such as "core of their reality," "as they really are," and "in God's eyes" is evocative of the "true" identity known only to God because of its individual createdness. It is not seen by those Merton is discussing, perhaps because they are preoccupied and unable to see, or perhaps it is not seen because *haecceity* in its fullness is known only to God, for it is a constitutive element of our very being and existence and therefore unknowable in completeness.

Mary Beth Ingham believes that Merton was significantly transformed by the spiritual realization of this insight from Scotus.[50] We can see in his reflection on the joys of being a human being and a member of the human race—that is, the race in which God became incarnate—an embrace, perhaps of a mystical sort, of the radical nature of *haecceitas* that reflects God's love in each dimension of creation.[51] In that same section of *Conjectures*, Merton describes a "spark within us" as that which stands "at the center of our being." It is "a point of nothingness which is untouched by sin and by illusion, a point of pure truth, a point or spark which belongs entirely to God, which is never at our disposal, from which God disposes of our lives."[52] Merton continues, "It is so to speak His name written in us, as our poverty, as our indigence, as our dependence, as our sonship."[53]

There is a sense in which the deliberateness of the tone reveals a concrete reality that is presumed by Merton to be a constitutive element of our very being and relatedness to God. Scotus explains that this *haecceitas* is in fact something akin to the condition for the possibility for relationship. In this respect, the "spark within us" echoes, not only Eckhart's sermons, but also a particularly Scotist outlook that might be the result of his influence on Merton. There is first the sense of Scotus's principle of individuation present in this line of thought, but there is also a more nuanced and complicated feature of Scotus's thought, namely, the doctrine of the univocity of being, as we saw above. This dimension of Merton's reflection that features the "spark's" universality, as when he writes, "it is in everybody," is certainly compatible with aspects of Scotus's philosophical and theological intuitions that elsewhere permeate Merton's work.

Discovering Ourselves with Merton and Scotus

Who am I, and who is God? These questions stand at the core of every person's life and spiritual journey. Recognizing that, from an early point in Merton's own journey of faith, he was influenced by the Franciscan tradition in addressing these points, we are now left to set foot on our unique path toward discovering the answers. It is natural to seek some method or procedure according to which one might systematically or more easily discover one's true self, but Merton cautions against that way of thinking. Using one of his many synonyms for the true self, this time saying "inner self," Merton explains,

> It is clear that there is and can be no special planned technique for discovering and awakening one's inner self,

because the inner self is, first of all, a spontaneity that is nothing if not free. . . . The inner self is not a part of our being, like a motor in a car. It is our entire substantial reality itself, on its highest and most personal and most existential level.[54]

James Finley puts it this way:

Here methods, techniques, ideas, and spiritualities of themselves are of little use. We must not stand in the burning house with a dictionary thinking we are safe because we are frantically looking up the definition for a fire extinguisher! Merton once told me that so few of us are willing to become people of prayer because so few of us are willing to go beyond definitions and concepts to grasp life itself.[55]

The true self, Merton asserts, is not simply an accidental or compartmental aspect of our identity or being but the entirety of our being, as Scotus also states. So it's not a matter of looking more closely from without or keeping in mind a list of criteria against which to search for matching elements in ourselves. Our true self can only be discovered in relationship to God, so contemplation, prayer, and awareness of the Divine is the only answer.

Merton, as Scotus before him, maintains a very Christ-centered sense of what the journey looks like. In *New Seeds*, Merton explains that the act of contemplation—that prayer that allows us to draw nearer to God and thereby to ourselves—is not some "out of this world" experience but the most grounded and this-worldly reality that we can imagine. This is the case because God has intended it to be, by becoming one like us through the Incarnation. God continues to dwell near to us, too. Merton writes,

Our discovery of God is, in a way, God's discovery of us. We cannot go to heaven to find Him because we have no way of knowing where heaven is or what it is. He comes down from heaven and finds us. He looks at us from the depths of His own infinite actuality, which is everywhere, and His seeing us gives us a new being and a new mind in which we also discover Him. We only know him in so far as we are known by Him, and our contemplation of Him is a participation in His contemplation of Himself. We become contemplatives when God discovers himself in us. . . . In order to know and love God as He is, we must have God dwelling in us in a new way, not only in His creative power but in His mercy, not only in His greatness but in His littleness, by which He empties Himself and comes down to us to be empty in our emptiness, and so fill us in His fullness.[56]

The authentic quest to discover our true selves and to discover God, who is already always closer to us than we are to ourselves, means that we are changed by the experience. Just as Christ has changed history in entering the world in a unique way as part of creation, so too our discovery of God in discovering ourselves should change us: "In seeking to awaken the inner self, we must try to learn how this relationship is entirely new and how it gives us a completely different view of things."[57]

Like Finley's person with a dictionary, focused on definitions, concepts, techniques, and methods, and like Merton's people who are unwilling to surrender to true life in the Divine, are we unable to move forward in discovering ourselves and God because of our own expectations, limitations, and desire for control? *If only I knew more, understood more, or experienced more, then I would be able to find my true self,* one might say. Yet knowledge, understanding, and experience don't mean much without love and relationship. And they are not the means by which one comes to discover one's true self. William Shannon explains that there are, according to Merton, only two ways to discover the true self.

The discovery of the real self is achieved (1) through death, which Merton conceives not so much as the separation of the soul from the body, but as the disappearance of the external self and the emergence of the real self, or (2) through contemplation, which is the renouncing of our "petty selves" to find "our true selves beyond ourselves in others and above all in Christ." Contemplation is the letting go of the false self—which is why it is a kind of death, a death that takes place during life.[58]

Are we able to die to ourselves and so live in Christ, draw near to God, and discover ourselves? The journey begins with and returns to prayer. The path is one of life-changing relationship with God and others. The self is what we really, truly are before God—and nothing more.

CHAPTER 6

The General Dance: Franciscan Christology and the Christ of Thomas Merton

Why did God become human? This has been a question that lies at the heart of Christian reflection on faith for millennia. How we answer this question shapes the way we view God, creation, salvation, and sin. There has been a longstanding and popular tradition that argues God would not have become incarnate as a human if Adam and Eve—that is, humanity in general—had not sinned. In other words, holders of this view of the Incarnation believe that it was first and foremost the human need for redemption for our sinfulness that explains why the Word became flesh. Among those best known for holding this view stands St. Anselm of Canterbury (ca. 1033–1109), who is most often cited as the exemplar of the satisfaction or atonement approaches to Christology. Put in simple terms, the idea is that the primary reason God became human was to "fix the mess" we humans caused by our finitude and sinfulness.

Not everybody has held or holds that position. I, for one, never found that theory satisfying, because it seems to suggest that human beings, generally—and through our sin, specifically—are responsible for God's action in some way. How can it be that our sin, something that is objectively bad or evil, is the cause for what Christians hold to be the greatest good in all of history? This doesn't seem to make sense.

Thomas Merton felt similarly and offers a different picture of the reason for the Incarnation, one that centers on God's absolute freedom, goodness, and love. While there are other sources that converge to inform Merton's Christology—among these are the Eastern Christian tradition, scripture, and others—I believe that one of the strongest influences in Merton's personal reflections on Christ is the Franciscan tradition. As with the development of his notion of the true self, Merton was similarly influenced by the thought of John Duns Scotus on the Incarnation. Scotus, who was not the first to express this view but remains one of the iconic contributors to this tradition, argued that the Incarnation was predestined by God from all eternity. This frees God to be God, for God's actions are no longer subject to the sinfulness of humanity, a view that should strike the average believer as suspicious from the outset as will become clearer in the following two sections. Additionally, this approach decenters human sin and focuses instead on the infinite and unconditional love of God.

In addition to the influence of Scotus, the thought of Scotus's Franciscan predecessor, Bonaventure, also appears to have influenced Merton's reflections on Christ. Although Bonaventure did not hold the same view of the Incarnation as did Scotus (Bonaventure, together with his contemporary Thomas Aquinas and Anselm before them, believed that the Incarnation would not have occurred if Adam and Eve had not sinned), Bonaventure did maintain a strong sense of divine *kenosis* or the "self-emptying" or humbling of God in becoming human. Throughout Merton's writings on Christ, this same sense of *kenosis* comes through clearly.

In this chapter we will look at the ways in which Merton's Christology was shaped by the thought of Scotus and Bonaventure. Rather than side with the popular view on the reason for the Incarnation, Merton found in the theology of Scotus a concrete expression of what he intuitively held to be true about the reason for the Word becoming flesh. In considering the *kenosis* of God in the Incarnation, Merton carries forward the tradition of reflecting on God's radical humility and love that is found in the thought of Bonaventure and others.

John Duns Scotus on the Incarnation

John Duns Scotus has long been identified as one of the major contributors to a minority position on the reason for the Incarnation. Commonly referred to as the supralapsarian school, this perspective suggests that the reason for the Incarnation should be considered apart from human sinfulness or "the fall." Beraud de Saint-Maurice has termed these two approaches the "anthropocentric" and the "Christocentric" schools.[1] The anthropocentric school asserts the subordination of the Incarnation to the fall of humanity. In other words, Christ is said to enjoy an occasional or conditional predestination that is dependent on human sinfulness. The Christocentric school adheres to the thesis that if Adam had remained faithful and had not sinned, the Word would have still become incarnate.[2] A position that can be traced back to medieval monk Rupert of Deutz (ca. 1075–1129) and is seen in the thought of certain figures during the thirteenth century, the Christocentric position has come to be associated most closely with John Duns Scotus and, at times (mistakenly), referred to as "the Franciscan Thesis."[3] Scotus generally agrees with the position as he would have inherited it from his supralapsarian predecessors. However, his adoption of that position comes from a slightly different perspective than that of Rupert and others.

Mary Beth Ingham summarizes Scotus's motivation rather simply, suggesting two primary reasons that he held for the Christocentric view. The first reason is that the motivation for the Incarnation can be explained apart from sin. The second reason is that divine intentionality and desire are compromised by the notion that the Incarnation was the result of human sin. In other words, the highest act of divine presence in our world could not be caused by sin.[4]

Unlike those thinkers, such as Rupert of Deutz or former chancellor of Oxford University Robert Grosseteste (ca. 1168–1253), who began their supralapsarian inquiry and contributions to the minority Christocentric school with a hypothetical or counterfactual consideration of what God might have done *if* Adam had *not* sinned, Scotus began with the actual present order as opposed to some other possible but nonexistent situation. This marks the most significant contribution Scotus makes to the Christocentric school, namely, that the Word was predestined to become incarnate from all eternity.[5] The way he goes about presenting his argument is to make a distinction between the predestination of all creation to glory (including human beings) and the need for redemption caused by human sinfulness. In other words, "The ultimate end of creation is God's own goodness as a perfection to be communicated to creatures; it is to share that goodness with others that God has created, and in sharing His perfection He receives glory from His handiwork."[6] The focus, therefore, is shifted from the need to repair the problem caused by sin to consideration of what God's plan for creation is and how God intended that to be accomplished. Scotus explains in his *Ordinatio* that

> predestination consists in foreordaining someone first of all to glory and then to other things which are ordered to glory. Now the human nature in Christ was predestined to be glorified, and in order to be glorified, it was predestined to be united to the Word, in as much as such glory as it was

granted would never have been conferred on this nature had it not been so united.[7]

Scotus makes the point that the reason for the Incarnation rests in the need for all of creation to be glorified and share in God's goodness. This comes to us directly from scripture in Paul's letter to the Romans, in which we read, "For the creation was subjected to futility, not of its own will but by the will of the one who subjected it, in hope that the creation itself will be set free from its bondage to decay and will obtain the freedom of the glory of the children of God" (Rom 8:20–21). This is accomplished through the unity of the Word and human nature. This sensibility follows the ancient notion of recapitulation (*anakepheliasis*) of creation to God found in Patristic writing such as that of Irenaeus.

To further emphasize the repugnancy of sin as the reason for the Incarnation, while highlighting the redemptive quality of the Incarnation in light of human fallenness (something that Scotus does not shirk), Scotus continues,

> If [men and women] had not sinned, of course, there would have been no need of redemption. Still it does not seem to be solely because of the redemption that God predestined this soul to such glory, since the redemption or the glory of the souls to be redeemed is not comparable to the glory of the soul of Christ. Neither is it likely that the highest good in the whole of creation is something that merely chanced to take place, and that only because of some lesser good. Nor is it probable that God predestined Adam to such a good before he predestined Christ. Yet all of this would follow, yes, and even something more absurd. If the predestination of Christ's soul was for the sole purpose of redeeming others, it would follow that in foreordaining Adam to glory, God would have had to foresee him as having fallen into sin before he could have predestined Christ to glory.[8]

Scotus does not deny the redemptive action of the Incarnation but instead subordinates it as a secondary effect.[9] The primary purpose, motivation, and effect of the Incarnation is the predestination of all creation to glory in various orders, which requires the unity of human nature and the Word. Therefore, for Scotus the question of sin is immaterial insofar as the primary motivation for the Incarnation and the predestination of Christ are concerned. The Incarnation was inevitable because of God's love for creation. Or, as George Kilcourse once summarized it so well, "Scotus's cosmic Christ was not an afterthought of God, but God's first thought, the paradigm of creation, revealing the innate capacity of the human person to be fulfilled in love."[10]

Merton's View of the Incarnation

Thomas Merton found this perspective extremely compelling. The influence of Scotus's thought, already explored above in terms of *haecceitas* and the true self, comes through Merton's work strongly at various points. Likewise, the Christological outlook that Merton appropriates and reflects upon is Christocentric and certainly indebted to the thought of Scotus. Additionally, Merton might have been influenced further by his reading of Robert Grosseteste, Scotus's predecessor in the supralapsarian school, during his time at St. Bonaventure.[11] There are two texts of Merton's that illustrate the Scotist, Christocentric, and supralapsarian view of the Incarnation well. The first, *New Seeds of Contemplation*, is also the fecund location of Merton's engagement with Scotus's *haecceity* in his effort to elucidate what one's identity really is. The second, *The New Man*, is a text that is often overlooked by Merton scholars, perhaps because so many view it, as one critic wrote, as "a book mixing autobiographical soliloquy with pages of dry notes."[12] One notable exception is Christopher Pramuk, who, in his recent study of Merton's sophiological Christology, writes, "*The New Man* reflects Merton's masterful ability to weave together a theological vision from a dizzying range of sources," among which is counted Scotus.[13] I suggest that, although Merton was indeed concurrently influenced by several sources, the place of Scotus in his theology of the Incarnation deserves particular consideration, if not pride of place.

The last chapter of *New Seeds*, "The General Dance," is a key example of the presence of Scotus's influence in Merton's Christological thought. In the second paragraph of the chapter, Merton writes,

> The Lord made the world and made man in order that He Himself might descend into the world, that He Himself might become Man. When He regarded the world He was about to make He saw His wisdom, as a man-child, "playing in the world, playing before Him at all times." And He reflected, "My delights are to be with the children of men." The world was not made as a prison for fallen spirits who were rejected by God: this is the Gnostic error. The world was made as a temple, a paradise, into which God Himself would descend to dwell familiarly with the spirits He had placed there to tend it for Him.[14]

This reflection on divine intentionality with a strong sense of cosmic Christology echoes Scotus's own concern about the absolute present order in place of earlier supralapsarian perspectives on the Incarnation that were largely counterfactual or hypothetical in nature. Merton asserts that the Incarnation, God's own descent into the world to live as a human person, was part of the plan for creation from the beginning. The distinction might not at first be clear, but it is of notable importance that the starting point of Merton's reflection—and that of Scotus before him—on the *reason* for the Incarnation is God's intentionality in opposition to the much more popular supralapsarian view that relied on the question, "What if Adam had not sinned?"[15] This is further emphasized by Merton's association of this assertion with a reflection on the Genesis accounts of humanity's creation. Merton sees in God's decision to create men and women in God's image and likeness an expression of the cosmic Christocentricity of creation as a whole. "God creates things by seeing them in His own Logos," Merton writes of the second person of the Trinity's place in the act of creation.[16] Here we recall the hymnic creation verse in the letter to the Colossians: "He is the image of the invisible God, the firstborn of all creation; for in him all things in heaven and on earth were created, things visible and invisible" (Col 1:15–16). Christ is the center and the "blueprint" for creation, through him and in whom all is created, from the beginning. Merton, citing the letter to the Colossians in part, explains, "The Word of God Himself was the 'firstborn of every creature.' He 'in Whom all things consist' was not only to walk with man in the breeze after noon, but would also become Man, and dwell with man as a brother."[17]

Like Scotus, Merton does not artificially separate creation from the fall of humanity in sin, thereby segregating the creative act of God from the redemptive and saving act of the Incarnation. Instead, they are intimately tied together as one and the same thing. Scotus maintained that it was God's predestination of all creation to glory (therefore, Christ preceding) in divine love that was the reason for the Incarnation. Likewise, Merton holds a similar view of the relationship between divine love in the predestination of all creation to glory and the reason for the Incarnation.

> The Lord would not only love His creation as Father, but He would enter into His creation, emptying Himself, hiding Himself, as if He were not God but a creature. Why should He do this? Because He loved His creatures, and because He could not bear that His creatures should merely adore Him as distant, remote, transcendent and all powerful.[18]

Love holds primacy in the cosmic Christology of Merton as it similarly does in Scotus's doctrine of the absolute predestination of Christ.

Merton sees in the kenotic and cosmically Christocentric dimensions of the Incarnation certain implications for every human person. In a wonderfully summarizing journal entry on March 25, 1960 (which happened to be the Feast of the Annunciation), about different approaches to a theology of the Incarnation, Merton wrote,

> One thing Christ has said: "He who sees me sees the Father also." In emptying Himself to come into the world, God has not simply kept in reserve, in a safe place, His reality and manifested a kind of shadow or symbol of Himself. He has emptied Himself and is all in Christ. Invisibilis in suis; visibilis in nostris [Invisible in his own; visible in ours]. Christ is not simply the tip of the little finger of the Godhead, moving in the world, easily withdrawn, never threatened, never really risking anything. God has acted and given Himself totally, without division, in the Incarnation. He has become not only one of us but even our very selves.[19]

Merton not only holds Christ as the true God-as-human but also sees in the very action of God's becoming human a key element of Christian faith, for it is through Christ that we are able to see God as God truly is—humble, loving, forgiving, and poor. To say "Christ" is, at one and the same time, to say this is who God is and this is who *we are called to be*. For Merton, Christ is the center of everything, a view he notes in his 1965 journal when he writes that "Christ" is "at the center and heart of all reality, as a source of grace and love."[20]

Bonaventure likewise affirms the centrality of Christ, as when he wrote at the end of his life, "It is necessary to begin with the center, that is, with Christ. For He is the Mediator between God and humanity, holding the central position in all things, as will become clear."[21] In his famous spiritual mediation, *The Journey of the Soul into God*, Bonaventure ties together the centrality of Christ, the humbling of God in the Incarnation,

and the meaning this has for humanity in a way that antici-
pates Merton's own views.

> When in Christ, the Son of God, who is by nature the image
> of the invisible God, our mind contemplates our humanity
> so wonderfully exalted and so ineffably united, and when
> it sees at one time in one Being the first and the last, the
> highest and the lowest, the circumference and the center,
> the Alpha and the Omega, the caused and the cause, the
> Creator and the creature, that is, the book written within
> and without, it reaches something perfect.[22]

Like Bonaventure who saw Christ as the key, the centerpiece
of all reality and faith, Merton recognized the tremendous significance of Christ for him as an individual human being and
member of creation, as well as for the whole human family. In
a 1965 journal entry, Merton enthusiastically tied together the
humility of God in the *kenosis* of the Incarnation with what it
means to be truly, authentically human.

> The joy that I am *man*! This fact, that I am a man, is a theo-
> logical truth and mystery. God became man in Christ. In
> becoming what I am He united me to Himself and made
> me His epiphany, so that now I am meant to reveal Him,
> and my very existence as true man depends on this, that by
> my freedom I obey His light, thus enabling Him to reveal
> Himself in me. And the first to see this revelation is my
> own self. I am His mission to myself and through myself to
> all men. How can I see Him or receive Him if I despise or
> fear what I am—man? How can I love what I am—man—if
> I hate man in others?[23]

George Kilcourse, in discussing Merton's "turn to the kenotic
Christ," summarizes this type of Christological insight well:
"The achievement of Thomas Merton was his discovery in the
humanity of Christ of a paradigm for our religious self-under-
standing."[24] There is, in passages such as this, an ethical tone to
Merton's view that God's decision to become a human being

necessarily says something about each and every human person and his or her inherent dignity and value. All ethical consideration arises from a realization that who God is in Christ is the model for authentic human living and that revelation is only made possible by God's free and humble decision to empty God's self to become one like us out of love. In this spirit, Merton wrote, "And indeed, if Christ became Man, it is because He wanted to be any man and every man. If we believe in the Incarnation of the Son of God, there should be no one on earth in whom we are not prepared to see, in mystery, the presence of Christ."[25] It should come, then, as no surprise that this passage appears in *New Seeds* at the very end of the book, within Merton's closing reflection on the true self and false self, which, as we have already seen, is deeply indebted to Scotus's doctrine of *haecceitas*. That Merton's reflection on the *haecceity* of each person bears such close proximity to his supralapsarian consideration of the reason for the Incarnation in *New Seeds* is not likely a chance occurrence but instead another attestation of Scotus's influence on Merton's thought.

Another noteworthy instance of Merton's indebtedness to Scotus concerning his unique contributions to a supralapsarian approach to the Incarnation is found in the sixth chapter of *The New Man*, titled "The Second Adam." Merton takes an explicitly scriptural starting point in this reflection, offering insight into the meaning of the term "second Adam" as found in Paul's writing. He begins the chapter with a refutation of an overly simplistic consideration of the term "second Adam."

> To say no more would be to imply, as preachers so often imply, that Adam was, so to speak a "first attempt" that failed, and that the Lord was compelled to make good this first "failure" with a second attempt which succeeded, and which would not even have been necessary if the first had not failed. In this view, Christ would be in every sense "second" to Adam, except, of course, for the fact that He is God. He would be, in other words, an "afterthought."[26]

Certainly, Merton continues, this is not what the New Testament authors mean. Furthermore, Merton takes this opportunity to again repeat Scotus's concern about the absolute present order and not simply a hypothetical consideration of the Incarnation, this time drawing on scripture as the source for this supralapsarian interpretation. "Quite apart from the speculative argument that divides scholastic theologians on the question whether there would have been an Incarnation if Adam had not sinned, the New Testament writers clearly see Adam as completely subordinated and secondary to Christ; from the very beginning, Adam points to Christ."[27]

Merton's supralapsarian and Christocentric reflection on the motive for the Incarnation serves as the starting point for further consideration of the implications of the Incarnation in understanding the meaning of human existence and creation. This portion of Merton's Christological, and subsequently anthropological, engagement bears distinctively Pauline marks. Beyond the language of "second Adam," Merton draws on texts such as Colossians 1:15–17, as he did in *New Seeds*, from which we again see his interest in connecting the event of the Incarnation with the act of creation. Christ, for Merton as for Scotus, is the exemplar, model, and center of all creation. As such, Christ comes "before Adam not only because He is more perfect, has a more exalted dignity, a greater power, but also because in Him Adam is created, like everything else in heaven and on earth."[28] This cosmic Christology at the center of Merton's reflection reveals, as Ilia Delio notes, "a mystic who has plumbed the depth of divine mystery to enter the heart of humanity and the heart of the world."[29] This mystical expression of Christological doctrine finds further elucidation in Merton's meditation on the character of creation in light of the Incarnation.

> Creation is created and sustained in Him and by Him. And when He enters into it, He will simply make clear the fact that He is already, and has always been, the center

and the life and the meaning of a universe that exists only by His will. To us no doubt, this all seems very strange, because all the Gospel narratives of the Incarnation suggest that God enters into His own world as a stranger and an alien. But that is because we have our own peculiar ideas of proprietorship and possession. The hiddenness, the unobtrusiveness, the simplicity of Christ as Man are simply another manifestation of the simplicity, the unobtrusiveness and hiddenness of God Himself, living and acting in the world.[30]

This mystical consideration of the cosmic Christ in and through whom creation comes into being reflects Scotus's primacy of Christ in a particular way but also mirrors the more general Franciscan tradition of the humility of God, which is an influence in the kenotic impulse that Merton's Christology tends to emulate.[31]

Following Scotus, Merton does not dismiss or diminish the redemptive value of the Incarnation but instead subordinates it as an effect of the Incarnation and not the cause. Merton describes the reparation of the fall in terms of "the reorientation of all human life" expressed in terms of the parable of the lost sheep.[32] "The Second Adam comes down to find man in the depths of confusion, in the moral chaos and disintegration into which he has been plunged by the sins of the first Adam and of all our other ancestors. Christ finds Adam, the 'human race,' like the Lost Sheep and carries him back by the way he came in his wandering from the truth."[33] Through the Incarnation, this reorientation of human living—from sin to truth and from death to life—is accomplished. It is accomplished through the very act of God's recapitulation, the return of all creation back to God in Christ, but also through the reminder of who *we are* in Christ. Merton maintains that the notion of the false self is closely linked to the concept of original sin or, to put it another way, original forgetfulness. We no longer recall who it is we really are; we have forgotten our true self.

Like the lost sheep, we are on the wrong path. In God's very living, walking, and breathing among us, we are shown who it is we are by seeing and knowing who God is. In this way, an effect of the redemption that comes through the event of the Incarnation is, to return to the title of Merton's book, that we are made *new men* and *women*.

CHAPTER 7

Paradise Consciousness: Modern Spirituality of Creation in a Franciscan Key

Unlike other aspects of Thomas Merton's life, thought, and writing, the Franciscan hue that colors his understanding of creation does not appear to have arisen from studying certain texts or being mentored by Franciscan friars. Instead, Merton's awareness of the created world as it really is—deeply interconnected by the Spirit of God and foundationally interdependent in a way that humanity oftentimes chooses to ignore—seems to have emerged from within his heart and from an early age. In a sense, it might not be quite accurate to describe Merton's spirituality of creation as "Franciscan" per se for that reason. Yet, I believe that there is something distinctive about the echoes found in Merton's writing and reflection that can only be described as Franciscan in the truest and most unique way.

The similarities between the Franciscan theological tradition on the topic of creation and Merton's own outlook might otherwise be viewed as coincidental if taken by themselves. However, situated within the broader context of Merton's

Franciscan disposition and affinity, one is left with an appreciation for the possibility that Merton arrived at this consciousness of creation in a Franciscan "key." Kathleen Deignan has
put it in another way: "In true Franciscan spirit, Merton could
sense the 'angelic transparency of everything, of pure, simple
and total light.'"[1] Creation therefore stands as a theme alongside other examples of the way the Franciscan tradition influenced Merton's worldview and spirituality, if only in a slightly
more subtle way than his understanding of the true self or the
Incarnation.

The spirituality of creation that is found throughout Merton's journals, letters, and other writings can be understood
in terms of a threefold movement. First, Merton begins to see
in a new way. This is a consciousness, an awakening, and an
eye-opening movement from the seclusion of one's human selfishness and self-centeredness toward a realization of the harmony of creation and humanity's call to become aware of that
symphonic tune. In a way different than his evolving interest
in and gradual appropriation of other Christian theological and
spiritual doctrines (which required serious study and deliberate reflection), Merton's awareness of creation and the way it
spoke to him can be seen in his work from the outset. There
are hints of this sensitivity and appreciation for the mountains,
trees, animals, insects, and elements of nature in his earliest
journals and correspondence. As Merton became more exposed
to the Christian tradition, sought Baptism, and discerned a
call to religious life, his consciousness blossomed in ways that
might rightly be described as mystical. The Franciscan spiritual tradition, particularly as developed in Bonaventure's
understanding of contemplation, offers a concrete approach to
understanding this creation mysticism and the ongoing process
of seeing the world anew.

Second, in addition to a growing consciousness of the created order, Merton also understood each element of the created
order as a vestige of God. The term "vestige" is used in modern

English to refer to something that has disappeared or to some part of an organism that no longer functions in a practical way. In theological discourse, "vestige" is more closely tied to the original Latin root, *vestigium*, which means "footprint." The medieval Franciscan Bonaventure was best known for developing a theology of creation that highlighted the ways in which everything that was created by God was, in a sense, a vestige of the Creator. In other words, everything that exists reflects or points back to its Creator. Each tree, blade of grass, bird, and so forth bears the imprint (*vestigium*) of the God who lovingly willed that aspect of the created order into existence. Merton holds a similar view of creation. A telling acknowledgment of this view and its connection to the Franciscan tradition appears in a 1967 letter Merton wrote to a young man who had sent him a letter asking several questions. "My idea of the world: first of all the world as God's good creation. I have the good fortune to live in close contact with nature, how should I not love this world, and love it with passion? I understand the joy of St. Francis amid the creatures! God manifests himself in his creation, and everything that he has made speaks of him."[2] We will take a closer look at Bonaventure's theology of vestiges and the passages from Merton's writing on creation that offer similar reflections, which will help us appreciate better this significant theme in the twentieth-century monk's thought.

Third, Merton's reflections on creation exhibit a recognition of what has been in recent years called a "kinship model of creation." A deeply Franciscan theological and spiritual tradition, this outlook can be traced back to Francis of Assisi himself and found at various points in the writings of Franciscan thinkers over the course of eight hundred years.[3] While Francis exemplifies this paradigm and is perhaps the best-known proponent of this intuitive understanding of our deeply ingrained relationship with the rest of the created order, the kinship model finds its roots in both the Hebrew and Christian scriptures. It is difficult to establish a causal relationship between the Franciscan contribution to a theology of kinship and Merton's consistent reflection in that key. But such a connection is not really necessary. Rather, what is important here is to see how Merton's own approach—whether independently intuited, garnered from scripture, or directly influenced by the Franciscan tradition—aligns with and echoes this unique way of looking at creation and our place as part of that same creation.

In this chapter, we will take a look at these three movements in Merton's thought, alongside their echoes within the Franciscan tradition. There is no clear linear stage of development or straight path to follow in tracing these themes in Merton's writings or in the Franciscan tradition. This is perhaps why so few have delved into this aspect of Merton's thought. Rather, all three of these spiritual and theological movements intertwine with each other, ebb and flow throughout Merton's writings, and develop over the course of his lifetime. It is my hope that in exploring these aspects of Merton's modern spirituality of creation, we might become attuned to the sound of the Franciscan key in which Merton's own outlook was played and then open our eyes, see the vestiges of God present everywhere, and recognize our kinship with the rest of creation.

Merton's Paradise Consciousness

As we have already seen from the biographical sketch of Merton's life in chapter 2, his discernment of a vocational call to Franciscan life in chapter 3, and his ultimate arrival at the gate of the Abbey of Gethsemani by way of St. Bonaventure University in chapter 4, it is clear that Merton did not experience a singular conversion in life and worldview.[4] Instead, he grew to appreciate his call from God, the Christian call to engage the world, and the relationship that humanity has with the rest of the created order slowly and over time. Toward what would ultimately be the end of his life, Merton began to become aware of the emerging "ecological movement" of the

1960s, a movement marked by the publication of iconic books such as Rachel Carson's *Silent Spring* (1962) and Roderick Nash's *Wilderness and the American Mind* (1967).[5] Merton read both of these texts and corresponded with many other people concerned about the sense of urgency the postindustrial and postwar age brought to the ecological landscape of the United States at the time.

There might be an understandable temptation to interpret Merton's more explicit engagement with and reflection on the environment during the 1960s as a sign of a new awareness of creation. However, as Patrick O'Connell explains in a 2010 article about the sources of Merton's environmental spirituality,

> while the sense of urgency was new, Merton's recognition that a commitment to cherish and protect the environment is an integral dimension of the Christian life was rooted in his deep appreciation of the sacramentality of the natural world, of creation as a sign of the Creator, that was already developing at the time of his conversion in 1938 and continued to deepen as he immersed himself in the resources of the Christian theological and spiritual tradition throughout the course of his monastic life.[6]

Among these "resources of the Christian theological and spiritual tradition" in which Merton would become immersed during his time before *and* after his entrance into the monastery stand those thinkers and texts of Franciscan intellectual tradition.

O'Connell points out that among the first mentions of St. Francis in Merton's journal is a reference to the saint's sermon to the birds. On September 26, 1939, Merton wrote,

> Saint Francis in his sermon to the birds told them first of all how grateful the birds must be to God who gave them their coats of fine feathers for which they did not have to toil and spin, and for giving them the air as their element.

So they should never, then, be ungrateful to him: but they should go everywhere praising him.

Thus first he told them what they already knew, of the great love and goodness of God. After that he told them never to be ungrateful to God, but always to praise him and glorify His Name.[7]

There is a sense in which Merton's early journal entry on Francis is a superficial reading of the saint's actions, which is not an uncommon understanding. The context for the story highlights the respect Francis has for other-than-human animals in presupposing that they would listen to the proclaimed Word of God without protest, whereas human beings often choose to ignore it outright. Nevertheless, that Merton was moved to consider this Franciscan episode and record it points to the early association that the new convert made between the Franciscan tradition and creation, which O'Connell observes in his study.

It is clear that Merton's awareness of creation grew during his time reading more about the Franciscan tradition and other Christian sources, but there are also other indicators that Merton might have had an even earlier sensitivity to the natural world around him. Kathleen Deignan has suggested that Merton's father played an early and formative role in his ability to see the world through the lens of paradise consciousness.

His father's mentorship influenced his abidingly vivid sense of geography and the confluence of art and nature in his sensibility. He inherited his father's intense and disciplined way of looking at the world, which Merton would later translate into a painterliness of language in describing it. Such training in "natural contemplation" became the foundation of his psychic life, and the ground of his experience of the divine, such that at an early age his religious instinct went skyward.[8]

Like O'Connell and Deignan, Monica Weis recognized the significant and dynamic history of Merton's growing awareness of creation. She structures her book *The Environmental Vision of Thomas Merton* (2011) in a way that seeks to trace the contours of Merton's lifelong experience of ecological conversion. Like Deignan, Weis also suggests that Merton's artist father played a formative role in the future monk's "learning to see" the world around him.[9] In addition to his father's influence, Weis argues that clues from Merton's childhood, particularly those preserved in a journal kept by his mother titled *Tom's Book*, offer us invaluable insight into the creational outlook of the young boy. Weis explains,

> It is not unreasonable to believe that at least some of [Merton's] outdoor time was spent near his father's painting sites and that patterns of light and color—from nature and from the canvas—became part of Merton's informal schooling. "When we go out," writes his mother, "he seems conscious of everything. Sometimes he puts up his arms and cries out 'Oh Sun! Oh joli!' Often he throws himself on the ground to see the 'cunnin' little ants' (where he learned that expression, I do not know!)."[10]

Even as a little boy, with the inherited artist's eye of his father and the instructive support of his mother, Merton seemed entranced by the beauty of God's creation.

During the time in which Merton's discernment of a possible call to religious life reached its climax—between the withdrawal of his application to the Franciscans and his entrance into the Trappist community—his paradise consciousness blossomed in noticeable ways. One strikingly illustrative episode took place when Merton was riding a train through the Delaware Valley back to St. Bonaventure University in January 1941. Here he began to consider his thoughts while glancing out the window during his last trip on the same route in 1938 and noted that three years earlier he had not yet acquired the "philosophical words" to express his experience. This time, however, he "found something else" that revealed his keen awareness of God's intention that human persons discover their true self, in part, through relationship with the rest of the created order.

> It suddenly struck me as a painfully offensive thing for me to ride whirling through those rocky valleys in a train exclaiming "I know all these hills!" What do I know of them, or they of me?
>
> It suddenly occurred to me that these real hills must be, to me, because of the peculiarity of my position, peculiarly, very painfully abstract.
>
> What position?
>
> I am sealed up in an air-conditioned train, whirled past the hills and the ice-jammed banks of the river and the woods streaked with white filaments of brick, and cliffs white with icicles.
>
> In order to know these hills, I ought to set foot upon their earth in quietness, perhaps. At least that seemed something painfully necessary at the time. Instead I go through in the sealed train, looking out from behind glass. I am cut off entirely from the hills and they are fairly abstract. What do I know of them, or they of me? There is no necessity for me to know them, or for them to know me. If I am to know those hills, if their rock faces are to be more than blanks, perhaps I have to climb them, be lost in their woods. However, it is a terrible thing to ride encased in the glass, sterile, train asking the hills who they are, and being cut off from any real answer in a sealed tube of scientifically cleaned and heated air, not the same air as fills the bitter, hostile woods outside. When the hills go to answer, they are defeated; so is the questioner. The answer can't get through the glass.[11]

The sense in which Merton "saw" the hills and recognized the world of the natural realm outside the technologically enabled enclosure of his train car offers us a glimpse at the power of sight and how one learns to *really* see. Drawing on the twentieth-century mystic Simone Weil, Weis explains that this "learning to see" is the process of recognizing the sacrament of creation, within which we human beings are participants. "Traditionally, *sacrament* has been defined as a visible sign that reveals and communicates grace," Weis writes. "Yet, insists Weil, whether or not one finds God, the act of looking and waiting with open eyes is essential to realizing our full human potential."[12] Furthermore, Weis rightly asserts that, over the course of his entire life, "each event and place expanded Merton's belief in the value of *seeing* the uniqueness of each creature and acknowledging the sacredness of place."[13]

Merton's more in-depth theological reflection on the environment and the natural world would only continue to expand his horizon, something that was made possible through his increasing commitment to contemplation. But what sort of contemplation? For someone who spent a great deal of his life reflecting on, writing about, and practicing contemplation, the practice remained an elusive category that was difficult for Merton to succinctly identify. Later in his writings, Merton spent as much time describing what "contemplation is not" as he did in striving to articulate a positive concept. Part of the difficulty in describing what contemplation is in a precise manner stems from the variety of traditions that incorporate some sort of meditative, prayerful, or similar practice. Even within Christianity, the diversity of religious communities contributes a number of ways to approach the practice. One way that the Franciscan tradition presents the meaning and practice of contemplation can help us appreciate better the way Merton's paradise consciousness developed over time.

As I introduced in my first book, *Dating God: Live and Love in the Way of St. Francis* (2012), contemplation in the Franciscan tradition can be a lot like the experience of conversion that takes place when we enter into a new relationship. When we enter into a new relationship, make a new friend, date a new partner, give birth to a new child, or form some other significant bond with another person, rarely are our lives changed in discrete, particular, and compartmentalized ways. Instead, something about us shifts. Something about the way we see the world is now informed by that relationship, and we can no longer go back to seeing things exactly the same way again. Maybe we are drawn to a new hobby or interest. Perhaps we look at art with a new eye or hear music with a new ear. Such is also the case with God. The more deeply we enter into relationship with the Creator, the more our outlook on the world changes.

The medieval Franciscan Bonaventure wrote about contemplation in his famous treatise *Itinerarium Mentis in Deum* ("The Soul's Journey into God"), a text that Merton studied with great interest and enthusiasm during his time studying with Father Philotheus Boehner at St. Bonaventure (he even ends *The Seven Storey Mountain* with an encouragement to his readers that they look up the text). Interestingly, most Christian spiritual writers used the Latin word *contemplatio*, which means "to see, to gaze, to focus," and from which we get our word "contemplation." However, Bonaventure was deliberate in using the Latin word *speculatio* instead. It might not seem such an earth-shattering difference, especially given that both Latin words are typically translated into the English editions as "contemplation." Yet, as with so much that is rendered into one language from another, a great deal is often lost in translation. Unlike *contemplatio* and its meaning—related to gazing or focusing—*speculatio* is tied to the Latin word *speculum*, which is a noun meaning "a mirror." Bonaventure, inspired by the life and example of Francis of Assisi, understood contemplation to be about reflection. On one level, it could mean reflection on God, like "contemplation" in its traditional understanding. Yet, on a deeper level, Bonaventure is talking about the reflection *of God* in *our world*. Closely tied to his use of *speculatio*, Bonaventure uses another Latin word to talk about *how* God is reflected in creation: he describes these instances as vestiges (*vestigia*), an aspect of Franciscan creation spirituality that we will explore in greater detail a little later in this chapter.

What is significant for us about this use of *speculatio* is that it suggests contemplation in a Franciscan key is not about our searching for God in particular times and dedicated places. Rather, Franciscan contemplation is about learning to see how God is always already right before us, reflected in all aspects of creation. We need to see the world anew, not because God is hidden and waiting for us to take our turn in a "spiritual hide-and-seek," but because God is always "it" and at play around us. In other words, God is not hiding; God's footprints are *everywhere*. We are usually the ones with our heads in the sand or hands over our eyes. We are usually the ones, like Merton in the air-conditioned train car, sequestered from the day-to-day mystical experience of reconnecting to the rest of the created order, and thereby we are less aware of God's enduring closeness to us and the rest of creation than we could be. A Franciscan approach to contemplation challenges us not to let contemplation, the gazing at God, become just another thing we have to do. We need to let our relationship with God transform us to see the whole world in new and life-giving ways.

Drawing on the insight of St. Augustine, Bonaventure, in his *Itinerarium Mentis in Deum*, describes what sin means in terms of sight and vision:

> In the initial state of creation, man was made fit for the quiet of contemplation, and therefore God placed him in a paradise of delights (Gen 2:15). But turning from the true light to changeable good, man was bent over by his own fault, and the entire human race by original sin, which infected human nature in two ways: the mind with ignorance and the flesh with concupiscence. As a result, man, blinded and bent over, sits in darkness and does not see the light of heaven unless knowledge with wisdom come to his aid against ignorance.[14]

To talk about Merton's increasing awareness of the natural world, his growing concern about environmental crises, and his developing paradise consciousness is to talk about his standing up straight to see the true light of God in the world around him. Like all human persons, Merton had the capacity from the beginning to recognize the reflection of the Creator in creation, but with time, sin and selfishness would obscure that view. To learn to see the world anew, to have your eyes opened to God in creation, is another way of talking about becoming an everyday mystic in the tradition of Franciscan contemplation.

Discovering the "Footprints" of God in Creation

With a growing awareness of creation and an increasingly new way of looking at the world, Merton's ongoing ecological conversion included the recognition of the vestiges of God. On occasion he would use a term from Bonaventure directly, such as when he wrote, "This is the reality I need, the vestige of God in His creatures,"[15] but more often than not it was a subtler expression of God's personal mark in each aspect of creation that appeared in Merton's writings. Weis explains how Merton's increasing awareness of his surroundings, his commitment to contemplation, and his emergent interest in the ecological concerns of his day led him to more explicitly see each aspect of creation as a vestige of the Creator.

> Finding God in creatures is not, as Merton first believed, merely a stepping stone to God, but rather a bursting forth, an ongoing encounter with the Divine. Once he discovers how "landscape is important for contemplation," once he is permitted to wander in the woods, along the lakes, and on the knobs beyond the confines of the enclosure, Merton's capacity for contemplation expands. Each foray into nature, occasionally accompanied by a sudden and

profound spiritual insight, is an invitation to discover more
deeply his vocation.[16]

We can see this encounter with the "mirrors of God," the vestiges of creation, throughout Merton's writings. For example,
on the day after the Feast of St. Francis of Assisi in 1957, Merton
wrote in his journal about the impact of discovering a flock of
birds and the way "looking into this world of birds" led him
to feel close to God.

> The warblers are coming through now. Very hard to iden-
> tify them all, even with field glasses and a bird book. (Have
> seen at least one that is definitely not in the bird book.)
> Watching one which I took to be a Tennessee warbler. A
> beautiful, neat, prim looking thing—seeing this beautiful
> thing which people do not usually see, looking into this
> world of birds, which is not concerned with us or with
> our problems. I felt very closer to God or felt religious awe
> anyway. Watching those birds was as food for meditation
> or as mystical reading. Perhaps better. Also the beautiful,
> unidentified red flower or fruit I found on a bud yesterday.
> I found a bird in the woods yesterday on the feast of St.
> Francis. Those things say so much more than words Mark
> was saying, "The birds don't know they have names."
> Watching them I thought: who cares what they are called?
> But do I have the courage not to care? Why not be like
> Adam, in a new world of my own, and call them by my
> own names? That would still mean that I thought names
> were important. No name and no word to identify the
> beauty and reality of those birds today, is the gift of God
> to me in letting me see them.[17]

Even in Merton's earliest journal entries, there was a deeply
Franciscan sense of the way all aspects of the created order
bear the mark of the Creator and reflect the divine love and
intention of creation. This comes across in his lengthy September 26, 1939, entry that began with his musings about St.
Francis and the birds. It continues with a recognition of how

the Augustinian emphasis on the right ordering of love and valuation of created things vis-à-vis God, which is picked up by Bonaventure, bolsters an appreciation for the way in which everything is a vestige of God when this or that thing is not loved for itself but loved in proper relationship to the Creator.

> Loving the tree, not for itself, we are able to achieve the imaginative self-identification with it poets and Saints both seek after and we love it in something of the same kind of way as Saint Francis loved and understood the birds and all living creatures.
>
> But we cannot possess or enjoy or love trees for what they are in themselves alone, for in themselves alone they are really nothing, or very uninteresting. The soul cannot enjoy things, it can only enjoy itself or the love of God. It cannot enjoy trees: but God and his mercy and love are everywhere in the air, in the trees, in our hearts. So we can be struck with love and sympathy and understanding for the Godliness that is in all things around us, that proclaim the immense and unfailing love of their creator.[18]

The following year, on December 4, 1940, Merton copied a lengthy passage from Bonaventure's *Itinerarium Mentis in Deum*, in which the way to God is first and foremost found in the created order, not (as some gnostics and others might attest) outside of it. This passage from Merton's journal includes the original Latin that translates, "The very universe is a kind of ladder for ascending to God, and that in certain things there is *a trace*, or *image*, of the *spiritual* in certain *corporal* things, and of the *eternal* in certain *temporal* things, and of certain things *inside us* in certain things *outside us*."[19]

While Bonaventure's concept of *vestigia* in his theology of creation was clearly influential in Merton's understanding of the "footprints of God" in creation, he wasn't the only Franciscan source that inspired the modern monk. Another lesser-known thirteenth-century Franciscan figure factors into Merton's environmental spirituality and creational worldview.

This is Blessed Angela of Foligno, who was a member of the Third Order or "secular Franciscans," just as Merton was. She lived in the late thirteenth century and was regarded in her time as a mystic and was a frequently sought-after spiritual director. In her famous book *The Memorial*, Angela recounts to a friar who served as her scribe the events of her spiritual journey and visions. At one point, Angela recalls being in Assisi when she had a particularly powerful experience of God's presence. She heard the voice of God say to her, "My sweet daughter, no creature can give you this consolation, only I alone." Angela explains that this experience was one of great intimacy, revealing to her God's closeness and care for her. She continued to recall her vision:

> Afterward [God] added: "I want to show you something of my power." And immediately the eyes of my soul were opened, and in a vision I beheld the fullness of God in which I beheld and comprehended the whole of creation, that is, what is on this side and what is beyond the sea, the abyss, the sea itself, and everything else. And in everything that I saw, I could perceive nothing except the presence and the power of God, and in a manner totally indescribable. And my soul in an excess of wonder cried out: "This world is pregnant with God!" Wherefore I understood how small is the whole of creation—that is, what is on this side and what is beyond the sea, the abyss, the sea itself, and everything else—but the power of God fills it all to overflowing.[20]

It doesn't take much effort to see the kindred sensibility in the mystical writings of Bonaventure and Angela, for they both bear a powerful awareness of God's presence in and through creation.

Merton was familiar with the life and writings of Angela. He actually delivered a conference to the monks in formation in 1965 on the theme of Angela's mystical thought and embrace of the evangelical life after the example of St. Francis.

Few people today are familiar with Angela of Foligno, though there has been significant scholarly and popular work done on her thought in recent decades. It is astounding that Merton could, in the 1960s, speak so intelligently about Angela in a professional setting such as the formation conferences he regularly delivered. Despite all this, Merton claimed in his journal on April 13, 1965, that "in the evening I talked foolishly of Angela of Foligno."[21] While Merton was certainly not a medieval scholar who specialized in the thought of Angela, his presentation is succinct, insightful, and largely true to what contemporary scholarship suggests by way of interpretation. At one point, Merton says,

> So one of the things that is very interesting here is that in the height of her mystical love of God she comes to love everything, every being in God, which is something that tends to be left aside in this. Often you find in these mystical assents that everything vanishes, [the mystics] just love God alone, everything else drops out. Now here's this idea of loving every being in God, the goodness of creation and the goodness of the world and the goodness of what God has made and so forth.[22]

Merton sees in Angela, despite her reputation for being eccentric and therefore often dismissed by "serious scholars" (here we might recognize a latent, if not overt, academic misogyny), wisdom that is valuable for today. This wisdom includes the need for Christians to be drawn into the mystery of God's good creation, moving evermore closely toward a new vision of the world such that God's imprint or vestige can be seen everywhere and among all things.

The Kinship of All Creation

Among the many contributions the Franciscan tradition has made to theological reflection on creation, the most significant is perhaps that concept of the kinship of all creation. Oftentimes this aspect of the Franciscan spiritual and theological heritage is reduced to a caricature of "St. Francis in the birdbath" or the little poor man from Assisi talking with wolves and birds. In truth, the importance of kinship as the model for how God intends humanity to relate to the rest of creation cannot be overstated, and the sources for this way of viewing the world date back to St. Francis himself.

As I have written elsewhere, Francis of Assisi's understanding of a theology of creation was in no way systematic or scholarly.[23] Ilia Delio, building on the work of earlier thinkers such as Ewert Cousins, suggests that a good way to understand Francis's experience of creation was as a "nature mystic." Delio writes,

> A nature mystic is one whose mystical experiences involve an appreciation of creation as God's handiwork; nature manifests the divine. Francis's nature mysticism included a consciousness of God with the appropriate religious attitudes of awe and gratitude . . . he took spontaneous joy in the material world, singing its praises like a troubadour poet. With a disarming sense of immediacy, he felt himself part of the family of creation.[24]

While not expressed in the scholastic categories of his day, the thought of Francis of Assisi as articulated in his own writings—prayers, rules of life, and letters—and in the writings of the early Franciscans about Francis reveals a theology of creation that is easily identifiable with the kinship model.

There is perhaps no more accessible example of this characteristic of Franciscan thought than that of Francis's "The Canticle of the Creatures."[25] Eric Doyle explains, "As a prayer of praise to God the Creator, 'The Canticle' is a sublime expression of the authentic Christian attitude to creation, which is to accept and love creatures as they are."[26] What makes Francis's attitude toward creation "authentically Christian," to borrow Doyle's phrase, is precisely this innate sensitivity to the universal kinship of all creation as experienced in the mystical

and fraternal worldview of the *poverello*. The brilliance of the
canticle is multilayered, staged as it is in overlapping strata
of increasing agency within creation.[27] All dimensions of the
created world (with the exception of nonhuman animals)—
planetary bodies, weather phenomena, elemental features of
the earth, vegetation, human beings, and death—are included
in this hymnic reflection of the interrelationship of creation.
Although nonhuman animals are not expressly included in this
canticle, Francis's reverence for all creatures shines through in
the more hagiographical sources and the earliest traditions of
the Franciscan movement.

Doyle continues to explain well the place of the created
order for Francis as it is seen in this famous hymn of praise.

> Nature for Francis was not just a reflection of human activ-
> ity and reactions, because this would have been to destroy
> the unique value of other creatures. They are not mirrors
> of us, but like us, they reflect God. He began with equality:
> we are all created . . . we are all brethren. Francis believed
> the doctrine of creation with his whole heart. It told him
> that the entire universe—the self and the total environment
> to which the self belongs (microcosm and macrocosm)—is
> the product of the highest creative power, the creativity of
> Transcendent Love.[28]

How does one come to this realization, or reach this degree
of understanding? Doyle insists that "the mystical experience
which gave birth to The Canticle was a creative encounter with
reality."[29] To put it another way, through prayer and a deep
appreciation of God's revelation in scripture (as St. Bonaventure
will later attribute this gift), Francis became prophetic in his
ability to see the world as it really is—to truly see reality. This
reality, this truth in creation, is God's loving act of bringing into
and sustaining all things in existence.[30] Francis of Assisi did not
need to be a professor of theology at the University of Paris
to come to this conclusion. His inspired worldview, shaped

as it was by his total surrender to God's grace and Gospel life, allowed him to see this truth: all of creation is one family.

Keith Warner has written on this very subject. A Franciscan friar and an environmental scientist, Warner asserts that Francis did indeed have an explicitly familial sense of creation, one that we can call a "kinship model" of creation. For Warner, this means three things for a Franciscan understanding of creation: it celebrates relationship, it promotes courtesy, and it reflects a commitment to the practice of penance.[31] Warner explains what this might mean for Franciscans and those inspired by Francis's view of creation today.

> We can imitate him by being environmental peacemakers. Just as Francis built peace in the relationship between the bishop and mayor by singing The Canticle of the Creatures, we can bring reconciliation to the conflicts around us by practicing and promoting respect for the existence and well-being of others. By honoring both parties in a conflictual situation we invite others to adopt a stance of respect and to acknowledge the right of others to exist. Direct confrontation of personal and corporate greed can be ineffectual. I believe that by encouraging others to acknowledge, respect and enjoy the relationships they have with others, that greed can be replaced with courtesy, and this seems fully consistent with Francis' approach.[32]

Becoming "environmental peacemakers" is indeed a novel way to approach our vocational call as brothers and sisters to creation. How is it that we advocate for the "least among us," particularly when the least among us includes the earth, endangered species, rainforests, or the ocean? Following the example of Francis's fraternal worldview, his kinship theology of creation, we might help reconcile not just the broken relationships among the world's men and women but also the broken relationship all of humanity shares with the rest of creation.

The renowned Brazilian theologian and former Franciscan friar Leonardo Boff has also observed this creational model of kinship in the thought and practice of Francis of Assisi. Boff goes so far as to suggest that, in opposition to other models of creation, Francis was in fact "the living embodiment of another paradigm, one of a spirit that acts in kinship, one that is filled with compassion and respect before each representative of the cosmic and planetary community."[33] Unlike some of the other Franciscan theologians and environmentalists, Boff offers what appears to be a more radical interpretation of Francis's worldview. Boff suggests that what Francis innately discovered was really an intuitive sense of classical paganism. The term "paganism" is off-putting, for it conjures images of heresy, polytheism, and non-Christian religiosity. However, Boff believes that throughout Christian history, the Church has (necessarily perhaps) had to struggle to define itself against traditionally pagan cultures. In an effort to maintain something resembling orthodox Christian faith in the face of paganistic heterodoxy, anything that hinted of pre-Christian pagan religion was effectively squashed. As a result, the previously ubiquitous notion of divinity found in all aspects of the cosmos, and all of creation reflecting something beyond itself, was categorized under the genus of pagan and suppressed for fear of heterodoxy. Boff believes that Francis was, in some way, able to transcend the limitations of the human-centered, popular worldview of Christendom in order to see the sacred indwelling of creation around him. He explains,

> St. Francis brought this whole age of purgation to an end. Eyes recovered their innocence. Now one could contemplate God and the splendor of God's grace and glory in the extensive wealth of creation, which is the great sacrament of God and Christ. Intuitively and without any previous theological training, Francis reclaimed the truth of paganism: this world is not mute, not lifeless, not empty; it speaks and is full of movement, love, purpose, and beckonings

from the Divinity. It can be the place for encountering God and God's spirit, through the world itself, its energies, its profusion of sound, color, and movement.[34]

Boff goes on to note that all of the biographies of Francis written after his death, including those works by Bonaventure and Thomas of Celano, as well as *The Legend of the Three Companions*, *The Legend of Perugia*, and *The Mirror of Perfection*, portray Francis as having existed in a unique relationship with all creatures and the entire creation.

Francis's way of living in the world was one of intimate relationship. He lived *with* the world and not above and against it as others so commonly do. Boff explains that for Francis, nothing was simply available for human possession or consumption, but instead there existed only God's magisterial creation that is related to all other parts of creation in a divine interconnectedness. Boff puts this in another, more poetic way: "Everything makes up a grand symphony—and God is the conductor."[35]

As Merton's paradise consciousness grew and his awareness of the vestiges of God in creation became clearer, there was also the dawning realization of his deeply ingrained relationship to the rest of creation. As with the Franciscan notion of "vestige," the term "kinship" is used less frequently than it is implied in the writings of Merton. There are times, such as on November 4, 1964, in a journal entry, when Merton does use the term explicitly. Talking again about the birds near the monastery, Merton wrote,

> In the afternoon, lots of pretty little myrtle warblers were playing and diving for insects in the low pine branches over my head, so close I could almost touch them. I was awed at their loveliness, their quick flight, etc. Sense of total kinship with them as if they and I were of the same nature, and as if that nature were nothing but love. And what else but love keeps us all together in being?[36]

There is a deeply metaphysical quality to Merton's reflection on the kinship he recognizes with the birds he sees flying and diving. It is the God scripture calls "love" (1 Jn 4:8) that creates, and it is this same God-as-love that sustains all of creation in existence.

Merton came to realize more and more, particularly later in his life when he moved into the hermitage full time, that his place in the created order—and by extension the place of all women and men—only made sense according to the radical Christian conviction that we are interconnected and interdependent on the most fundamental levels. From the beginning, God did not create separate castes within the natural world, humans occupying a place of primacy and superiority over and against the rest of the nonhuman universe. Merton would never deny that human beings were special in some ways, including in terms of moral agency and the ability to choose between entering into and forsaking a relationship with one another. Yet there was a refreshing sense of the interrelational dimension to our existence found throughout Merton's reflections on the Christian meaning of the human person and creation. Highlighting this awareness, Merton writes, "How absolutely true, and how central a truth, that we are purely and simply *part of nature*, though we are the part which recognizes God."[37]

In coming to see that we are part of nature, members of the family of creation, like all plants and animals, elements and minerals, and terrestrial and planetary bodies, Merton became acutely aware of what Francis of Assisi intuited nearly eight centuries earlier in his "The Canticle of the Creatures," namely, that humanity is not the only aspect of creation that is capable of praising God. As early as the late 1940s and early 1950s, Merton included a telling passage that illustrates this sentiment in what would become published as *The Sign of Jonas*.

> But now I am under the sky, away from all the noise.
> The birds are all silent now except some quiet bluebirds.

> The frogs have begun singing their pleasure in all the
> waters and in the warm green places where the sunshine
> is wonderful. Praise Christ, all you living creatures. For
> Him you and I were created. With every breath we love
> Him. My psalms fulfill your dim, unconscious song, O
> brothers in this wood.[38]

Instead of claiming that only human beings can praise God,
Merton speaks to his "brothers in this wood" as a fellow sup-
plicant before God, offering up his prayers in a complemen-
tary and fulfilling way alongside his other-than-human kin of
creation.

It is not only animals that Merton considers in this light.
There is a familiarity Merton detects when reflecting on his
relationship to the elemental aspects of creation: wind, water,
light, darkness, and so on. Also in *The Sign of Jonas*, we have an
early example of this attentiveness to the environment that is
both his home and his familial landscape when he writes, "It
is a strange awakening to find the sky inside you and beneath
you and above you and all around you so that your spirit is
one with the sky, and all is positive night."[39] Strange though
the awakening may be for Merton, it is yet another glimpse
into the deepening awareness that Merton experienced during
the course of his life.

Furthermore, the kinship model of creation operative in
Merton's spirituality informed his ethical outlook as much as
anything else. This is something that grew from a seed of his
spiritual environment in the early years into a large tree that
shaded his social justice concerns near the end of his life. In one
journal entry, Merton wrote, "We do not realize that the fields
and the trees have fought and still fight for their respective
places on this map—which, by natural right, belong entirely
to the trees."[40] Here Merton seems to ascribe to trees (one of
his favorite aspects of the nonhuman created order alongside
birds) a sense of moral agency and subjectivity. They—the

trees—have *a natural right* to exist and to be recognized as inherently valuable.

The ethical dimension of Merton's thought about creation, rooted as it was in the sense of kinship so naturally a part of his spiritual horizon, blossomed into full bloom when he began reading the work of Rachel Carson, Roderick Nash, and others in the 1960s.[41] In a brief review essay (which appeared in the June 1968 issue of *The Catholic Worker*) about Nash's book *Wilderness and the American Mind* (1967), Merton expounds on the importance of the historical development of popular conceptualizations of "wilderness" and "nature" in the United States up to that time. This remains an important consideration for us today. As we face even greater ecological crises due to the rapid advances in technology and the widespread subjugation of "nature" for human interest, the idea of "ecological conscience" as introduced by Aldo Leopold and adopted by Merton becomes even more urgent.

> Also Leopold brought into clear focus one of the most important moral discoveries of our time. This can be called the *ecological conscience*. The ecological conscience is centered in the awareness of *man's true place as a dependent member of the biotic community*. Man must become fully aware of his *dependence* on a balance which he is not only free to destroy but which he has already begun to destroy. He must recognize his obligations toward the other members of that vital community. And incidentally, since he tends to destroy nature in his frantic efforts to exterminate other members of his own species, it would not hurt if he had a little more respect for human life too. The respect for life, the affirmation of *all life*, is basic to the ecological conscience. In the words of Albert Schweitzer: *"A man is ethical only when life as such is sacred to him, that of plants and animals as well as that of his fellow man."*[42]

Here we see the nexus of Merton's threefold movement of creation spirituality play out in an integrated critique and admonition near what would ultimately be the end of his life. He calls for an "awareness," a growing consciousness that arises from a renewed sense of each person's "ecological conscience," as Leopold puts it. Drawing on Schweitzer, Merton reiterates the sacredness of all life—human, plant, and animal—and implies this is true because God is the source and sustainer of all creation. Finally, we see repeated the affirmation that human beings are part of an interdependent community that requires balance, care, respect, and support.

Merton's paradise consciousness, awareness of God's created vestiges, and celebration of humanity's kinship with all of creation bear a remarkable resemblance to and are, in part, indebted to the Franciscan spiritual and theological tradition. There still remain numerous examples to explore that would further illustrate this aspect of the Franciscan influence in Merton's life, thought, and writings. Among these are Merton's poetry and abundant journal entries that simply cannot be included in a book of this size.[43] However, I hope that this chapter has sparked an enthusiasm for seeing the world anew, recognizing the "footprints of God," and embracing one's identity as a sister or brother of creation.

PART IV

Engaging
the World

Seeing the World as It Really Is: Prophecy at the Heart of the Christian Vocation

Although Thomas Merton died at far too young an age, his influence, insight, wisdom, challenge, and humanity continue to be present in the prophetic voice he left behind. There are times that I read the sage words and reflections of this twentieth-century monk and feel as though his voice is responding to the immediate and urgent needs of our time. His insight into prayer and spirituality, criticism of violence and discrimination, and genuine interest in interreligious dialogue and interfaith experiences still touch the hearts and lives of women and men of our age. And surely the relevance and appeal of his thought and writings will continue to inspire generations to come. I believe, above all else, that the reason his spirit continues to live on in this way, long after his bodily death, is because Thomas Merton was a prophet.

By prophet I do not mean, as Merton himself once dismissed, one who has certain magical abilities as in "the sense of sudden illuminations as to what is going to happen at some future moment."[1] Instead, I recognize in Merton the prophetic life and voice that he called others to adopt, "in the sense that we are so one with the Holy Spirit that we are already going in the direction the Spirit is going."[2] A prophet, as Merton attests, is not some kind of fortune-teller or a predictor of what is to come but someone whose life is so open to God's Spirit that she or he cannot help but begin to see the world in a new way. In an essay addressed to poets, he wrote, "To prophesy is not to predict, but to seize upon reality in its moment of highest expectation and tension toward the new."[3] What distinguishes prophets from other people, even other people of faith, is that they can begin to see the world as God sees it; or to put it another way, prophets see the world as it really is.

Just as with other aspects of Merton's life, thought, and writing, there were many influences that came together to inform and shape the modern monk's outlook on and understanding of prophecy and its central place in the Christian life. Among those influential sources stands the Franciscan tradition, particularly as it was developed in the thought of Bonaventure. To understand what that means and the implications that arise from such a way of living in the world, we need to look a little closer at the meaning of prophecy and the prophetic vocation, especially as Bonaventure understood it. In doing so, it is my hope that we might not only come to a deeper appreciation for the prophetic legacy that Merton leaves us in his writings but especially come to see how we can follow Merton's own example and become the much-needed prophets of our own time.

The Prophetic Vocation

Unlike the more colloquial use of the word "vocation," whether in the secular world to discuss a trade and career path or in the religious context to refer to a state of life (e.g., marriage, religious life, single life, etc.), Merton's notion of vocation is much more capacious. As we saw in chapter 5, Merton recognized that each person was individually created into existence with a particular identity known to God fully and known to us partially as the "true self." In this sense, everybody has a calling (a *vocare*, meaning "to call" in Latin, which is the root word for our English term "vocation") from God to be the person each was created to be, which is an entirely unique, unrepeatable, and wholly loved identity. Yet Merton also wrote about a more universal sense of a vocation. This sense of the term referred to what was shared among the baptized, what each Christian was called to do and be in light of our communal commitment to following the Gospel. To talk about a prophetic vocation is to talk in this more general way, as a characteristic of our collective Christian identity. Its manifestation will necessarily appear differently in the lives of various people by virtue of the differences in lifestyle, social location, familial commitments, religious profession, and so on. But a general call for all Christians to be prophets in the world is universal.

Not everybody, however, lives up to this call, just as not everybody lives to each aspect of baptized life. Nevertheless, when someone does respond, usually unwittingly or unconsciously, they are immediately recognized as "different from the pack."

We see this differentiation going back to the prophets of the Hebrew scriptures. Those called by the Lord to speak the truth in society and within the faith community are remembered because of their stance within the community and the message they proclaimed. What is both comforting and discomfiting at the same time is that none of these historic prophets appear to have wanted to accept the call they had received. Jeremiah is one of my favorite examples, in large part because his main excuse is that he is too young. We read at the beginning of Jeremiah the call that echoes each of the prophets of Israel:

> Now the word of the LORD came to me saying, "Before I formed you in the womb I knew you, and before you were born I consecrated you; I appointed you a prophet to the nations." Then I said, "Ah, Lord GOD! Truly I do not know how to speak, for I am only a boy." But the LORD said to me, "Do not say, 'I am only a boy'; for you shall go to all to whom I send you, and you shall speak whatever I command you. Do not be afraid of them, for I am with you to deliver you, says the LORD." (Jer 1:4–8)

As someone who entered the Franciscan Order at the relatively young age of twenty-one, right after graduating from college, I can appreciate Jeremiah's hesitancy and insecurity with regard to what is being asked of him. To commit one's self to religious life today, something that Merton describes time and again as a prophetic stance in the world, is an intimidating venture in a culture that is not always supportive of such a choice—one that, like Merton's own experience in his time, is also filled with both euphoric highs and surprising lows. It makes perfect sense to me that Jeremiah, while still in his youth, would instinctively resist the call of the Lord.

Merton, coincidentally, was also struck by Jeremiah's story of call and resistance. In the retreat he gave at the Abbey of Gethsemani for religious sisters in the late 1960s, the text of which was later published as *The Springs of Contemplation*, Merton writes, "Read the prophets in the Old Testament. Their biggest problem was that they were prophets. Jeremiah didn't want to be a prophet. In some sense, we're in the same boat. God lays on us the burden of feeling the contradictions in our world and Church and exposing them, insofar as we are honestly able to do that."[4] Merton sees in Jeremiah an example for all of us. We, too, are called to be prophets in our time, but most reject that possibility outright. This is not necessarily done consciously or with malice, but in order to live a prophetic vocation, one's story must be God's story, which is the narrative of faith and not one of the many other competing narratives of the world.

As we have already noted, one of the medieval figures that deeply influenced Merton's thought and theological worldview early on was Bonaventure, the thirteenth-century Franciscan friar, saint, and Doctor of the Church.[5] Bonaventure had a lot to say about prophecy, particularly in terms of how St. Francis exemplified the prophetic vocation in both word and deed. Merton's understanding of prophecy was very likely shaped, if in implicit ways, by Bonaventure's theology. Merton even mentions St. Francis, as did Bonaventure, in his retreat to the sisters, *The Springs of Contemplation*, in which he writes, "For him, too, there is a radical break with the world into a prophetic and free life."[6]

In his presentation of St. Francis as prophet, Bonaventure compares the medieval Italian saint to John the Baptist, the great herald of Christ, who is generally hailed within Christianity as one of the greatest prophets of history. John's particular greatness stems from his proximity to Jesus, both chronologically and spiritually, since he is the most immediate forerunner of the Lord and, according to the New Testament canon, the first to recognize the Lord for who he really is. The way Bonaventure highlights the meaning of prophecy is rooted in the tradition of the great prophets of the Hebrew scriptures. It is not, as Merton rejected earlier, the notion of one's ability to foretell the future but instead to see reality *as it truly is*. In this sense, the meaning of prophecy is more in line with the Greek word *propheteia*, which bears the connotation "to speak forth" more than it signifies "foretelling" or something magical.[7] The ability "to speak forth" was unique among the charisms that St. Paul names in his epistolary, not because of the content so much as the grounding for what was being proclaimed. The grounding of one's prophetic pronouncements came from the appropriation of the scriptural narrative—that is another way to talk about embracing God's story. Bonaventure insists that a prophet is one who focuses his or her life on scripture and, over time and by way of divine inspiration, comes to arrive at its spiritual and fuller sense.[8] In short, we become prophets when we become people of scripture imbued with God's revelation in a way that shades and shapes our perception. It is only then that a prophet can begin to see with "God's eyes."

This is what we might say is the formative process for becoming a Christian prophet, something that Merton described in his comments to the sisters published in *The Springs of Contemplation*. Time and again he returns to the importance of scripture and the role of the Holy Spirit in shaping the outlook of women and men who follow their call to live out the Christian prophetic vocation. But this is not the end of the story. Prophets, as one might recall about any of the famous (or even not-so-famous) prophets in the tradition, do not keep silent and do not keep their way of seeing the world to themselves. As if unable to contain the pain of seeing the incongruity recognized in the way people live in the world contrasted with the way God intends the human family to live in this life, the prophet speaks out against the increasingly more recognizable instances of injustice, pain, suffering, abuse, and other troubles in the world. The true prophet, like all of his or her prophetic predecessors, necessarily becomes a marginal person because this way of seeing reality inevitably pushes one to the edges of the socially acceptable and of the status quo. It should come as no surprise that prophets are often viewed as outsiders. In truth they could live no other way. They enter the realm of what some postcolonial theorists have recently taken to calling the "location of the surplus," or that marginal space from which a different perspective is gained because that marginal space does not align with nor is it subsumed into the predominant power system or structure of a given society, institution, or place.

Prophets become a nuisance to those who have vested interests in the maintenance of power or control because they point out the disconnections between the ways those in power or those with authority act and the way God intends the human family to relate to one another and the rest of creation. Merton made this point well when he said that "the prophetic struggle with the world is the struggle of the Cross against worldly power."[9] This struggle with the world and against worldly power will inevitably result in friction and suspicion on the part of those whose identity and interests are threatened by the prophet's public acknowledgment of the incongruity of lived reality versus the reality God intends. Merton sees this as inherently painful for those who follow the call of the Holy Spirit to become prophets in their time: "To live prophetically, you've got to be questioning and looking at factors behind the facts. You've got to be aware that there are contradictions. In a certain sense, our prophetic vocation consists in hurting from the contradictions in society. This is a real cross in our lives today. For we ourselves are partly responsible."[10] This is not simply a societal issue for Merton but something that affects the prophet personally and ecclesiastically, for the more we start to see the world as it really is and observe the ways in which we consistently fall short of God's loving desire, the more we see the inherent contradictions in our own lives, in the world, and in the Church.

Thomas Merton's Prophetic Legacy

This was the sort of prophet that Thomas Merton was and continues to be long past his earthly death. He was able, with time, to see more and more of what God's vision for the world was and how the way in which humanity exercised its collective freedom in myriad ways was far afield from that divine intention. It didn't happen overnight. The prophetic legacy he leaves us and from which we continue to glean inspiration arose out of a life of conversion, a life committed—in imperfect, finite ways—to following the call of the Holy Spirit.

I am certainly not the first to highlight Merton's prophetic legacy as one of the central gifts the twentieth-century monk has left us. From Gerald Twomey's tellingly titled 1978 collection of essays *Thomas Merton: Prophet in the Belly of a Paradox* to the more recent volumes including Paul Dekar's *Thomas Merton: Twentieth-Century Wisdom for Twenty-First-Century Living* and Mario Aguilar's *Thomas Merton: Contemplation and Political Action*, scholars and enthusiasts of Merton's life and work have identified the threads of prophetic intuition and proclamation that continue to speak to the pressing concerns and unsettling times of our own day.[11] Along with these authors, I am continually struck by the insight that emerges from the writing of a man whose social location (a member of a cloistered monastic community in Kentucky) and personal identity (a white, highly educated, celibate, Roman Catholic cleric) would appear far too removed from the experiences of those whose struggles with justice, violence, and power today are most pressing. Yet his ability to cut to the heart of the matter is reflective of the true prophetic heritage from which it arises.

Many people might be quick to assume that, because Merton was a cloistered monk remotely situated in relationship to the urgent concerns about the economy, justice, race, and violence of his day, he was less able to respond to the "signs of the time."[12] However, in light of what we know about true prophets in the Christian tradition, it was precisely this lifestyle and location that provided the very condition of the possibility for fostering his prophetic vocation.[13] There is much to be said for his lived example of a life devoted, at least in principle, to prayer, study (especially of scripture), and reflection that ultimately cultivated an environment capable of imbuing God's narrative in his heart and mind. In a sense it is a real spiritual luxury to live in a milieu so singularly dedicated to living the Gospel. In truth, each monk in the monastery—just as each person in any walk of life—must willingly respond in freedom to the Holy Spirit's call. Therefore, simply being a member of a religious order is not enough without the commitment of the individual to *live* the life. Nevertheless, the conditions of religious life are intentionally designed to enable a person to let God's story become more and more that person's story, to let scripture become the pacemaker, and to allow prayer to guide the thoughts and actions of each member of that community.

In the case of Merton, this spiritual landscape within which he was located, a terrain shaped by daily recitation of the psalms, hearing scripture, and celebrating the Church's liturgies, was an ideal locale for the formation of a prophet. Removed, in part, from the more common distractions of life in his time, Merton could—if he so chose—focus more dedicatedly on becoming a person of scripture, a man whose own story began to look a lot more like God's story, and a monk whose eyes could glimpse the world with some of God's vision of reality.

In the beginning, this was not the case. Merton's most popular books and essays early on do not reflect the thought of someone whom we could call a prophet. He was more like a "prophet in training" (something to which we should all aspire in our own ways). His focus was on the life of prayer and scripture, and his writing reflected it. The texts *Seeds of Contemplation* and *The Sign of Jonas* reveal a Christian grappling with the meaning of evangelical life in the modern world.[14] But it was these periods of intense gazing and spiritual struggle that enabled the later Merton—the author of *Conjectures of a Guilty Bystander* and *The Cold War Letters*—to become who he was.[15] By the time his eyes were opened to the condition of the world in which he recognized himself as a fellow citizen with the rest of humanity, Merton was already at the margin of society, living an ancient monastic life in a complex modern time. His location was, without his knowing it, a place of theological and social "surplus," a place at once removed from the systems of status quo and the ordinary.

With years of living a life of scripture, having become saturated daily with the inspired Word of God, Merton looked out of his monastery at the World around him and saw the disconnection between what God intended and the way his sisters and brothers were living. The disjunction appeared in stark relief because of the injustices and abuses of his time made manifest in racial inequality, international threats of violence and war, economic disparity, and so many other iterations of systemic sin. With this vision of what God intended for the human family placed in contrast alongside his vision of reality, Merton could not help but cry out and call attention to the problems. He did this the best way he knew how: through writing.

Merton's writing is the medium by which his prophetic legacy is passed on from one generation to the next. The entire written corpus provides us with a holistic vision of his lifelong conversion from idealistic young monk to prophet. At times subtle, the shift in emphasis that is generally expressed as a move from solitude and contemplation toward social justice and interreligious dialogue is not as fragmented or demarcated as some would have us think. In embracing the prophetic vocation one doesn't move away from a life of prayer and scripture but is instead sustained in one's authentic Christian call precisely through that faithful living of modern discipleship. This is important to remember. Merton could not be a prophet without a continued personal and, on some level, communal commitment to a life of prayer and scripture. He could, of course, have been a so-called secular radical, perhaps even committed to many of the same concerns. But as we know and Merton affirmed, to be a prophet requires one's life to be transformed by the Holy Spirit and one's story to be aligned with God's story in scripture. Merton's prophetic legacy transcends the sectarian or ideological strictures that generally limit other well-meaning peoples' concerns; God's concerns are not limited to partisan interests but touch on the well-being of all people and the entirety of creation.

The Need for Prophets in Our Own Day

In what would be one of the last few addresses of his life, Thomas Merton gave an informal and unscripted talk on monasticism to some monks in Calcutta, India, in October 1968. Throughout the short reflection, the often-eloquent monk struggled to find the words and the images he needed to express the feelings he wished to convey. He was moved by the fundamental unity that connected all human persons together beyond the superficial distinctions, cultural variation, perceived differences, and other things that separate people from one another. He concluded that address with the affirmation that "we are already one. But we imagine that we are not. What we have to recover is our original unity. What we have to be is what we are."[16] This realization that there is an intrinsic feature of our existence that binds us together in an inseparable way is in part an articulation of the scriptural vision of humanity that reflects reality as it really is. This is, in the truest sense, a prophetic expression of who we are as human beings. All the exterior differences and struggles to divide people are iterations of worldly narratives that do not align with God's vision of reality.

In the same talk, Merton makes it abundantly clear that he recognizes the prophetic dimension of what he is saying, while at the same time he reaches beyond his own experience to call his audience—to call us—to follow that divine impulse toward being prophets in our day. Merton explains what this entails:

> And so I stand among you as one who offers a small message of hope, that first, there are always people who dare to seek on the margin of society, who are not dependent on social acceptance, not dependent on social routine, and

prefer a kind of free-floating existence under a state of risk.
And among these people, if they are faithful to their own
calling, to their own vocation, and to their own message
from God, communication on the deepest level is possible.[17]

As discussed above, Merton was very aware of the marginal
lifestyle that being a true prophet necessarily entailed. In one
sense he warns his hearers of what to expect, while in another
sense he encourages them, nevertheless, to be "faithful to their
own calling, to their own vocation." This is a message for you
and me as much as it was for the monks in Calcutta more than
four decades ago. We need prophets in our own day that are
willing, in whatever state of life such people find themselves,
to follow the example of Merton and become people committed to prayer and scripture in ways that enable transformation
from a worldview shaped by the narratives of our cultures and
societies to a vision of reality as it really is from the vantage
point of God.

Do we "dare to seek on the margin of society" in an effort
to cry out for justice in our world? Are we willing to follow the
direction of the Holy Spirit in our actions and words? Can we
become people of prayer and scripture in our various states of
life, from the married and committed partnerships to those in
communal religious orders? This is our task today, to follow
in the footprints of Thomas Merton in discovering who we are
and in discovering what God has in store for all of us. There
are, as Merton says above, inherent risks that come with this
embrace of our call: the risks of marginalization, the risks of
upsetting the status quo, and the risks of doing what is right
and just.

Merton's prophetic legacy can only continue in the lives,
words, and actions of you and me. What better way to celebrate
his one hundredth birthday than to commit ourselves to following more closely the prophetic call that all Christians have
received on the day of our Baptism? Just as Merton ultimately
gained that spiritual clarity through prayer and scripture that

opened his eyes to God's vision, may we too continually strive to see the world as it really is and become the much-needed prophets in our own day.

CHAPTER 9

No Longer Strangers: Thomas Merton and Franciscan Interreligious Dialogue

Hidden within Thomas Merton's 1966 text *Conjectures of a Guilty Bystander* stands a telling passage only seven paragraphs long that presents perhaps the most succinct expression of Merton's model and inspiration for interreligious dialogue. He begins this section with a quotation from Eulogius, an Orthodox Metropolitan, and notes its significance in his life. "'Men like St. Seraphim [of Sarov], St. Francis of Assisi, and many others accomplished in their life the union of the churches.' This profound and simple statement . . . gives the key to ecumenism for monks, and indeed for everyone."[1] As we have seen throughout the previous chapters, Merton's admiration for the Franciscan tradition shaped his theological and spiritual outlook from early on and continued to influence his way of looking at the world long after he entered the Trappist Order. While others have drawn attention to the ways in which St. Francis remained an important figure in Merton's life and work,[2] exploration of the particular way the Franciscan charism affected, and perhaps directed, Merton's approach to interreligious dialogue has been overlooked. What's more striking is the similarity in the method, outlook, and practice utilized by both Francis and Merton.

It is clear from the quotation above and elsewhere in his writings that Merton held Francis as a paragon of interreligious dialogue in the forefront of his interreligious and ecumenical consciousness. Another example of Merton's recognition of and appreciation for Francis's example of interreligious dialogue appears at the end of an important essay on peace titled "The Christian in World Crisis: Reflections on the Moral Climate of the 1960s," which was inspired by Pope John XXIII's encyclical letter *Pacem in Terris*. Merton wrote in the conclusion, "The whole climate of the encyclical, in its love of man and of the world, and in its radiant hopefulness, is Franciscan."[3] He continued, acknowledging his familiarity with Francis's revolutionary instruction to his brothers in the earliest rule for the Franciscan way of life:

> Anyone familiar with the writings of St. Francis and with his life is aware that the Saint was always urging his Friars to be at peace with each other and to go among men as peacemakers. A remarkable chapter on missions among the Saracens (First Rule of St. Francis, C. 16) anticipates the ecumenical ideas of our own time, even though it was written in the age of crusades.[4]

After this paragraph Merton cites in whole the section from Francis's *Regula non bullata*, which we will take a closer look at later in this chapter. It is striking to see the explicit acknowledgment of Francis's example in such an important essay at such a significant time in Merton's own emerging consciousness of the need for authentic interreligious and ecumenical dialogue and relationship.

In an age that continues to be shaped by misunderstanding, fear, skepticism, and violence—often in the name of religion— the wisdom of Francis and Merton continues to be as relevant as ever. Despite being more connected across space and time than ever before, we remain separated from one another by isolating disparities in wealth, a lack of understanding, differences in culture, and a general ignorance about and absence of respect for the religious traditions and personal commitments of others. This chapter explores the connection between the nearly eight-hundred-year-old Franciscan tradition of peaceful interreligious dialogue that has arisen from the Franciscan movement and its impact on the twentieth-century monk, while highlighting the present-day implications for hearing the voice of the stranger in our midst and abroad.

First, we will look at Franciscan interreligious dialogue. Since every interreligious experience is rooted in a particular historical setting, I will present a brief historical context. Without an appreciation for the ecclesiastical and sociopolitical world serving as a backdrop to the interreligious experience of Francis, the full significance of hearing the other is lost. Next, I will present a summary of Francis's interreligious encounter with the sultan in Egypt. The most famous of Francis's interreligious encounters, this will serve as a case study. From our examination of Francis's encounter with the sultan, I will suggest three characteristics that arise from our methodological reflection that will allow us to locate the operative hermeneutic in the work of Francis.

Second, I will use the three characteristics of Franciscan interreligious dialogue identified in the first section as a lens through which to examine the interreligious work of Merton. As we will see, Merton's interreligious encounters bear a strong resemblance to Francis's meeting with the sultan. Through his own words and actions, Merton expresses the

Franciscan spirit of peaceful and authentic encounter with the "stranger."

At the end of the chapter, I will suggest considering our present time as not that different from those of Merton decades ago and Francis centuries earlier. I will examine the contemporary relevance of the model for interreligious dialogue that Francis and Merton leave to us and show how an adoption of the method of Francis and Merton might open new pathways for interreligious dialogue today. As twenty-first-century citizens, we are inheritors of a rich tradition shaped by these two prophetic voices that continue to speak with great pertinence today. We are better able to hear the voice of the stranger in our own day aided by their wisdom and guided by their example.

Setting Up the Story of Francis and Franciscan Interreligious Dialogue

In April 1213, Pope Innocent III released his encyclical *Quia maior*, which introduced his plan for the fifth crusade (1217–1221). As the second crusade called by Innocent III—his first was from 1202 to 1204—this endeavor was seen as the final step in recapturing the Holy Land and was doubtless the talk of the town. The two hallmarks of *Quia maior* were the general call for everyone in Christendom to support the effort and the encyclical's great detail concerning the manner in which this fifth crusade was to be launched. Whereas the preceding crusades had been launched largely because of the activity of the emperors, the fifth crusade was an effort completely of Innocent III.

In addition to the somewhat unique nature of the crusade being called by the pope, its announcement through a papal encyclical presented a new theological dimension to understanding the purpose of the crusade. No longer was a crusade to be interpreted, however superficially, as an act of civil authority or aggression. Innocent III's encyclical placed the papacy and all of Christendom behind the effort.[5] Innocent III set the plan in motion, but it would be ordinary Christians who would pay the bill, staff the army, and pray for military success. Further developing a theological purpose for the crusade, Innocent III declared that this effort was part of God's divine command.[6] Horrifically, this view was rooted in Innocent III's understanding that the Gospel call to "love one's neighbor" compelled Christians to liberate their fellow Christians in the Holy Land, "who are being held in the hands of the perfidious Saracens in dire imprisonment and are weighed down by the yoke of most severe slavery," he wrote.[7] The operative hermeneutic of the time was one of fear, relegating Muslims to otherness and viewing these women and men as absolute strangers. By excluding Muslim men and women from the Christian obligation to "love one's neighbor," they were dehumanized.

This attitude of the dehumanized other had been developing for nearly a century by this time. Innocent III was greatly influenced by the theology and preaching of Bernard of Clairvaux, who believed that while God could easily liberate the Holy Land from the Saracens, God had provided an opportunity for all Christians to prove themselves faithful to Christ by becoming involved in the crusade.[8] Not only was the defeat of the Muslims a matter of military strategy, but it was also viewed as God's will. Evidence of similar disdain for Muslims exists among chroniclers of the time such as in the writing of Bishop Jacques de Vitry, who, in addition to providing a personal account of Francis's encounter with the sultan, describes the Saracens as "sacrilegious disciples of [the] Antichrist."[9] The general attitude of the time was one of great hostility toward Muslims.

The Beginning of
Franciscan Interreligious Dialogue

Revolutionary in lifestyle and ambitious in scope, Francis of
Assisi's first rule of life for the Order of Friars Minor, tentatively
approved by Pope Innocent III, included a chapter dedicated
solely to the way the friars were to engage non-Christians.
Francis's desire, articulated in summary at the onset of his
rule, was simply to live the Gospel of Jesus Christ.[10] It is clear
that the experience of Gospel living informed the lens through
which Francis viewed his world. Beginning with the famous
encounter with the leper, when Francis himself recognized
his own need for conversion, and continuing throughout his
earthly journey, Francis set an example for Christian engagement with the "stranger." Nowhere in his writings is this
example more clear than in the chapter of his way of life that
instructs his followers on how to encounter the strangers of
his time: the Muslims and other nonbelievers.

Chapter 16 of the *Regula non bullata*, titled "Those Who
Are Going among the Saracens and Other Nonbelievers,"[11]
resulted from the experience of Francis and his companions
in their peaceful mission among the Saracens in 1219.[12] At a
time when the Christian world was rallying support for and
contributing to the efforts of the fifth crusade, Francis—initially
motivated by zeal for the gift of martyrdom, and later inspired
to promote peaceful resolution to war[13]—traveled to Egypt
with a few of his companions to preach to the Muslims and
oppose the crusade.[14]

His journey began in 1212, prior to the formal launching
of the fifth crusade. Strongly moved to preach the message
of the Gospel to the Muslims, Francis set out on a journey
to Syria and shortly afterward to Morocco, but his mission
was cut short due to travel complications and poor health.[15]
Francis would eventually succeed with his plan and reach
Damietta. Upon arriving, having traveled to Egypt with Italian

crusaders, Francis saw the devastation of battle and the inevitable defeat that lay ahead for the Christian army. While staying in the crusaders' camp, Francis challenged the crusaders to consider whether their engagement in battle with the Saracens was really the will of God. Francis's most famous biographer, Thomas of Celano, suggests that the crusaders were warned by Francis that their losses in battle were the result of their disregard for the true will of God, that of peacemaking and not war. Francis's espousal of nonviolence and his efforts to dissuade violent action by the crusaders speaks volumes of the countercultural position embraced by this man from Assisi. According to scholar Jan Hoeberichts, "Francis occupied an exceptional position among his contemporaries with regard to the crusades and the attitude they expressed towards the Saracens and Islam. This is all the more striking since virtually the entire church from high to low was committed to the crusade."[16]

Francis de Beer suggests that "Francis's attitude appears strange, to say the least."[17] Certainly Francis's opposition to the direction the Church and the political world was moving was seen as odd, considering his loyalty to the Church and its leadership. However, his commitment to following the Gospel trumped even his steadfast fidelity to the Church.

Having preached to the crusaders, Francis left the protection of their camp to go among the Saracens. His vision of universal fraternity and connectedness as children of God allowed him to approach the Saracens, viewing them not as "enemy" but as friend, remembering the call of Christ to "love your enemies and do good to those who hate you."[18] Jesus' command to love was for Francis a central truth, and by radically adhering to this truth, he was an example to his followers of what it meant to follow Christ by living as a *frater minor* (lesser brother). Becoming vulnerable to the point of risking his very life, Francis humbly lived as a brother to all.

Along with his companion Brother Illuminato, Francis crossed the Saracen threshold and requested permission to see the sultan. They were at first denied, but after persistent requests, they were seized, beaten, and eventually taken to Sultan Malik al-Kamil. The Saracens most likely thought Francis and Illuminato were negotiators sent by the crusaders in response to the sultan's earlier attempt at calling a truce.[19] However, Francis had come on his own with his own agenda: a message of peace.

This message included preaching the Gospel to the sultan in a way that was respectful and inviting. Francis never insulted or denigrated Islam—as his contemporaries were known to do—but his disarming approach created an atmosphere of conversation and dialogue. It is believed that Francis and his companion spent up to three weeks with the sultan and his advisors discussing religious matters and sharing their experiences.

Malik al-Kamil was known to be a kind and just man in his own right. His attentive listening to Francis, and that he graciously allowed a Christian to preach in his court, demonstrates the openness to dialogue the sultan had toward a humble man who posed no threat and sought peace amid violence. Jacques de Vitry chronicles this experience of openness as he notes,

> When the cruel beast [the Sultan] saw Francis, he recognized him as a man of God and changed his attitude into one of gentleness, and for some days he listened very attentively to Francis as he preached the faith of Christ to him and his followers. . . . At the end he said to Francis: "Pray for me, that God may deign to reveal to me the law and the faith which is more pleasing to Him."[20]

When the time had come for Francis and his companion to depart from the sultan's court, Malik al-Kamil showed his admiration and affection for the *poverello* in a personal request for a prayer. As Kathleen Warren notes, the sultan was sincerely moved by Francis's goodness and sincere desire to promote peace and truth among the Christians and Saracens.[21]

The sultan was surely aware that Francis saw the Muslims as children of God and his brothers and sisters. Francis de Beer identifies this encounter, signified by the sultan's prayer request, as a moment when Francis transcended "the cloister of Christianity" and invited the sultan to likewise transcend his own boundaries.[22] While the sultan was not yet ready to make that move, it was clear that a seed was planted and "a dialogue was initiated which transcended all quarrels, discussions, and arguments. And no one could go any further: neither Francis nor the Sultan. One must wait for the hour of the Spirit. And the suspense has lasted for centuries."[23]

Three Insights from Francis of Assisi's Experience

A question naturally arises concerning the manner with which Francis was able to engage in such peaceful dialogue: how did Francis do this? To appreciate the significance of Francis's encounter with the sultan, and his entire interreligious attitude, we must first explore his method. In the interest of brevity, I suggest three factors that operate concurrently throughout Francis's interreligious encounter with the sultan that form the foundation of what we might today call "Franciscan interreligious dialogue." These factors are as follows:

1. The radical adhering to the evangelical value of solidarity
2. The preferential option for the discovery of common faith
3. The position of minority rooted in a commitment to lifelong conversion

While the person and charism of Francis of Assisi cannot be limited to these three attributes, in naming them we might

nevertheless establish a starting point from which an analysis
of Franciscan interreligious dialogue can advance.

The Franciscan movement, rooted in Gospel living, has
always collectively embodied the notion of fraternity. The
quintessential expression of this principle is found in Francis's
most famous writing, "The Canticle of the Creatures."[24] Here
Francis expresses his radical worldview of the interconnectedness of all creation stemming from the one, loving God. While
this Franciscan expression has often been diluted to a caricature
of the *poverello* and a birdbath, its most honest reading suggests
an intense appreciation for the gift of life and existence shared
by all. Beyond the poetry of "The Canticle of the Creatures,"
this view is found in the living example of Christian charity of
Francis encountering the sultan. From prayer to praxis, Francis
saw himself as another blessed creature of God, in many ways
no different from the sultan and the Saracens. In understanding
himself as brother to all, Francis transcended the boundary of
"us" versus "them" categories and embraced the marginalized
and abused outcasts of his day.

There is a strong temptation to romanticize this encounter and neglect the sacrifice and vulnerability of Francis. His
decision to welcome the sultan and other Muslims into his
life as brothers and sisters was in stark contrast to the policies
and practice of the Church and the social order of his day. In
choosing to stand in solidarity beside the Muslims, he moved
outside the comfort of inclusion to live at the margins and
became better able to hear the voice of the "stranger" because
he had become a stranger to his own culture.

Our second characteristic, the preferential option for the
discovery of common faith, is found explicitly in Francis's rule
of life. The recent work of Franciscan scholar Laurent Gallant
has shed a great deal of light on the true meaning of Francis's
sixteenth chapter of the *Regula non bullata*. The text has always
been interpreted to have an ecumenical tone and understood
as the product of the experiences of Francis and his brothers'

mission among the Saracens.[25] Take, for example, verse 6, concerning how the friars are to live spiritually among the Saracens: "One way is not to engage in arguments or disputes, but to be subject to every human creature for God's sake and to acknowledge that they are Christians."[26] The significance of Gallant's study is the extent to which Francis's directive expresses a preferential option for the discovery of common faith. While previously acknowledged as explicit instructions for his followers to encounter the stranger, the method of dialogue seems to have been skewed over time.

The traditional translation, influenced by the proliferation of copied manuscripts that include the addition of the word "in" (*ut credant* in *Deum omnipotentem*), has been understood as instructing evangelization efforts to promote Christianity among the Muslims.[27] Verse 7 has been read as, "The other way is to announce the Word of God, when they see it pleases the Lord, in order that [unbelievers] may believe *in almighty God, the Father, the Son and the Holy Spirit, the Creator of all.*"[28] This reading suggests an exclusively Christian approach toward encountering the other. Gallant believes that this is a copyist error that dates back to at least the seventeenth century and has reoccurred in every major edition since. Gallant posits that this error was easily overlooked and replicated because of the possible influence of and resemblance to the Christian creed.[29] The familiarity of the copyists with the Christian creed (which begins *Credo* in *Deum omnipotentem*) would naturally lead them to "correct" the written rule of Francis by inserting the word "in." Subsequently, this copying error has led to the diminishing of the radical example of interreligious dialogue over several centuries.

Serious textual criticism of the manuscript tradition has only been explored since the middle of the twentieth century, beginning with the work of scholars such as David Flood and Thadee Matura.[30] Gallant's revisiting of the *Regula non bullata* text is the most recent contribution to this field. His reading of the text suggests a more radical—and curiously more "Franciscan" in the fraternal sense—expression of Francis's desire that the friars meet the stranger on common ground. Gallant asserts that Francis's instruction in verse 7 be read as follows:

> in order that they may believe
> 1. that almighty God [in which they already believe] is Father, Son, and Holy Spirit,
> 2. that the Creator of all [in which they also already believe] is the Son [i.e., God's creating Word], who is Redeemer and Savior.[31]

This interpretation suggests an effort to unite the Muslim and Christian through doctrinal agreement as a starting point. The establishment of common doctrinal ground is the first step of a two-tiered enterprise. The second step is the explication of the Christian conception of "almighty God" as Trinity, and that "Creator of all" includes the Son. This second step is only possible built on the foundation of the preferential option for the discovery of common faith. Francis's goal here was not to preach exclusive Christian dogma to the Muslims and other nonbelievers. Rather, by discovering articles of faith shared by both groups, a peaceful conversation rooted in solidarity can begin. Gallant also observes that historians and theologians of the Franciscan movement often emphasize Francis's "acute conscience of the presence of God and of the working of the Spirit in all human beings. This shared Christian-Muslim belief in ['almighty God'] and 'Creator of all' would certainly be an example of common faith."[32]

In many ways our third category suggests the most original and classically "Franciscan" of the three characteristics found in Francis's encounter and his vision that his brothers were to follow. The position of minority rooted in a commitment to lifelong conversion is also the most organic and dynamic of the three, which further complicates a systematic analysis of his interreligious approach.

Francis held that in order to live a truly authentic form of Gospel life, one was never to place one's self above another. In chapter 6 of the *Regula non bullata*, Francis remarks that this attitude is to be held even among the brothers: "Let no one be called 'prior,' but let everyone in general be called a lesser brother. Let one wash the feet of the other."[33]

Minority is not synonymous with passivity. Rather, Francis viewed a life as minor when one courageously stood against the power differentials that divided the people of his day. A product of his time, Francis was all too familiar with the medieval authoritarian structures that made up his world. Even with the rise of the merchant class in the thirteenth century, Francis could not escape the social pressure to achieve some sort of noble status. As a young man both he and his father desired that Francis become a successful knight. It was not until the beginning of his conversion in 1206 that Francis began seeking a life of minority. Thomas of Celano describes his outward change in appearance: "He who once enjoyed wearing scarlet robes now traveled about half-clothed."[34]

The humility that naturally accompanies such a state of living helped to create a nonthreatening space for dialogue. If one is not interested in winning, being correct, or ranking above another, then one is not a threat. The sultan had nothing to fear from Francis. The way Francis lived his life demonstrated his willingness to be subordinate to every other person for God's sake. Francis recognized himself as a sinner and therefore knew of his own need for continued conversion, garnering a great deal of patience for those whom he encountered. While considering what was so nonthreatening about Francis, Franciscan theologian Kenneth Himes said, "It was the fact that no one ever had to fear Francis. Francis never sought to dominate, manipulate, or coerce anyone. No person ever looked into the eyes of Francis and saw a lust for power or control."[35]

In many ways these characteristics of "Franciscan interreligious dialogue" show but a snapshot of the complex and inspiring charism they aim to convey. It is my hope that by articulating these factors, we might better appreciate the Franciscan spirit that so touched and influenced Thomas Merton.

Thomas Merton's Interreligious Dialogue

As we have already seen, the occurrence of Merton's frequent and direct references to Francis of Assisi throughout his written corpus alone testifies to his conscious reflection on the medieval saint. However, what's more is the strong resemblance of Merton's implicit worldview to that of Francis. While their historic contexts are separated by centuries, their core principles remain powerfully parallel. Simply put, the lifelong significance of Francis and Franciscan spirituality for Merton helped shape the way he viewed those of other faiths. Similarly, we see this in other areas of his life. His prayer, poetry, and other writings often maintain a style that reflects Franciscan views of Christology, environmental theology, Trinity, human relationship, poverty, and humility, to name a few. It seems appropriate to name Franciscan interreligious dialogue as a major source of Merton's own interreligious approach and include it as part of the ways in which the Franciscan tradition had carried over into Merton's life, thought, and writings.

Here we will explore just a sample of Merton's interreligious work through the lens of Franciscan interreligious dialogue as outlined above. It is my hope that, after careful consideration, we can affirm the resemblance to and likely influence of Franciscan interreligious dialogue in Merton's life and work.

The Radical Adhering to the Evangelical Value of Solidarity

For Francis, fraternity summarized his radical living in solidarity with all of humanity and creation. Abstracted in the vernacular poetry and prayer of "The Canticle of the Creatures" and exemplified in the encounter with the sultan, Francis's starting point rested in the faithful recognition of his relationship to the other. Merton shares a similar starting point for his interreligious encounters. Best articulated as openness and eremitical prayerfulness, Merton's radical adherence to solidarity with the other stood as a foundation for his interreligious work.

Authentic Gospel living is not based on the building up of toleration and an emphasis on individuality, as was the emerging tendency at the dawn of postmodernity toward the end of Merton's life. Rather, Merton asserted the need for unity and the end of division, envisioning a community like the Acts of the Apostles describes: "They devoted themselves to the apostles' teaching and fellowship, to the breaking of bread and the prayers. . . . All who believed were together and had all things in common" (Acts 2:42, 44). It is this ardent faithfulness to the Gospel that we can describe as radical adherence to solidarity.

If we look to the text from which came the title for this conference, Merton's essay "A Letter to Pablo Antonio Cuadra concerning Giants," we see an assertive critique of those unwilling to stand in solidarity with the rest of humanity.[36] He names the affluent antagonist the "tourist." Merton opines, "He cannot possibly realize that the stranger has something very valuable, something irreplaceable to give him. . . . The tourist lacks nothing except brothers. For him these do not exist. The tourist never meets anyone, never encounters anyone, never finds the brother in the stranger."[37] While this is an explicit polemic aimed at the United States, it is perhaps an implicit reference to when the young Merton was something of a globetrotter himself and much less open to the stranger. Rooted in his own experience, Merton can empathize with—and in turn criticize—the "tourist," challenging the Western citizen to growth in the evangelical life.

Merton's own spiritual maturation led to his identification with the rest of humanity. Seeking a life of solidarity in which he might live in a way other than the "society of isolated

individuals," Merton recognized that Christians are called to
build communities of persons and not collections of individuals.[38] Concerning the world of isolated individuals, Merton
explains, "They do not know that reality is to be sought not
in division but in unity, for we are 'members one of another'
. . . the [one] who lives in division is not a person but only an
'individual.'"[39]

Solidarity appears as a recurring theme throughout Merton's work. For Merton, solidarity is seen as openness to both
God and humanity. William Apel describes this feature as "one
of the greatest lessons we can gather from Merton's life."[40]
What's more, placing Merton's response of solidarity within
the context of his time, we see, as Allan McMillan put so well,
"Merton had insights not typical to the times in which they
occurred and his learning had an experiential base."[41] McMillan goes on to suggest "seven lessons" learned by Merton
during his interreligious encounters. The fourth such lesson
is that of solidarity, "that one cannot understand the depth of
feelings and faith experiences of another person unless one
has experienced and wrestled with them in his or her own
life. This compassion, this willingness to 'suffer with' *the other*
opens us to the appreciation of the greatness of how other
people respond to the Divine call."[42] This position of solidarity, while not necessarily present in the behavior and writing
of the young Merton, is a recurring characteristic of the later
Merton's interreligious modus operandi.

Merton's interreligious efforts were made at a time marked
by great suspicion of outsiders. Long before the Second Vatican Council's "Declaration on Religious Freedom" (*Dignitatis
Humanae*) and the "Constitution on the Church in the Modern World" (*Gaudium et Spes*), Merton chose to stand with the
"stranger" and to engage the "other," setting himself outside
the popular limit of any interreligious encounter endorsed
by his peers, culture, and Church. His decision to embrace a
position of solidarity risked the rejection of some, to be open to

all. Merton knew his own identity was inescapably intertwined with the rest of humanity. He says in *New Seeds of Contemplation*, "I must look for my identity, somehow, not only in God but in other men [and women]. I will never be able to find myself if I isolate myself from the rest of [hu]mankind as if I were a different kind of being."[43]

The Preferential Option for the Discovery of Common Faith

With a worldview shaped by the desire to form a community of persons as opposed to a collection of individuals, Merton moves from a foundation of solidarity with the "other" or "stranger" to engage in interreligious encounters. At this point the preferential option for the discovery of common faith emerges with force. Returning to *Conjectures of a Guilty Bystander*, we observe Merton's explicit expression of this characteristic: "The more I am able to affirm others, to say 'yes' to them in myself, by discovering them in myself and myself in them, the more real I am. I am fully real if my own heart says *yes* to *everyone*. I will be a better Catholic, not if I can *refute* every shade of Protestantism [or other faiths], but if I can affirm the truth in it and still go further."[44] Merton, like Francis, recognized that true dialogue could never be based on proselytizing or evangelization in the narrow sense. Both Francis and Merton reflect the truth that God dwells in each person, and each saw the need to affirm that truth in the "stranger" as paramount to fruitful dialogue.

Merton's relationship with D. T. Suzuki illustrates this well. In a journal entry dated April 11, 1959, Merton reflects on the experience of a spiritual encounter with Suzuki.

> Thus if I tried badly and bluntly to "convert" Suzuki, that is, make him "accept" formulas regarding the faith that are accepted by the average American Catholic, I would, in fact, not "convert" him at all, but simply confuse and

> (in a cultural sense) degrade him. Not that he does not
> need the Sacraments, etc. but that is an entirely different
> question. On the contrary—if I can meet him on a common
> ground of spiritual Truth, where we share a real and deep
> experience of God, and where we know in humility our
> own deepest selves . . . then I certainly think Christ would
> be present and glorified in both of us and this would lead
> to a *conversion of us both*.[45]

Those who knew Merton, such as Amiya Chakravarty, Glenn
Hinson, D. T. Suzuki, and John Wu, have commented on his
ability to engage with members of other faiths through his
openness to their experience. Merton expresses in *Mystics and
Zen Masters* that the true meaning of "catholic" includes "a
readiness to enter into dialogue with all that is pure, wise,
profound and humane in every kind of culture."[46] He spends
much of this volume drawing connections between Christianity and Zen Buddhism, which remains one of his most
explicit examples of the preferential option for the discovery
of common faith.

Mystics and Zen Masters chronicles Merton's step-by-step
exploration of Eastern spirituality through the lens of common faith. He highlights his discovery of existential similarities among Christians and the "stranger" in various ways.
Merton cannot help but identify the ways that Zen Buddhism
corresponds to Christianity. He compares the tea ceremony
with Franciscan simplicity;[47] "Buddhahood" with passages
in 1 Corinthians;[48] the Zen notion that "zero equals infinity"
with John of the Cross's "*todo y nada*" (all and nothing);[49] the
tradition of Kung Tzu with the tradition of St. Benedict;[50] the
wisdom of the *Tao Te Ching* as resembling the Sermon on the
Mount;[51] the philosophical insights of *Hsiao Ching* reflecting
Christian Neoplatonic thought like that of Pseudo-Dionysius;[52]
and so on. Following Francis, Merton's modus operandi is that
of a preference for the discovery of that which unites humanity

in God, or as Merton often described it, "the Hidden Ground of love."

This ongoing quest to identify with those of other beliefs through the discovery of common faith led Merton to return to the metaphor of the "tourist." Like Merton's own growth from naive Catholic convert to interreligious ambassador par excellence, he calls the "tourists" of the world to find themselves in the "other" and in "strangers" who are most unlike them. In doing so, they will have made a successful pilgrimage. Merton says, "It was in this spirit that St. Francis went on pilgrimage—on his own original kind of 'crusade'—to meet the [sultan]; as a messenger not of violence, not of arrogant power, but of humility, simplicity and love."[53] Merton refers us to his pilgrimage guide and model with the hope that we too will emulate St. Francis.

The Position of Minority Rooted in a Commitment to Lifelong Conversion

Finally, we examine how Merton emulated Francis's position of minority rooted in a commitment to lifelong conversion. Lawrence Cunningham suggests that Merton's most radical conversion, or "series of conversions," occurred through the 1950s and reached a climax with the 1966 publication of *Conjectures of a Guilty Bystander*.[54] Any reader of his life work will notice the gradual shift in emphasis from internal reflection to include external action. One struggle that remained constant for Merton was discerning the relationship between his vocation to the eremitical life and the call to engage the world. Eventually, and most explicitly, the nexus of monk and prophet became manifest in his strong interreligious interest and peace activism of the 1960s.

Like Francis, who has often been depicted as something of a "playboy" in his youth, one might say that Merton lived a rather pleasure-seeking life during his early years. Outlined

in *The Seven Storey Mountain*, Merton's initial conversion to
Catholic Christianity took shape in a manner much like Francis's own. A clear liminal experience marked the beginning of
the conversions of both Francis and Merton. I say "beginning"
because both men saw this process as an ongoing experience
of reorientation upward toward God and outward toward the
rest of humanity after the pattern of the Gospel. As Lawrence
Cunningham has noted, this experience of conversion continued to shape Merton's life and lead him toward the "stranger"
through interreligious dialogue.

Those familiar with Merton's life and work know of his
struggles with ego. In a strikingly honest passage in *New Seeds
of Contemplation*, Merton prays, "Give me humility in which
alone is rest, and deliver me from pride which is the heaviest
of burdens. And possess my whole heart and soul with the
simplicity of love."[55] The almost instant fame resulting from the
bestselling success of his autobiography early in his religious
life, and his subsequent battle with egotism, is an example
of his struggle to find balance, humility, and vocational clarity. Merton discovered the answer to his dilemma in the full
embrace of his vocation to solitude.

Contemplation is many things for Merton. Much of his
writing expresses his struggle to specifically identify its meaning. Merton describes contemplation as that which is beyond
all other forms of experience, as that which reaches out to the
inexpressible God, as an awareness of the gift of our contingent
existence, and finally as a response to God.[56] Contemplation
is understood in varied ways, but every perspective views
contemplation as an ongoing process. To experience contemplation, Merton tells us that continual divesting of our ego,
self-centeredness, and sinfulness is necessary to recognize that
in our true poverty we are free to more perfectly follow Christ.
This experience of humility beckons an awareness of the poverty and need of those around us. In turn, such a process of

ongoing conversion, or contemplation, leads one upward to God and outward toward the rest of humanity.

Francis's mendicant life of minority is reflected in Merton's monastic life of contemplation. Minority encompasses those aspects of the *vita evangelica* (poverty, chastity, and obedience) common to religious life. It is also a conscious renunciation of power and status. It requires voluntary subordination of one's self for the sake of solidarity and communion with the other. Reaching the state of minority is a process of ongoing conversion. Another way to appreciate Francis's minority and Merton's contemplation is to consider these terms as describing two sides of the same coin. Francis's minority most accurately describes the manifestation of the process of ongoing conversion, whereas Merton's contemplation summarizes the action (or lack thereof) of the process.

The dynamic result of this ongoing process of conversion is the discovery of one's true identity. In order to hear the "voice of the stranger" and authentically encounter the other, I must know who I am. An oft-cited fruit of Merton's life of contemplation is the emergence of his conceptualization of the "true self." Merton finds the "true self" in God's image of him rather than in his own skewed perception. To find who he is, Merton must find who God is. "In order to know and love God as He is, we must have God dwelling in us in a new way, not only in His creative power but in His mercy, not only in his greatness but in His littleness, by which He empties Himself and comes down to us to be empty in our emptiness, and so fill us in His fullness."[57] The act of God's *kenosis* that Merton describes serves as a model for his own life. It is the Incarnation that articulates God's choice to live out a position of minority among us. Discovering and following this example, we live as our true selves. Through contemplation and openness to ongoing conversion from the false self, we discover who we really are in who God really is. To live the life of the Gospel is to live a life of self-emptying service, finding God in our emptiness and poverty. From that position of minority, we, like Merton and Francis, are able to authentically encounter the "stranger" and to hear his or her voice.

No Longer Strangers:
Hearing the Voice of the Other

We continue to live in a world of strangers. While technology, science, travel, and other forms of discovery have shaped our contemporary culture to appear unlike Francis's thirteenth-century Italy and even Merton's early twentieth-century United States, some aspects of life transcend the boundaries of geography and time. Unfortunately, we, like Francis and Merton, find ourselves in a world of broken humanity. The ongoing struggles of the human condition call us to help advance reconciliation and dialogue.

We are challenged daily by threats of violence, war, unrest, discrimination, inequality, racism, and other forms of injustice. In an age marked by the overt presence of religious pluralism and secular governments, openness to other people, cultures, and religious expressions is surprisingly sparse. It is even difficult to recognize the faux form of acceptance Merton decries as a "society of isolated individuals," when violence erupts in the form of genocide in Sudan, authoritarian oppression and coercion in China, political unrest in Kenya, terrorist attacks in Britain and Spain, school shootings in the United States, utter chaos in Iraq, turbulence in Afghanistan, and in manifold manifestations in every corner of the globe. As citizens of a postmodern, globalized, twenty-first-century world, we have much to learn about seeing, hearing, and loving the "stranger." For, as Merton reflects in his masterful and poetic essay "Day of a Stranger," we *too* are strangers.[58] The stranger can be a negative image of isolation, marginalization, and difference, or it can represent the embrace of one's "true self." Patrick

O'Connell has written about a renowned essay by Merton in which Merton describes an "ordinary" day:

> In describing his day, Merton presents his life as a unique way of experiencing a common humanity. The word "stranger" in the title might initially suggest someone whose way of life is strange or exotic, but eventually it takes on the connotations of one who does not fit in, whose identity cannot be defined by a public role, a recognized place in society at large or monastic society in particular, cannot, in fact, be defined at all. Merton takes pains to dispel the impression of strangeness in the first sense by emphasizing that in fundamental ways his life is no different from anybody else's, but this very ordinariness protects and nurtures the mystery of identity that unfolds throughout the description of the day.[59]

The strangeness of being a stranger can be cast in either of these lights: exclusion or embrace. The exclusive nature of the stranger emerges in the marginalization, the stereotyping, the misunderstanding, and the willful ignorance of the shared humanity of the other. The embracing light of strangeness is— as Merton models after the example of Francis—what results from simply being who it is that you are before God. Embracing one's true self is the way to recognize that our strangeness is simply another name for the humanity we share, the hidden ground of love, and the relationship we share in Christ that precedes our recognition or acknowledgment of that reality.

I believe we can benefit greatly from Franciscan interreligious dialogue and Merton's model of and contribution to that tradition. Following the lead of Francis and Merton, and learning from their examples, we might move from living in a society of isolated individuals and exclusive strangers to living an expression of God's kingdom with our sisters and brothers.

Both Francis and Merton speak a prophetic word to us today. Francis maps the path to hear the voice of the stranger, while Merton demonstrates that the path can still be traveled.

Both exemplars of interreligious dialogue embody the three characteristics outlined above, and our desire to emulate their model of interreligious dialogue must lead us to similar embodiment of these characteristics. If we hope to effect change in our world, we must first be willing to change ourselves.

The change required of us is essential to implementing Franciscan interreligious dialogue. This change is not a matter of exterior practice, political affiliation, social networking, branding, or the use of fashionable and politically correct buzzwords. The change demanded of us is internal, foundational, and spiritual. It is the adoption of a new way to live our lives; it is the willingness to rethink our worldview; and it is revisioning the way we see God in our world and in one another.

The new way to live our lives is found in the embodiment of the position of minority rooted in a commitment to lifelong conversion. When capital gain and power over others are the measures of success, voluntarily embracing minority is indeed a novel way to live. Francis demonstrates that authentic Christian living is rooted in becoming subject to our brothers and sisters and, by doing so, avoiding the pitfalls of power and unjust authority. Merton teaches us that it is God who models the greatest example of humility through the Incarnation, and it is through contemplation that we come to see this more clearly. The lives of Francis and Merton show us that this is not an overnight process. Rather, we must remain committed to the process of lifelong conversion that draws us nearer to God and each other.

The willingness to rethink our worldview is located in the embodiment of the preferential option for the discovery of common faith. When winning and advancing at the expense of another is broadly accepted and preferred in our society, seeking to form connections and identifying similarities with others is a radical paradigm shift. Francis started at the level of the other, wherever that might be. Instead of condemning the differences of the stranger, Francis embraced the shared faith and experiences of those he encountered. Likewise, Merton saw a reflection of God in the faith and life of those different from him.

Revisioning the way we see God in our world and in one another is manifest in the radical adherence to the evangelical value of solidarity. When our society defines our personal identities by what makes us different, we must uncover the truth of God's presence on earth—that all citizens of this world share our humanity. Francis saw his life as interdependent and connected to every other aspect of God's creation. This fraternal view of the universe marks a path for us toward a global community. Merton saw the intrinsic value of each person as an interrelated participant in God's creation. He walked Francis's path away from understanding society as a collection of individuals toward the Christian experience of a community of persons.

The opportunity for the internal, foundational, and spiritual transformation placed before us today is an invitation to radically change the way we encounter all whom we meet. Embodying the characteristics of Francis and Merton's method of interreligious dialogue will allow us to become the new prophetic voices our world so desperately needs. We can become the voices that announce the possibility of a world that welcomes, no longer strangers, but brothers and sisters all.

Scott Thomas makes the argument that Franciscan interreligious dialogue speaks a message to today's world that confirms tolerance and appreciation for the religious sensibilities and traditions of others but is not based on, nor leads to, skepticism, relativism, or syncretism. Rather, authentically hearing the voice of the stranger is the fruit of remaining firmly rooted in one's own religious tradition with a genuine openness to encountering the other.[60]

Thomas Merton's work in the early and middle part of the twentieth century demonstrates the life-giving nature of a tradition that speaks to our contemporary world as much as it did some eight hundred years ago. Merton saw the great need for valid religious renewal in order to maintain any semblance of relevance in our modern world.[61] Franciscan interreligious dialogue provides a schema for ecumenical relevance in a broken and divided world. I believe that this powerful model of authentic encounter with "the other" informed the action of Merton over time and possesses the possibility to steer our interreligious efforts in a positive direction today.

Some will dismiss Francis and Merton as irrelevant to their lives because of the extraordinary nature of their work. Some will suggest that both Francis and Merton lived and acted in another time, in another place, and in another manner foreign to the time, locations, and issues of today. Some will suggest that the challenge of engaging in authentic dialogue is too difficult.

The last objection, if only a flaccid excuse, is somewhat honest. It is difficult to engage in authentic dialogue, to change our image of "other or stranger" to "brother or sister." This experience demands a comprehensive change in lifestyle, worldview, and communication. It is, as our third characteristic of Franciscan interreligious dialogue suggests, truly a process of lifelong conversion that requires our commitment to relationship.

Like Francis and Merton, we must answer the call to enter into this relationship wholeheartedly, risking much for the sake of another. We are shown a way of solidarity, seeking common faith and lifelong humility. We are asked to change and be God's instruments of change in the world. Only then will our ears be open to hear the voices of the strangers, and our hearts be open to love and to be loved by them.

CHAPTER 10

Becoming Instruments of Peace: How Francis and Merton Challenge Us to Live Today

Although Francis of Assisi did not write the prayer that has come to be so closely associated with his name and legacy (the so-called Peace Prayer of St. Francis was written and published in French during the early twentieth century by an anonymous author), the theme, goal, and flow of the prayer does reflect the spirit of the *poverello* in the truest sense. Francis sought to live in such a way as to shine the light of Christ for those who were in darkness, offer a sign of faith for those in doubt, bring joy to the sad, console the grieving, understand the misunderstood, and love the unloved. In a phrase, Francis really did pray with his whole life, in word and in deed, to *become an instrument of peace*.

As we saw in the last chapter, Francis's experience in Damietta during his peaceful interreligious encounter with

Sultan Malik al-Kamil was one of the most concrete and powerful examples of his commitment to peacemaking. Merton
not only recognized the interreligious spirit in the lived model
of Francis but also seems to have had a rich appreciation for
the ways that the encounter in Egypt was reflected in various
other encounters with women and men throughout his life. At
the beginning of chapter 9, we read that Merton wrote in the
early 1960s that "anyone familiar with the writings of St. Francis and with his life is aware that the Saint was always urging
his Friars to be at peace with each other and to go among men
as peacemakers."[1] This is simply one instance when Merton
explicitly highlights Francis's enduring significance as a model
of Christian living. But we are left with a question: in what way
does this become embodied in the life, thought, and writing
of Merton?

This chapter is an exploration of the ways Francis of Assisi
and Thomas Merton understood peacemaking and its place
in the life of Christian discipleship. At times, such as in the
quotation above where he highlights Francis directly as an
influence and guide, Merton is overt in his acknowledgment
of the role the Franciscan tradition has played in the development of his understanding of peace, peacemaking, and the
Christian vocation. However, most times he does not identify
Francis or the Franciscan tradition by name. In this sense, the
Franciscan inspiration in his life, thought, and writings bears a
closer resemblance to his "paradise consciousness" as we saw
in chapter 7. Merton's sense of peacemaking and its intrinsic
place in authentic Christian living takes the shape of Francis's
challenging vision.

The structure of this chapter is threefold. First, we will take
a look at how Francis of Assisi's life and writings, as well as
the tradition that followed, provide us with a unique notion
of peace and peacemaking. For the saint from Assisi, it was
rooted in his notion of *evangelical poverty*, which stood at the
heart of his whole life project of following in the footprints of

Jesus Christ. Second, we will see how Thomas Merton gradually became aware of the absolute centrality of peacemaking in Christian life. His commitment to peace and justice, informed as it was by his increasingly prophetic vision of God's intention for humanity and all creation, compelled him to shift his glance from an interior life of prayer and solitude toward an outward focus on social justice, civil rights, nonviolence, and what we might call "contemplation in action." Finally, we will see how peacemaking is a dimension of the human vocation, which extends even beyond baptized Christians to include all women and men, in the worldviews of both Francis and Merton.

Francis of Assisi: Poverty, Power, and Peacemaking

It is not surprising that when most people think of Francis of Assisi and the religious movement that bears his name, the subject of poverty usually comes to the forefront of their minds. The Franciscan scholar Michael Robson explains that "a radically new dimension was brought to the history of religious life in the western Church by Francis's renunciation of all forms of ownership and his rejection of the customary forms of economic support for a community of friars. He and his followers lived in both individual and corporate poverty, a significant departure by a religious community."[2] It is true that poverty played a significant role in what became Francis's way of living the Gospel. But, as we saw back in chapter 1, the notion of poverty in the life and vision of Francis is more complicated than most people realize.

In recent years, scholars in the United States and Europe have uncovered some of the complexities that shade the meaning of poverty in Francis's choice to follow in the footprints of Christ. For example, the French historian Jacques Dalarun has spent much of his academic career trying to disentangle the complicated portrayals of Francis that are passed on through

the centuries in the mixed collection of hagiography (narratives about the lives or holiness of saints) and historical fact
that appear in the early sources, legends, and chronicles of
the thirteenth and early fourteenth centuries.[3] In his *Francis
of Assisi and Power*, Dalarun studies the tradition and textual
evidence, arguing in turn that what was really the fundamental
issue at stake for Francis in his particularly idiosyncratic way
of life, "according to the pattern of the Holy Gospel,"[4] was not
poverty as an *end in itself* (something we began to discuss in
chapter 1) but rather poverty as a strategy for the *renunciation
of power*. Dalarun explains, in sum, what we can expect to find
in Francis's writings:

> [Francis] chose to establish in a rule of religious life the
> condition shared by the most powerless classes in the soci-
> ety of his time: destitution, precariousness, itinerancy, and
> manual labor. He showed a loathing for all forms of power
> that went far beyond the scorn of the world as found in
> the monastic and ascetic tradition. With Francis, there is
> less of a merely visible break with the world; at the heart
> of his life there is instead more intransigence toward any
> compromise with the world and its powers.[5]

The idea that Francis was interested in renouncing power is
not necessarily an intuitive interpretation. But if we look at the
earliest concrete expression of his vision for living the Gospel
contained in the *Regula non bullata* (the "Rule without papal
approval" completed in 1221), we see inscribed explicit references to power and its exercise, as well as passages that allude
to the intended social location of the friars who would come
after him. One of the most direct references to power in the
Regula non bullata appears in the fifth chapter:

> Likewise, let none of the brothers exercise any power or
> any form of domination [*potestatem vel dominationem*] in
> this way, especially among themselves. For, if the Lord
> says in the Gospel, "the rulers of the Gentiles lord it over

them and the great ones [*maiores*] make their authority over them felt" (Mt 20:26–28), it will not be this way among the brothers. And whoever will wish to become greater [*maior*] among them, let him be their minister and servant [*minister et servus*]. And let he who is greater [*maior*] among them become the least [*minor*].[6]

This is followed closely by a similarly striking passage in the next chapter of the *Regula*: "Let no one be called 'prior,' but let everyone in general be called a lesser brother. Let one wash the feet of another."[7]

Power and evangelical poverty are intimately connected in Francis of Assisi's way of discipleship. Dalarun explains that "the 'lesser' model advocated by the Poverello in his very first fraternity was in no way that of an urban 'bourgeois' religious life, but a joining in the conditions of the *most powerless*, who can be identified through the concrete study of their living conditions—for example, the seasonal agricultural worker."[8] For Francis, everything about the Gospel life was rooted in the inherent relationality of the human person as the *imago Dei* ("image of God"). Just as God humbled Godself to become human like us in the person of Jesus of Nazareth, and then proceeded to live in the world according to the priority of service, love, peace, and reconciliation, so too all people are called to do likewise. The humility of the Incarnation and the poverty of Christ served as Francis's template.[9] Francis desired that nothing should get in the way of one's ability to embrace and relate to others, just as Christ allowed nothing to get in the way of his embrace and relationality to others.

The embrace of evangelical poverty that is tied to renouncing power after the model God laid out for humanity in the Incarnation is the foundation for peacemaking. For Francis, peacemaking was, plain and simple, to live as God intended human beings to live among one another within the broader context of the created universe. God provided the highest example of this way of going about the world in the life, death,

and resurrection of Jesus Christ. It falls to us, those who live
so many centuries after Jesus, to look at the Gospel and adopt
the Christian narrative of human relating as our own. As we
saw in the last chapter, this inherently peaceful way of being in
the world that Francis so closely associated with the example
of Christ was written down in his instructions to the brothers
who desired to go into the world as missionaries: "One way
is not to engage in arguments or disputes, but to be subject to
every human creature for God's sake and to acknowledge that
they are Christians."[10] At the core of Francis's understanding
of what it means to be a peacemaker is the commitment to take
down any barriers we intentionally or inadvertently put up
between ourselves and others that prevent us from entering
into honest, humble, and meaningful relationships with others.

This vision of peacemaking, of continuously working to
enter more and more into unencumbered relationships with
other women and men by meeting them where they are and
revealing our true selves to the other, is very challenging for us
today. We live in a time and within a society that is individual-
istic and self-centered. Additionally, the proliferation of techno-
logical means of communication and social media has created
a new type of wall between us and the other, while simulta-
neously convincing us that we are "more connected" and "in
touch" with family, friends, and strangers. Franciscan peacemaking requires a self-awareness that unsettles our everyday
obliviousness to the words and actions we engage in that place
barriers between people and stifle genuine relationships.

Thomas Merton:
Becoming an Instrument of Peace

Given how well Thomas Merton is known today for his antiwar, civil rights, and social justice writings in the 1960s, it can
be difficult to recall that he had not always been so interested
in or convinced of the need for engagement with the emerging

peace movements of his day. There was indeed a marked shift, as many biographers and Merton scholars have noted, in the final decade of his life, which has been frequently characterized as his "turn toward the world." Through his correspondence with women and men involved in the antiwar, civil rights, and peace movements, Merton came to a clearer sense of the obligation he had as a Christian to speak out against the injustices in his time, reflecting again the prophetic vision we briefly explored in chapter 8. As in his becoming a prophet over time, and his growing paradise consciousness and embrace of interreligious dialogue, his focus on peacemaking and its central place in the Christian life did not happen overnight.

The gradual increase of attention Merton began to pay in writing to the violence and injustice in the United States and abroad raised the ire of some of his readers and concerned many of his religious superiors in the Cistercian Order. William Shannon has pointed out that in 1961, "much to the astonishment of the many people who had admired [Merton] for all he had said on spirituality and contemplation, Thomas Merton seemed suddenly to be turning to politics, writing about war and other social issues, challenging his readers to responsibility and action. . . . Many of his faithful followers were scandalized and bewildered by this change in direction."[11]

While there had always been seeds of social consciousness and incredulity toward violent action in Merton's worldview, something about the nexus of the Vietnam War, the civil rights movement, the ecumenical and interreligious shift in the Church, and his increasing ecological awareness led to a break from the singular focus on the interior spiritual life toward the praxis of Christian *living*.

This comes across clearly in what amounts to Merton's first "major publication" on nonviolence, peacemaking, and war. In 1961, he wrote an article for Dorothy Day's *The Catholic Worker* newspaper titled "The Root of War Is Fear." It was later included in his revised *New Seeds of Contemplation*, but in that version several paragraphs were not included because the religious censors of Merton's community had not seen and approved them. Among those parts left out of the book is the following paragraph, which expresses succinctly and powerfully the vision Merton had for the whole Christian community.

> Christians must become active in every possible way, mobilizing all their resources for the fight against war. First of all there is much to be studied, much to be learned. Peace is to be preached, nonviolence is to be explained as a practical method, and not left to be mocked as an outlet for crackpots who want to make a show of themselves. Prayer and sacrifice must be used as the most effective spiritual weapons in the war against war, and like all weapons they must be used with deliberate aim: not just with a vague aspiration for peace and security, but against violence and against war. This implies that we are also willing to sacrifice and restrain our own instinct for violence and aggressiveness in our relations with other people. We may never succeed in this campaign but whether we succeed or not the duty is evident. It is the great Christian task of our time.[12]

Part of the work of Christian discipleship, Merton explains, is to in effect "do one's homework" when it comes to right action ("orthopraxis") in Gospel living. One can sense in Merton's words an outlook that bears some similarity to that of Francis of Assisi. Nonviolence and peacemaking for Merton includes— or, perhaps, is built upon—our willingness to "sacrifice and restrain our own instinct for violence and aggressiveness in our relations with other people." In other words, nonviolence and peacemaking mean nothing if we continue to put up barriers between us and others, between people who are called by the Creator to be in humble, honest, and direct relationship. Violence is always an instance of breaking relationship with another.

For Merton, nonviolence was an integrative dimension of Christian discipleship that, as Shannon describes it, "is an all-or-nothing reality. It embraces all of one's life and all of the responsibility flowing from one's particular way of life."[13] If your way of life is Christianity, then nonviolence is nonnegotiable. It doesn't appear that Merton necessarily saw the relationship between poverty and nonviolence in quite the same way that Francis did. But the grounding principle, which is the renunciation of power to enter more authentically into relationship with others and the rest of creation, is at the core of Merton's emphatic defense of Christian nonviolence. He wrote that nonviolence "is not out for the conversion of the wicked to the ideas of the good, but for the healing and reconciliation of man with himself, man the person and man the human family."[14] Elsewhere Merton wrote that, to engage in nonviolent action and advocate on behalf of peace, one had to start with the presupposition that humanity was—at least according to God's intention—foundationally united as creatures of a loving God.

Merton resisted the moniker "pacifist," arguing that he was—at least ideologically—a defender of the "Just War Theory," a longstanding tradition that claimed there could be a justifiable war fought if strict moral criteria were met. However, James Forest has claimed that Merton's writings on nonviolence suggested he was really a pacifist in practice. Forest wrote, "[Merton] was also a pacifist—someone who has renounced violence as a means in peacemaking—yet he often said he was against war only in practice, not in theory. . . . In an existential and temperamental sense, Merton was one of the most committed pacifists I have ever met. He saw war as one of the clearest examples of human estrangement from sanity and God."[15] In reading Merton's writing on Christian nonviolence, Forest understood correctly his prophetic vision of the way humanity has become estranged from itself and from God.

There are dozens of other examples that could be cited, but most important for us to appreciate here is that Merton's life moved along such a trajectory as to reflect, in his own unique and particular way, the principles of Gospel living that Francis of Assisi modeled centuries earlier. They both saw that the breaking of relationship—whether through the violent exercise of power caused by poverty or by physical force—is antithetical to true Christian living. Furthermore, while Francis and Merton exhorted other Christians to be peacemakers, both also came to a fuller understanding that peacemaking through nonviolent living in our world is not something reserved just for Christians. While not always easy to see at first in their respective writings, the medieval mendicant and the modern monk, each in their own time and place, realized that God's intention for humanity included the vocation of peacemaking.

The Vocation of Peacemaking

As we saw in the first chapter, there are many misconceptions or generalizations about Francis of Assisi and his perspectives on faith and the world. Oftentimes these are innocent caricatures, but they nevertheless mask the profound wisdom and power of Francis's worldview, convictions, and model of Christian living. One such example centers on the meaning of vocation and peacemaking. At the end of chapter 1, while we were looking at the composition of "The Canticle of the Creatures," I mentioned briefly that Francis wrote the second part of the canticle in response to a civil dispute between the mayor and the bishop of Assisi. Up until this point, the canticle was composed of nine verses that focused on the way in which various aspects of the created order praised God by being or doing what they were intended by the Creator to be or do. The sun, for example, gives praise to God by shining splendorous light; water gives praise to God by being "humble and precious and chaste"; fire gives praise to God through its warmth; and Mother Earth gives praise to God by "sustaining

and governing" all of the world. It is only at this point, at verse
ten of fourteen total verses, that Francis introduces human
beings into the song of praise and thanksgiving.

What follows in this very short reflection is startling for
both its brevity and its profundity. Francis cuts right to the
heart of what it means to be *truly human*, to give praise to God
through being and doing what God intended human beings
to be and do. Francis wrote,

> Praised be You, my Lord, through those who give pardon for
>   Your love,
> and bear infirmity and tribulation.
>
> Blessed are those who endure in peace
> for by You, Most High, shall they be crowned.

It is striking that love, forgiveness, and peacemaking—even
amid difficult times of infirmity and tribulation—are what
Francis highlights as the constitutive dimensions of the human
person. His "theological anthropology" (fancy theologian language for talking about what it means to be a human person
according to the Christian tradition) is not focused on humans
as "rational animals" as was that of ancient philosophers, nor
does Francis consider the technical advancement of human
creativity to be what allows us to praise God; no, it is simply
our ability to love, forgive, and be peacemakers.

Of course, there is hardly anything simple about loving,
forgiving, and making peace in the way that Francis of Assisi
is suggesting here (recall that he mentions doing so when times
are difficult—"infirmity and tribulation"). Yet, there is a welcome humility in recognizing that the playing field of human
existence is leveled in Francis's vision of how God sees us. It
is not one's intellectual prowess, athletic ability, or physical
beauty that glorifies God. Instead, it is our exercise of our free
will in choosing to be lovers, forgivers, and peacemakers that
in an ironic twist actually makes us very much like God.

This last statement—that we act *very much like God* when we love, forgive, and make peace—might require some unpacking. This is basically another way of saying that God doesn't lie to us and that if we take the dogma of the Incarnation seriously, that God became a human being like us, then how God acts as a human—loving the unlovable, forgiving the unforgivable, and bringing a peace the world cannot give (Jn 14:27)—is the most clear indication of how God *intends* for *all humans to act*. Jesus isn't just the fullest revelation of who God is but also the fullest revelation of *who we are* as women and men created in the image and likeness of God!

Francis of Assisi got that. He realized, even if he didn't express it in some sort of fancy theological language, that *all people* reflect their fullest humanity in following in the footprints of Jesus Christ. This doesn't necessarily mean that only those who explicitly express faith in Jesus Christ as do baptized Christians are fully human. No, it is those who love, forgive, and endure in peace, regardless of what they might encounter, who are fully human. Christians, we might say, have the most concrete illustration and a sure hope in what living one's full humanity looks like in the person of Jesus of Nazareth. What it means to give glory to God by living as the human beings God created us to be extends far beyond Christians to include all of the human family. True, Christian women and men have little or no excuse and should know better than to act against their true identity, but we are all part of the human family and the created order that was lovingly brought into existence by God. As trees give glory to God by being trees and bees give glory to God by being bees, you and I give glory to God by being human, which means to love, forgive, and be peacemakers.

This universal call to be peacemakers is something that resonates within Thomas Merton's vision of what it means to be a human person too. While Francis of Assisi never used the term "vocation" in describing this universal call for authentic human living, Merton's perspective on vocation is helpful in understanding better what he'll come to see as a constitutive dimension of the human person. Merton most succinctly identifies what he means by vocation in his book *No Man Is an Island*, in which we read,

> Each one of us has some kind of vocation. We are all called by God to share in His life and in His kingdom. Each one of us is called to a special place in the Kingdom. If we find that place we will be happy. If we do not find it, we can never be completely happy. For each one of us, there is only one thing necessary: to fulfill our own destiny, according to God's will, to be what God wants us to be.[16]

From the outset, Merton is identifying a universal quality or characteristic of the human condition in his reflection on vocation. *Every* person has a vocation, not just those who espouse the Christian narrative or those baptized into the Body of Christ in a special way. Instead, we draw on his constructive Christian anthropology, best summarized in his writings on the "true self" (explored in greater detail in chapter 5), which itself was informed so directly by the Franciscan tradition; thus, Merton posits vocation as an a priori condition of human existence. Merton's work reacts against the general social and ecclesial notions of vocation, each of which stem from either the popular notion that we are fabricators of our own identity or the longstanding Christian view of an external call (*vocare*) from the Divine.[17]

The Catholic Church has a venerable tradition of situating peacemaking at the center of Christian life. For example, this is the case in the United States Conference of Catholic Bishops' (USCCB) 1993 document *The Harvest of Justice Is Sown in Peace*. In this text, we see this latter, ecclesial notion of "vocation" in terms of peacemaking presented. Christian women and men, we read, receive a "call" from the Lord to be peacemakers that reflects authentic evangelical discipleship. In contrast to this claim, Merton immediately broadens the subject pool to include *all people* and grounds the concept of vocation in each individual's intrinsic identity or true self, which is created by and known to God.

This vocation or identity is not necessarily readily known or intuited.[18] This helps explain why it is not always easy to see peacemaking as so central to authentic human existence. The location of identity is found in its source: God. Merton explains,

> But whatever is in God is really identical with Him, for His infinite simplicity admits no division and no distinction. Therefore I cannot hope to find myself anywhere except in Him. Ultimately the only way that I can be myself is to become identified with Him in Whom is hidden the reason and fulfillment of my existence. Therefore there is only one problem on which all my existence, my peace and my happiness depend: to discover myself in discovering God. If I find Him I will find myself and if I find my true self I will find Him.[19]

Locating one's identity and vocation within God places the emphasis away from individual appropriation of some characteristic, construction of some habit, or longing for some goal, and instead it situates who we are in a place prior to our own discovery and positions vocation internally rather than in the realm of the external.

For Merton, vocation is not like a cloak put on from without or an identity forged at will but like an internal dimension of who we are in our deepest, truest self. This insight is grounded in Merton's theological anthropology (again, as we saw in chapter 5), his understanding of the human person broadly conceived, and is inexorably shaped by his notion of identity and God's creative act of the human person.[20] Robert Imperato has similarly identified a connection between Merton's intrinsic and a priori conception of human identity and vocation with the Trappist monk's social justice work and peacemaking. Imperato writes, "Throughout Merton's

writings on social issues, one feels—behind the particulars of
the issue—his commitment to the person. Turning from the
journals of Merton to his treatises on topics relating to peace,
the reader detects in Merton a more self-consciously rigorous
foundation. . . . Merton uses principles that are linked to his
intuition of the person."[21] This intuition of the human person
rests in Merton's theological conviction that all people are created in the image and likeness of God with inherent value and
dignity. Yet, like so much of our identity that appears hidden,
Merton believes we must discover this vocation deep within
our hearts, and contemporaneously, we find God.[22]

It is helpful to look at Merton's commentary on Pope John
XXIII's 1963 encyclical letter *Pacem in Terris*. Merton's commentary was written the same year and titled "The Christian
in World Crisis"; in it, we can gain additional appreciation
for Merton's claim that the vocation to be a peacemaker is
inherently situated within the divinely created identity of
every human person. From the beginning of his essay, Merton
focuses on John XXIII's universal address and later reiterates
that "the duty of working together for peace in this sense binds
not only public authority but all those to whom the Encyclical
is addressed: that is to say *everybody*."[23] While Merton does pick
up on the particular address to Christians in *Pacem in Terris*
and elsewhere, he always does so with the caveat that Christians have a "special obligation," because of their conscious
commitment to follow the Gospel, to be peacemakers.[24] The
universality of peacemaking plays a central role in Merton's
interpretation of the encyclical. "This [peacemaking] is not
a matter for a few individual consciences, it urgently binds
the conscience of every living man. It is not an individual
refinement of spirituality, a luxury of the soul, but a collective
obligation of the highest urgency, a universal and immediate
need which can no longer be ignored."[25] Later in his essay,
Merton contrasts the authority of *Pacem in Terris* with that of
violence-oriented or nation-state authority. The encyclical's

authority "rests on the objective reality of man"; it is rooted in the a priori human condition as created by God.[26]

While many Christian writers and the longstanding tradition of Catholic social teaching discuss the vocation of peacemaking in terms of Christian discipleship, Merton discusses what we might call the vocation of peacemaking in terms of his particular Christology, which was also deeply indebted to numerous Franciscan sources as we saw in chapter 6.[27] The grounding of Merton's notion of the human vocation as peacemaker in his Christology is not to be confused with the strictures of Christian confessional confines but is instead a call to interpret vocation and peacemaking through the lens of Christian anthropology with the understanding that, like Francis of Assisi, Merton recognized Jesus Christ as the fullest revelation both of what God is like and of what *the human person* is like. For it is Christ-as-human that most fully illustrates the universal human vocation as peacemaker. Merton insists that what we see passed down to us as originating in the *kerygma* (the New Testament Greek word for the earliest Christian preaching) and mediated through scripture is the "human nature, identical in all men [and women]" as perfected in the life, death, and resurrection of Christ.[28] When we see Christ as peacemaker, we see a reflection of our human vocation perfected.

Merton scholar Patrick O'Connell explains that this expansive sense of the human vocation as peacemaker beyond the confines of Christian discipleship or membership in the Christian Church is further bolstered in Merton's work by the monk's "conviction that the nonviolence of the gospel corresponds to the deepest needs, desires, and hopes of the human spirit."[29] For Merton, the reverse is also true. If peacemaking is a constitutive part of the human vocation as the image and likeness of God and one intrinsically oriented toward the Divine, then violence is in effect a denial of humanity's true identity, a distortion of our vocation.[30]

Merton, in something of a helpful interreligious move, saw in Mohandas Gandhi's writings and lived example a similar appreciation for the universality and intrinsic character of the vocation of peacemaking in all people. Each person has the capacity to live out this identity in truth, but one has to overcome the external distractions and irrational justifications toward violence. In the introduction to a collection of Gandhi's writings that he edited, Merton wrote,

> The spirit of non-violence sprang from an inner realization of spiritual unity in himself. The whole Gandhian concept of non-violent action and *satyagraha* is incomprehensible if it is thought to be a means of achieving unity rather than as the fruit of inner unity already achieved. . . . The first thing of all and the most important of all was the inner unity, the overcoming and healing of inner division, the consequent spiritual and personal freedom, of which national autonomy and liberty would only be consequences.[31]

Merton sees these values, these principles, and this nonviolent action arising from deep within the human person. He insists that these are universal and that whether one describes them in terms of Christian discipleship or as *satyagraha* (Gandhi's term for nonviolent resistance; it literally means "holding on to truth") or something else, they are inherent and prior to their multifarious descriptions.[32]

Illustrating this belief, Merton sent a brief acceptance address in response to being awarded the Pax Medal in 1963, because he was unable to attend the ceremony in person. He said quite simply, "This puts me in a rather awkward position of receiving a prize for doing what is only the plain and obvious duty of a reasonable human being who also happens to be a Christian. It is like getting a medal for going to work in the morning, or stopping at traffic lights, or paying one's bills."[33] While he was certainly expressing himself with a hint of jest, Merton's seemingly joking remarks might have been actually rooted in his conviction that the vocation of peacemaking is something *every* human person is called to live. It is at the heart of who we are as created in the image and likeness of God. When we discover our true selves and act according to that for which God has created us, we cannot help but live as peacemakers in the world.

The Challenge for Us Today

That peacemaking is an intrinsic part of our vocation to be authentically human might likely be an unexpected surprise to many. It is something that is often overlooked, either innocently or through willful ignorance, in both the Franciscan tradition and Merton's writings. The personal histories of both Francis of Assisi and Thomas Merton provide us with some comforting reassurance that we don't come to clarity about this aspect of our human existence overnight. For Francis and Merton, it took many years, lots of prayer, and genuine struggle to come to find the connection between God and the true self. Even though this sort of journey takes a long time (a lifetime to be exact), we have to start somewhere. Like Francis and Merton, the first challenge that this call to become instruments of peace presents to us is the need we have to more intentionally look at how we understand the human person. Returning to the insights of the Franciscan tradition channeled through Merton's creative reflections on the true self, we must ask ourselves, Who am I? And, where do I look for the answer to that question? Are we willing to confront the "false selves" that we present to the world and strive instead to step into that vulnerable place where we surrender control of our image and instead dare to embrace the *image and likeness* of God?

A second challenge for us is to look to Jesus Christ in the Gospel as *both* the fullest revelation of who God is *and* the fullest revelation of who we are. Just as Francis and Merton came to recognize in Jesus of Nazareth the love, forgiveness, and peace of God, so too we are challenged to respond to the call—the *vocare*, the vocation—to walk in the footprints of

Christ. This means that when we boldly proclaim ourselves to be Christians, those who bear the name "Christ," we are announcing to the world that the model for our being in the world is different from what various versions presented in the world might offer. Our model for authentic human living is Jesus Christ. But do we live up to our name as Christians? Can others look at us and know from our words and deeds that we know what it means to be a human person? Are others inspired to be more truly themselves in our presence, not because we are so great but because we know our weaknesses, embrace them, and continue to journey in life aiming only to love courageously, forgive unconditionally, and work for the peace that the world cannot give?

A third challenge is for us to consider how we view others. Those who advocate positions of pacifism, nonviolence, and peacemaking are often criticized for their idealism. Yet, isn't this "idealism" what Christians pray every day when they speak with their mouths the words of Jesus to his disciples? "Thy kingdom come, thy will be done." Indeed, what it means to be truly human is not something that comes easily. We have too many competing narratives and alternative gods in our lives, not the least of which is our own self-centeredness and selfishness, sometimes called original sin, for us to follow in the footprints of Christ with ease. But follow we must. This is not something that requires explicit profession of faith in Christ, but it does require concrete action that reflects a shift in worldview more in line with God's vision for true human action and living. This means that the way we look at others, evaluate them, judge them, exclude or marginalize them, ignore them, hold grudges against them, withhold love from them, or maintain a position of violence toward them must change. Christians who do these things cannot claim to be following Christ, nor can any human who isn't working for peace claim to be truly human. This is perhaps the most challenging aspect of taking seriously the legacies of Francis of Assisi and

Thomas Merton: we cannot simply go about living our lives in the ways we always have. Only in daring to hear and respond to the challenge Francis and Merton present to us can we really become instruments of peace.

CONCLUSION

Finding Francis
in
Unlikely
Places

That Thomas Merton had a Franciscan heart seemed an odd claim to make about the most famous Trappist monk of the last century. Yet, as I hoped to have shown in this book, the initial attraction to and continued influence of the Franciscan tradition indelibly shaped the worldview of Merton. In an age marked by the election of the first pope from the Society of Jesus, the first pope to come from South America, and the first pope to take the name "Francis" after St. Francis of Assisi, attention paid to the ways St. Francis appears in predictable and unpredictable ways is even more timely. This is perhaps just the latest example of how Francis continues to be found in unexpected places. Still, some might think it is an unlikely discovery to find Francis behind some of Merton's most famous ideas and texts, and yet this is what we have discovered here. It is my belief that the more we learn about what influenced Merton's thought process and experience of faith, the more we will be able to appreciate, study, appropriate, and follow his life, thought, and writing.

The necessary limitations of scope in an already lengthy book such as this prohibit even further investigation into the thought of Thomas Merton and the Franciscan influences behind it. For example, while we have taken a good look at some of Merton's more overtly Christian writings to discover the Franciscan sources behind many of them, we have not looked as closely at his poetry or literary essays. Among some of his most interesting essays one can find at times the explicit identification and at other times the spectral presence of Francis. Take, for instance, Merton's essays on Albert Camus. If one would initially think it unlikely to find Francis in Merton's thought generally, surely it would be even less likely to find the modern monk discussing the medieval saint in a text about the twentieth-century existentialist philosopher and playwright; yet, this is exactly what we find. In several places Merton writes about Francis and Camus, noting in one essay on Camus's notebooks that Camus had a particular admiration for Francis and the Franciscan Order. Merton contends that if Camus had gone a little deeper in his reflections on what about Francis's form of Christian living was so powerful, "he would have realized that the abstract God he could not believe in was not, and never had been, the living God of authentic Christianity."[1] For Merton, Francis of Assisi and his way of life provided something of an "antidote" for the atheism of Camus and likeminded others.

The Franciscan tradition was indeed one of the major influences in Merton's eclectic exploration of the Christian tradition. However, I contend that the Franciscan tradition was not simply one among many in an equal sense but one of the few most influential factors in Merton's theological, spiritual, and personal development. Appearing explicitly at every period of his life, Francis and the Franciscan tradition maintained a consistent pride of place alongside a few other key sources such as both the Desert and Eastern Fathers. Furthermore, Francis and the Franciscan tradition also appeared in less visible ways, behind the scenes of Merton's writing. And it is not difficult to see how this has played out in his life and thought.

From the earliest days of his religious conversion, Merton was drawn to a way of life that seemed to align naturally with his disposition and interests. When becoming a typical follower of Francis became ostensibly impossible, Merton consciously embraced his own version of a Franciscan life, committing to learn as much as he could about the tradition and live as close to that way of life as possible. Ultimately, it was by means of his pursuing this particular way of living in the Franciscan charism that Merton discovered his true monastic call and was encouraged along his way by those Franciscan friars he had come to love and admire at St. Bonaventure University.

In the decades that followed his entrance into the monastery, Merton's life, thought, and writings took on different shapes and forms but nevertheless retained a particularly Franciscan sense. This was not in contrast to the other sources Merton so famously engaged; rather, those threads of Franciscan thought and insight seem to have supplemented those other things Merton was exploring. What became Merton's notion of the true self, his understanding of the Incarnation, his relationship to creation, his embrace of the prophetic call, his interreligious efforts, and his views on war and peace all bore some Franciscan mark, albeit each in different ways.

Perhaps more than the theological and philosophical aspects of Merton's writing, it is the spiritual and prayerful dimensions of his thought and reflection guided by the Franciscan tradition that might speak to the hearts of women and men today. It was not according to some compelling argument or original theory that Merton felt Francis would have so significantly changed Albert Camus's worldview, but the simplicity of the medieval saint's embrace of the Gospel and understanding of God. I believe Merton could say this because he too—like Camus, Pope Francis, and billions of other people over the centuries—was drawn to the bare authenticity of the saint from Assisi. Merton takes this Franciscan inspiration and model and develops contemporary reflections into timely and relevant practices and ways of thinking that continue to call, challenge, and guide women and men today. Merton's life, thought, and writing have helped nurture my own Franciscan heart, and I hope that it has and will for you too.

Merton's Prayer to St. Francis of Assisi

SEPTEMBER 6, 1941

This prayer was composed at the beginning of Thomas Merton's last semester teaching at St. Bonaventure. Within four months, Merton will have found—in part—the answer to this prayer, having moved from St. Bonaventure to the Abbey of Gethsemani to become a postulant in the Order of Cistercians of the Strict Observance (O.C.S.O.), better known as the "Trappists." In addition to being an exemplary illustration of how Merton admired and respected St. Francis of Assisi during this time in his life and vocational discernment, this prayer highlights a number of perennial themes that are found within Merton's other journal entries, correspondence, and writings throughout his lifetime. A struggle Merton identifies here and elsewhere is that of pride and the desires he had for success, recognition, and literary renown. Additionally, an awareness of this tendency also prompts the discerning Merton to pray for humility, something he will also seek endlessly.

Holy Father Saint Francis

I believe that, in your immense and inexpressible love of Jesus Christ our Lord, you can look into my dumb, crooked soul and see what is there before I can say it in the selection of cheap, vulgar, stupid words presently about to flow from my inexpensive fountain pen. And because of the immensity of your burning and immaculate and humble love of Jesus My God, I know you will pray to him for me that I may be granted whatever I pray that may bring me to Him in love and humility.

Therefore I pray to you, Holy Father Saint Francis, first that I may be filled with tears and with the love of God, continually, not in order that I may delight in these things and be filled always with nothing but consolation, but in order that they may keep me silent from pride, and fill me with strength and desire to abandon the world altogether, even though I remain in the midst of it.

And when I am not filled with the strength of consolation, then, even more, do I need your prayers, Holy Father: because then the resolutions I made when I was full of love look as if they were about to be wrecked on my rocks of pride and fleshly self-love.

When I pray for suffering—and then get a cold, the world's most ridiculous disease; sneezing in church; running nose; sweat; no sense of devotion; very unpicturesque: what is the result? I am mad and impatient—and mad at myself for being impatient. But if I am mad at myself for being impatient it is a great new flourishing exercise of my pride and nothing else.

So then I go back to bed for a long nap after dinner, missing None, and I am mad at myself for doing that. Going to bed or not going to bed makes little difference to the love of God. But pride makes a lot of difference: and I am mad at myself because of pride—It would have been good if I hadn't gone to bed. I might still have a cold, which is gone. It doesn't matter. But I got mad and impatient, and that was a gross imperfection because it was nothing but pride.

Holy Father, take away, by your prayers, this pride; but for such pride, I would have something less absurd to write here. Because I am so aware of the absurdity is only a sign of more pride.

But for this pride, also, I wouldn't be so self-conscious about language to express what I feel: but that is only part of it. I wish I could write it better out of respect for God, Who gave me these small and very usual and familiar and unstartling and generous graces.

But I am also thinking it would be better to write about it in good words, not cheap words, so that the reader may (if it is ever read) respect me, *my* experience (as opposed to *the* experience, but it isn't *my* experience really, and if *I* claim respect for it, I lose all the good it brought me, of love and devotion to My Lord).

Yet, Holy Father, pray that I may write simply and straight anything I ever have to write, that no dishonor come to God through my writing rubbish about Him.

But if I am humble, I will write better, just by being humble. By being humble, I will write what is true, simply—and the simple truth is never rubbish and never scandalous—except to people in peculiar perplexities of pride themselves.

Holy Father Saint Francis, pray for me: for you will never refuse to hear prayers that will help me to come to Our Lord. Then pray for me that I may give as much as I can to the poor. And that soon I may be able to go hungry so that someone else may not suffer. And that I may laugh and sing when I am despised for God's love, and that I may dance and play when I am reviled for God's love, and called a mad man, and a fool and a crook.

Pray for me to be poor, meek; to hunger and thirst for justice, and be merciful; to be a peacemaker, clean of heart, to be reviled, to be persecuted for God's sake.

Pray for me, Holy Father Saint Francis, to do all these things although I have never gone hungry except for silly reasons (couldn't get my claws on the icebox) and never suffered except for silly reasons (hangovers; blisters from walking around all night in World's Fairs).

Pray for me, Holy Father Saint Francis, in all things to sing to God very humbly and childishly and sweetly, and not to be sore at myself when, instead of heroic temptations, I get nothing but silly and absurd and insulting and stupid temptations: who do I think I am? The others will come soon enough!

Only pray for me, my Father Saint Francis, to give up everything up for My Lord, to be the least of His children and the most insignificant of the poor for love only, and that in all things I may have grace to pray meekly and patiently and happily, and not in the confusion of pride, and the scruples pride puts in our heads and the fears pride freezes us with. Pray for me for enough humility to always pray for humility, poverty, and tears.

Through the merciful intercession of Christ Our Lord Who reigns eternally with the Father and the Holy Spirit, one God, the life and joy and bliss of all things and only object of all love! Amen.[1]

NOTES

Introduction: On "Merton's Heart"

1. Michael Downey, "Merton's Franciscan Heart," *Franciscan Studies* 55 (1998): 300.

2. This took place on the evening of February 19, 1941. Merton writes in his journal, "Tonight I was received into the Third Order, under the patronage of Saint Gregory. I was thinking [of] entering the Order long ago—last fall." See Thomas Merton, "February 19, 1941," in *Run to the Mountain: The Story of a Vocation*, ed. Patrick Hart, Journals of Thomas Merton 1, 1939–1941 (San Francisco: HarperSanFrancisco, 1995), 309. He also writes about this in Thomas Merton, *The Seven Storey Mountain: An Autobiography of Faith*, 50th anniversary ed. (New York: Harcourt Brace, 1998), 328. According to Merton's official biographer, Merton had been contemplating entering the Third Order as far back as his initial conversations with Father Thomas Plassmann about the possibility of teaching English at St. Bonaventure. See Michael Mott, *The Seven Mountains of Thomas Merton* (New York: Houghton Mifflin, 1993), 158.

3. Unpublished letter from Thomas Merton to Rev. Thomas Plassmann (May 31, 1955), Thomas Merton collection of Freidsam Memorial Library, St. Bonaventure University.

4. Letter from Thomas Merton to Anthony Bannon (February 2, 1966), in Thomas Merton, *Witness to Freedom: Letters in Times of Crisis*, ed. William Shannon (New York: Harcourt Brace, 1994), 164.

5. See David Golemboski, "Life of a Stranger: How Thomas Merton Pitched In by Dropping Out," *Merton Journal* 15 (2008): 19–24.

6. For more on this theme, see Fred Herron, "A Bricoleur in the Monastery: Merton's Tactics in a Nothing Place," *Merton Annual* 19 (2006): 114–27.

7. Second Vatican Council, *Nostra Aetate* ("Declaration on the Relation of the Church to Non-Christian Religions"), no. 2, in *The Documents of Vatican II: With Notes and Index* (Strathfield, Australia: St Pauls Publications, 2009), 387–88.

1. The Medieval Mendicant: Francis of Assisi

1. Francis of Assisi, "The Canticle of the Creatures," in *Francis of Assisi: Early Documents*, ed. Regis J. Armstrong, J. A. Wayne Hellmann, and William Short, 3 vols. (New York: New City Press,

1999–2001), 1:114–15. Further citations of this source will be noted as *FAED* followed by the volume and page number.

2. As it appeared in a 1992 special issue of *Time* magazine. This detail is cited in Lawrence Cunningham, *Francis of Assisi: Performing the Gospel Life* (Grand Rapids, MI: Eerdmans, 2004), vi.

3. Augustine Thompson, *Francis of Assisi: A New Biography* (Ithaca, NY: Cornell University Press, 2011); and André Vauchez, *Francis of Assisi: The Life and Afterlife of a Medieval Saint*, trans. Michael Cusato (New Haven, CT: Yale University Press, 2012).

4. Vauchez, *Francis of Assisi*, 7.

5. Thompson, *Francis of Assisi*, 8.

6. Dominic Monti, *Francis and His Brothers: A Popular History of the Franciscan Friars* (Cincinnati: St. Anthony Messenger Press, 2009), 10–11.

7. Thompson, *Francis of Assisi*, 10.

8. Paul Moses, *The Saint and the Sultan: The Crusades, Islam, and Francis of Assisi's Mission of Peace* (New York: Doubleday, 2009).

9. Moses, *The Saint and the Sultan*, 22.

10. Thomas of Celano, "The Life of Saint Francis," bk. 1, 2:17, in *FAED*, 1:195.

11. Francis of Assisi, "The Testament," 1–3, in *FAED*, 1:124.

12. Gustavo Gutiérrez, *A Theology of Liberation*, trans. Caridad Inda and John Eagleson (Maryknoll, NY: Orbis Books, 1988), 172. Themes in this section of the chapter were previously developed in an earlier essay. See Daniel Horan, "Profit or Prophet? A Franciscan Challenge to Millennials in Higher Education," *AFCU Journal* 8 (2011): 59–73.

13. Thomas of Celano, "The Life of Saint Francis" bk. 1, 3:6, in *FAED*, 1:187.

14. Ilia Delio, "Christian Life in a World of Change," *AFCU Journal* 7 (2010): 9.

15. Francis of Assisi, "A Letter to the Entire Order," 28–29, in *FAED*, 1:118.

16. Regis Armstrong and Ingrid Peterson, *The Franciscan Tradition* (Collegeville, MN: Liturgical Press, 2010), xi, xvii.

17. Bonaventure, "The Major Legend of Saint Francis," vol. 3, 3:1, in *FAED*, 2:542.

18. Francis of Assisi, "The Testament," 14, in *FAED*, 1:125.

19. Michael Cusato, "Francis and the Franciscan Movement (1181/2–1226)," in *The Cambridge Companion to Francis of Assisi*, ed. Michael Robson (New York: Cambridge University Press, 2012), 22.

20. Francis of Assisi, "The Earlier Rule (1221)," 7, in *FAED*, 1:68–69; and Francis of Assisi, "The Later Rule (1223)," 5, in *FAED*, 1:102–3. For more on the centrality of work in the early Franciscan movement, see David Flood, *Work for Everyone: Francis of Assisi and the Ethic of Service* (Quezon City, Philippines: CCFMC, 1997); and David Flood, *The Daily Labor of the Early Franciscans* (St. Bonaventure, NY: Franciscan Institute Publications, 2010).

21. Again see Francis of Assisi, "The Earlier Rule," 7, in *FAED*, 1:68–69; and Francis of Assisi, "The Later Rule," 5, in *FAED*, 1:102–3.

22. For examples of such accounts, see "The Legend of the Three Companions (1241–1247)," in *FAED*, 2:61–110; and "The Assisi Compilation (1244–1260)," in *FAED*, 2:113–230.

23. Cunningham, *Francis of Assisi*, 37.

24. Vauchez, *Francis of Assisi*, 59.

25. Honorius III, *Cum Secundum* (1220), in *FAED*, 1:561.

26. Thompson, *Francis of Assisi*, 103.

27. Cunningham, *Francis of Assisi*, 76.

28. Francis's health had been in steady decline for more than a year, and he came to realize that his health would not recover from the illness, maltreatment, and general ascetic effects that had long plagued the would-be saint's body. For more, see Thompson, *Francis of Assisi*, 113–15.

29. Thompson, *Francis of Assisi*, 114.

30. Ibid., 116.

31. Bonaventure, "The Major Legend of Saint Francis," vol. 3, 13:3, in *FAED*, 2:632.

32. Bonaventure, "The Major Legend of Saint Francis," vol. 3, 13:3, in *FAED*, 2:633.

33. Cunningham, *Francis of Assisi*, 83.

34. Francis of Assisi, "The Canticle of the Creatures," in *FAED*, 1:113–14.

35. Cunningham, *Francis of Assisi*, 112–13.

36. Francis of Assisi, "The Later Rule," in *FAED*, 1:100.

37. Gregory IX, *Mira Circa Nos*, in *FAED*, 1:565–69.

2. The Modern Monk: Thomas Merton

1. The biographer Jim Forest suggests at one point that the Mertons lived "close to destitution," although that is difficult to qualify and support. See Jim Forest, *Living with Wisdom: A Life of Thomas Merton*, rev. ed. (Maryknoll, NY: Orbis Books, 2008), 6.

2. I am grateful to Paul Pearson, director of the Thomas Merton Center at Bellarmine University, for bringing this to my attention. A

number of years ago he contacted the archivist at Bellevue Hospital in New York and looked into the policies concerning children at the hospital, and it was confirmed that a prohibition on children visiting wards such as the one in which Ruth was located was strictly enforced by the nurses of that time.

3. Thomas Merton, *The Seven Storey Mountain: An Autobiography of Faith*, 50th anniversary ed. (New York: Harcourt Brace, 1998), 16.

4. Ibid.

5. Forest, *Living with Wisdom*, 15–16.

6. Within the British educational system, the term "public school" bears the opposite meaning that it has in the United States. An English public school is a private, oftentimes boarding school.

7. Merton, *Seven Storey Mountain*, 130.

8. Michael Mott, *The Seven Mountains of Thomas Merton* (New York: Houghton Mifflin, 1993), 95.

9. For the text of Merton's master's thesis, see Thomas Merton, "Nature and Art in William Blake: An Essay in Interpretation," in *The Literary Essays of Thomas Merton*, ed. Patrick Hart (New York: New Directions, 1981), 385–453.

10. William H. Shannon, *Thomas Merton: An Introduction* (Cincinnati: St. Anthony Messenger Press, 2005), 5.

11. William Shannon, *Silent Lamp: The Thomas Merton Story* (New York: Crossroad, 1992), 130.

12. Shannon, *Silent Lamp*, 130.

13. Ibid., 138–39.

14. Ibid., 181.

15. Thomas Merton, "Letter to Pope John XXIII" (November 10, 1958), in *The Hidden Ground of Love: The Letters of Thomas Merton on Religious Experience and Social Concerns*, ed. William Shannon (New York: Farrar, Straus & Giroux, 1985), 482.

16. See Patrick Hart, "Foreword," in *The Asian Journal of Thomas Merton*, ed. Naomi Burton Stone, Patrick Hart, and James Laughlin (New York: New Directions, 1973), xxi–xxii.

17. Thomas Merton, "Marxism and Monastic Perspectives," in *Asian Journal of Thomas Merton*, 343.

18. See Mott, *Seven Mountains*, 564; and Forest, *Living with Wisdom*, 237.

3. The Rise and Fall of a Vocation

1. Thomas Merton, *The Seven Storey Mountain: An Autobiography of Faith*, 50th anniversary ed. (New York: Harcourt Brace, 1998), 29.

2. Merton, *Seven Storey Mountain*, 192.

3. Thomas Merton, "The White Pebble," in *Thomas Merton: Selected Essays*, ed. Patrick O'Connell (Maryknoll, NY: Orbis Books, 2013), 9.

4. See Charles Carpenter, *Theology as the Road to Holiness in St. Bonaventure* (New York: Paulist Press, 1999).

5. See Gregory LaNave, *Through Holiness to Wisdom: The Nature of Theology according to St. Bonaventure* (Rome: Istituto Storico dei Cappuccini, 2005).

6. Daniel Walsh, "The Metaphysics of Ideas according to Duns Scotus" (unpublished PhD diss., University of Toronto, 1934).

7. Merton, *Seven Storey Mountain*, 239–40.

8. Ibid., 241.

9. Michael Mott, *The Seven Mountains of Thomas Merton* (New York: Houghton Mifflin, 1993), 123.

10. Merton, *Seven Storey Mountain*, 241–42.

11. After the success of *The Seven Storey Mountain*, Walsh, in large part because of his friendship with Merton, was frequently invited to speak about his friend and former student. Merton later expressed his embarrassment that his former mentor had to suffer such requests, although Walsh never suggested it was a burden.

12. Merton, *Seven Storey Mountain*, 241.

13. Thomas Merton, "October 16, 1939," in *Run to the Mountain: The Story of a Vocation*, ed. Patrick Hart, Journals of Thomas Merton 1, 1939–1941 (San Francisco: HarperSanFrancisco, 1995), 58.

14. Thomas Merton, "October 4, 1939," in *Run to the Mountain*, 40.

15. Ibid., 59.

16. Ibid.

17. Thomas Merton, "[40.5] Letter to Robert Lax: February 16, 1940," in *When Prophecy Still Had a Voice: The Letters of Thomas Merton and Robert Lax*, ed. Arthur Biddle (Lexington, KY: University Press of Kentucky, 2001), 46.

18. See Merton, *Seven Storey Mountain*, 290–92.

19. Mott, *Seven Mountains*, 142.

20. Ibid., 154.

21. Ibid., 155.

22. Ibid.

23. Merton, *Seven Storey Mountain*, 324.

24. Ibid.

25. Ibid., 325.

26. Ibid., 316. Later Merton writes, "No matter what religious Order a man enters, whether its Rule be easy or strict in itself does not much matter; if his vocation is to be really fruitful it must cost him something, and must be a real sacrifice. . . . The truth of the matter is simply this: becoming a Franciscan, especially at this precise moment of history, meant absolutely no sacrifice at all, as far as I was concerned" (319–20).

27. Ibid., 316–17.

28. Ibid., 322.

29. Ibid., 323.

30. Mott, *Seven Mountains*, 155.

31. Merton, *Seven Storey Mountain*, 325.

32. Thomas Merton, "Letter to Anthony Bannon, February 12, 1966," in *The Road to Joy: Letters to New and Old Friends*, ed. Robert Daggy (New York: Harcourt Brace, 1989), 297.

33. Merton, *Seven Storey Mountain*, 326.

34. Thomas Merton, "[40.12] Letter to Robert Lax: July 24, 1940," in Biddle, *When Prophecy Still Had a Voice*, 54.

4. A Franciscan in Blue Jeans

1. In a rare personal admittance, Merton writes in his journal that "I don't know many people I ever knew it was possible to really revere. Father Thomas [Plassmann] is one." Thomas Merton, "February 4, 1941," in *Run to the Mountain: The Story of a Vocation*, ed. Patrick Hart, Journals of Thomas Merton 1, 1939–1941 (San Francisco: HarperSanFrancisco, 1995), 304.

2. Unpublished letter from Rev. Thomas Plassmann to Thomas Merton (September 7, 1940), Thomas Merton collection of Freidsam Memorial Library, St. Bonaventure University.

3. See Paul Spaeth, "On Manuscripts and Things: The Thomas Merton Archives at St. Bonaventure University," *Cithara: Essays in the Judaeo-Christian Tradition* 48 (November 2008): 31–37.

4. Spaeth, "On Manuscripts and Things," 34; and Michael Mott, *The Seven Mountains of Thomas Merton* (New York: Houghton Mifflin, 1993), 157.

5. Thomas Merton, "December 4, 1940," in *Run to the Mountain*, 271. He goes on in the same passage to talk about how he understood his entries in this journal to be written, ultimately, for publication: "Why would I write anything, if not to be read? This journal is written for publication. It is about time I realized that, and wrote it with some art. All that screaming last year, to convince myself a journal was worth writing, but not to be read. If a journal is written for publication, then you can tear pages out of it, emend it, correct it, write

with art. If it is a personal document, every emendation amounts to a crisis of conscience and a confession, not an artistic correction."

6. Thomas Merton, "Letter to Catherine de Hueck on November 10, 1941," in *Compassionate Fire: The Letters of Thomas Merton and Catherine de Hueck Doherty*, ed. Robert Wild (Notre Dame, IN: Ave Maria Press, 2009), 18.

7. Mott, *Seven Mountains*, 157.

8. Thomas Merton, *The Seven Storey Mountain: An Autobiography of Faith*, 50th anniversary ed. (New York: Harcourt Brace, 1998), 328.

9. Mott, *Seven Mountains*, 157 (italics added).

10. Thomas Merton, "Letter to Mark Van Doren, Lent 1941," in *The Road to Joy: Letters to New and Old Friends*, ed. Robert Daggy (New York: Harcourt Brace, 1989), 10.

11. Thomas Merton, "February 19, 1941," *in Run to the Mountain, 309.*

12. Mott, *Seven Mountains*, 158.

13. Thomas Merton, "August 3, 1949," in *Entering the Silence: Becoming a Monk and Writer*, ed. Jonathan Montaldo, Journals of Thomas Merton 2, 1941–1952 (San Francisco: HarperSanFrancisco, 1996), 343.

14. See Merton, *Seven Storey Mountain*, 262.

15. Thomas Merton, "Letter to Anthony Bannon, February 12, 1966," in *Road to Joy*, 298.

16. See William Shannon, "Herscher, Irenaeus," in *The Thomas Merton Encyclopedia*, ed. William H. Shannon, Christine M. Bochen, and Patrick F. O'Connell (Maryknoll, NY: Orbis Books, 2002), 200.

17. Thomas Merton, "August 16, 1964, Thirteenth Sunday after Pentecost," in *Dancing in the Water of Life: Seeking Peace in the Hermitage*, ed. Robert Daggy, Journals of Thomas Merton 5, 1963–1965 (San Francisco: HarperSanFrancisco, 1997), 136.

18. Thomas Merton, "Letter to Irenaeus Herscher, August 24, 1964," in *Road to Joy*, 296.

19. Merton, *Seven Storey Mountain*, 332.

20. Thomas Merton, "March 4, 1941," in *Run to the Mountain, 316.*

21. Unpublished letter from Thomas Merton to Rev. Irenaeus Herscher (February 20, 1959), Thomas Merton collection of Freidsam Memorial Library, St. Bonaventure University.

22. Thomas Merton, "Letter to Father Joseph Vann, September 19, 1940," in *Road to Joy*, 294.

23. Merton, *Seven Storey Mountain*, 365.

24. Thomas Merton, "Letter to Mark Van Doren, January 28, 1941," in *Road to Joy*, 9.

25. See Patrick O'Connell, "Franciscanism," in *Thomas Merton Encyclopedia*, 161; and Spaeth, "On Manuscripts and Things," 33–36.

26. Thomas Merton, "Letter to Naomi Burton [Stone], January 2, 1947," in *Witness to Freedom: Letters in Times of Crisis*, ed. William Shannon (New York: Harcourt Brace, 1994), 124.

27. Thomas Merton, "November 27, 1941," in *Run to the Mountain*, 456.

28. Thomas Merton, "November 28, 1941," in *Run to the Mountain*, 457.

29. Ibid., 458.

5. The "True Self": Getting to the Heart of Merton's Most Famous Insight

1. Francis of Assisi, "Admonition XIX: A Humble Servant of God," in *FAED*, 1:135. Merton's Latin citation reads, "*Nam quantum unusquisque est in oculis tuis, tantum est et non amplius, ait humilis sanctus Franciscus*" (For whatever a person is in your sight, he is only that, and no more, says humble Saint Francis), in *Run to the Mountain: The Story of a Vocation*, ed. Patrick Hart, Journals of Thomas Merton 1, 1939–1941 (San Francisco: HarperSanFrancisco, 1995), 398.

2. Thomas Merton, "September 3, 1941," in *Run to the Mountain*, 398.

3. James Finley, *Merton's Palace of Nowhere* (Notre Dame, IN: Ave Maria Press, 1978), 21 (italics added).

4. Ibid., 23.

5. Ibid., 27.

6. Thomas Merton, "September 19, 1946, Letter to Mark Van Doren," Mark Van Doren Collection, Butler Library of Columbia University, as cited in George Kilcourse, *Ace of Freedoms: Thomas Merton's Christ* (Notre Dame, IN: University of Notre Dame Press, 1993), 243.

7. For a study of Walsh's influence on Merton's theological outlook, see Robert Imperato, *Merton and Walsh on the Person* (Brookfield, WI: Liturgical Publications, 1987).

8. Michael Downey, "Merton's Franciscan Heart," *Franciscan Studies* 55 (1998): 300.

9. While it is beyond the scope of this chapter to examine these entries in full, the Boston College manuscript of *The Seven Storey Mountain* reveals page after page of Scotistic reflection. Even an initial examination of the original *The Seven Storey Mountain* manuscript illustrates the importance Scotus played in the thought of Merton

at this point in his life. For a transcription of the Boston College manuscript, see Andrea Neuhoff, "The Unedited Thomas Merton: Autobiography to Autohagiography" (unpublished undergraduate thesis, Reed College, May 2005), appendix A.

10. Michael Mott, *The Seven Mountains of Thomas Merton* (New York: Houghton Mifflin, 1993), 231.

11. Gerard Manley Hopkins, "July 19, 1872," in *Gerard Manley Hopkins: Poems and Prose*, ed. W. H. Gardner (New York: Penguin, 1985), 126.

12. Gerard Manley Hopkins, "Letter to Robert Bridges, February 20, 1875," in *Gerard Manley Hopkins*, 176.

13. For more on this, see Jim Forest, *Living with Wisdom: A Life of Thomas Merton*, rev. ed. (Maryknoll, NY: Orbis Books, 2008), 58–60.

14. Excerpts from Thomas Merton, "Duns Scotus," in *The Collected Poems of Thomas Merton* (New York: New Directions, 1977), 164–65. Merton wrote another poem in honor of Scotus titled "Hymn for the Feast of Duns Scotus," in *Collected Poems of Thomas Merton*, 198–99.

15. See, for example, the many references to Scotus in the journal entries contained in the second volume of Merton's journals. Thomas Merton, *Entering the Silence: Becoming a Monk and Writer*, ed. Jonathan Montaldo, Journals of Thomas Merton 2, 1941–1952 (San Francisco: HarperSanFrancisco, 1996). It should be noted that Montaldo mistakenly inserts "Erigena's" into the December 10, 1946, entry wherein Merton is describing his reading of John Duns Scotus's *Oxoniense III*, distinction 18—also known as the *Ordinatio*; John Scotus Erigena (the ninth-century Irish theologian) should not be confused with John Duns Scotus (the twelfth-century Franciscan).

16. See Thomas Merton, *New Seeds of Contemplation* (New York: New Directions, 1961). The book was originally published as *Seeds of Contemplation* (New York: New Directions, 1949), and later expanded into *New Seeds*. Due to the ease of availability of *New Seeds*, I have chosen to focus on that text and reference that edition throughout. For more on the development of the texts, see Donald Grayston, *Thomas Merton's Rewritings: The Five Versions of Seeds/New Seeds of Contemplation as a Key to the Development of His Thought* (New York: Edwin Mellen Press, 1989).

17. Richard Cross, *Duns Scotus* (New York: Oxford University Press, 1999), 3. There was an ordination on December 23, 1290, and had Scotus been old enough, it would seem likely that he would have been ordained at that time, thereby supporting the hypothesis that he was born between 1265 and 1266.

18. Mary Beth Ingham, *Scotus for Dunces: An Introduction to the Subtle Doctor* (St. Bonaventure, NY: Franciscan Institute Press, 2003), 15.

19. See John Duns Scotus, *De Primo Principio*, ed. Allan Wolter (Chicago: Franciscan Herald Press, 1982).

20. Ingham, *Scotus for Dunces*, 17.

21. Scotus rejects both the traditional Platonic and Aristotelian approaches in his *Lectura* II, d. 3, par. 1, q. 1. See the critical edition of this work: Ioannis Duns Scoti, *Opera Omnia*, ed. C. Balíc et al. (Vatican City: Typis Polyglottis Vaticanis, 1950). This portion of the *Lectura* is found in volume 18 (1982): 229–93. For an English translation, see John Duns Scotus, *Early Oxford Lecture on Individuation*, ed. Allan Wolter (St. Bonaventure, NY: Franciscan Institute Publications, 2005). (Further references to the *Lectura* will be noted by the Latin citation followed by the translation page number in parenthesis.) For more on this concept and Scotus's rejection of antecedent principles of individuation, see Allan Wolter, "Scotus's Individuation Theory," in *The Philosophical Theology of John Duns Scotus*, ed. Marilyn McCord Adams (Ithaca, NY: Cornell University Press, 1990), 68–97; and Kenan Osborne, "Incarnation, Individuality and Diversity: How Does Christ Reveal the Unique Value of Each Person and Thing?" *Cord* 45 (1995): 19–26.

22. Efrem Bettoni, *Duns Scotus: The Basic Principles of His Philosophy*, trans. Bernardine Bonansea (Washington, DC: Catholic University of America Press, 1961), 61.

23. Osborne, "Incarnation, Individuality and Diversity," 25.

24. Scotus, *Early Oxford Lecture*, xxi.

25. Ibid.

26. Kilcourse, *Ace of Freedoms*, 242–43.

27. Merton, *New Seeds of Contemplation*, 29–36.

28. Ibid., 29.

29. Scotus, *Lectura* II, d. 3, par. 1, q. 1 (15).

30. Merton, *New Seeds of Contemplation*, 29.

31. Ibid.

32. Scotus, *Lectura* II, d. 3, par. 1, q. 6 (70–97).

33. Merton, *New Seeds of Contemplation*, 31.

34. Ibid., 30 (italics added).

35. Robert McPartland, "Teaching 'Thisness': Guiding Students into Scotus's *Haecceitas* and the Poetry of Gerard Manley Hopkins and Thomas Merton," *AFCU Journal* 7 (2010): 57.

36. Merton, "September 3, 1941," 398.

37. Merton, *New Seeds of Contemplation*, 32.

38. Ibid.

39. Thomas Merton, unpublished typescript of *The Seven Storey Mountain*, Thomas Merton Collection, Burns Library, Boston College, 608. Hereafter cited as "Boston College manuscript."

40. Merton, *New Seeds of Contemplation*, 31.

41. Ibid., 33–34.

42. Ibid., 281.

43. Merton, "Boston College manuscript," 609.

44. Merton, *New Seeds of Contemplation*, 35.

45. See John Duns Scotus, *Ordinatio* I, d. 3, par. 1, q. 1–2, no. 25 (Vatican ed. III:16–17): "*Dico ergo primo quod non tantum haberi potest conceptus naturaliter in quo quasi per accidens concipitur Deus, puta in aliquot attibuto, sed etiam aliguis conceptus in quo per se et quidditative concipiatur Deus.*" [Therefore, I say that it is naturally possible to have not only a concept in which God is known incidentally, as it were, such as under the aspect of some attribute, but also one in which God is conceived in Godself and *quidditavely*].

46. Merton, *New Seeds of Contemplation*, 36.

47. See Meister Eckhart, "Sermon 48: Ein meister sprichet: alliu glichiu dinc minnent sich under einander," Meister Eckhart: The Essential Sermons, Commentaries, Treatises, and Defense, eds. Edmund Colledge and Bernard McGinn (New York: Paulist Press, 1981), esp. 198. For more on the posited influence of Eckhart on Merton's understanding of individuation, see Erlinda Paguio, "Blazing in the Spark of God: Thomas Merton's References to Meister Eckhart," *Merton Annual* 5 (1992): 247–62; Oliver Davies, "Thomas Merton and Meister Eckhart," *Merton Journal* 4 (1997): 15–24; Robert Faricy, "On Understanding Thomas Merton: Merton, Zen, and Eckhart," *Studies in Spirituality* 9 (1999): 189–202; and Thomas Merton, *An Introduction to Christian Mysticism*, ed. Patrick O'Connell, Initiation into the Monastic Tradition 3 (Kalamazoo, MI: Cistercian Publications, 2008).

48. For a sampling of scholarship on related and coextensive influences in Merton's thinking on individuation, see James Conner, "The Original Face in Buddhism and the True Self in Thomas Merton," *Cistercian Studies Quarterly* 22 (1987): 343–51; John Kennan, "The Limits of Thomas Merton's Understanding of Buddhism," in *Merton and Buddhism: Wisdom, Emptiness and Everyday Mind*, ed. Bonnie Bowman Thurston (Louisville, KY: Fons Vitae, 2007), 118–33, esp. 120–23; Jonathan Montaldo, ed., *Merton and Hesychasm: The Prayer of the Heart; The Eastern Church* (Louisville, KY: Fons Vitae, 2003); Elena Malits, "Signs and Sources of Spiritual Growth," in *The Legacy of Thomas Merton*, ed. Patrick Hart (Kalamazoo, MI: Cistercian Publications, 1986): 171–79; John Teahan, "A Dark and Empty Way: Thomas Merton and the Apophatic Tradition," *Journal of Religion*

58 (1978): 263–87; Christopher Pramuk, *Sophia: The Hidden Christ of Thomas Merton* (Collegeville, MN: Liturgical Press, 2009), 131–74; and Lawrence Cunningham, *Thomas Merton and the Monastic Vision* (Grand Rapids, MI: Eerdmans, 1999), 9–14, 19–46.

49. Thomas Merton, *Conjectures of a Guilty Bystander* (Garden City, NY: Image, 1968), 158.

50. Mary Beth Ingham, *Rejoicing in the Works of the Lord: Beauty in the Franciscan Tradition* (St. Bonaventure, NY: Franciscan Institute Publications, 2009), 30.

51. Merton, *Conjectures of a Guilty Bystander*, 157.

52. Ibid., 158.

53. Ibid.

54. Thomas Merton, *The Inner Experience: Notes on Contemplation*, ed. William Shannon (New York: HarperOne, 2003), 6.

55. Finley, *Merton's Palace of Nowhere*, 89.

56. Merton, *New Seeds of Contemplation*, 40.

57. Merton, *Inner Experience*, 19.

58. William Shannon, "Thomas Merton and the Discovery of the Real Self," in *The Message of Thomas Merton*, ed. Patrick Hart (Kalamazoo, MI: Cistercian Publications, 1981), 201.

6. The General Dance: Franciscan Christology and the Christ of Thomas Merton

1. Beraud de Saint-Maurice, *John Duns Scotus: A Teacher for Our Times*, trans. Columban Duffy (St. Bonaventure, NY: Franciscan Institute Publications, 1955), 241–42.

2. Ibid., 242, 249–50. See also Daniel Horan, "How Original Was Scotus on the Incarnation? Reconsidering the History of the Absolute Predestination of Christ in Light of Robert Grosseteste," *Heythrop Journal* 52 (2011): 374–91.

3. For recent examples that cast the supralapsarian or Christocentric tradition as "Franciscan," despite the well-documented heterogeneous history of Franciscan Christology, see Peter Dillard, "A Minor Matter? The Franciscan Thesis and Philosophical Theology," *Heythrop Journal* 50 (2009): 890–900; Richard Rohr, "The Franciscan Opinion," in *Stricken by God? Nonviolent Identification and the Victory of Christ*, ed. Brad Jersak and Michael Hardin (Grand Rapids, MI: Eerdmans, 2007), 206–12; Maximilian Mary Dean, *A Primer on the Absolute Primacy of Christ: Blessed John Duns Scotus and the Franciscan Thesis* (New Bedford, MA: Academy of the Immaculate, 2006); and Ilia Delio, "Revisiting the Franciscan Doctrine of Christ," *Theological Studies* 64 (2003): 3–23. For a response to some of this recent literature, see Daniel Horan, "Revisiting the Incarnation: Why the 'Franciscan

Thesis' Is Not So Franciscan and Why It Does Not Really Matter," *Cord* 59 (2009): 371–90.

4. Mary Beth Ingham, "John Duns Scotus: An Integrated Vision," in *The History of Franciscan Theology*, ed. Kenan Osborne (St. Bonaventure, NY: Franciscan Institute Publications, 1994), 219.

5. See Horan, "How Original Was Scotus?" 383–85.

6. Michael Meilach, *The Primacy of Christ: Doctrine and Life* (Chicago: Franciscan Herald Press, 1964), 38.

7. John Duns Scotus, *Ordinatio* III, d. 7, q. 3. English translation is from John Duns Scotus, *Four Questions on Mary*, ed. Allan Wolter (St. Bonaventure, NY: Franciscan Institute Publications, 2000), 21.

8. Scotus, *Ordinatio* III, d. 7, q. 3 (Scotus, *Four Questions on Mary*, 25).

9. For more on this distinction and Scotus's view on the redemptive quality of the Incarnation, see Richard Cross, *Duns Scotus* (New York: Oxford University Press, 1999), 129–32.

10. George Kilcourse, *Ace of Freedoms: Thomas Merton's Christ* (Notre Dame, IN: University of Notre Dame Press, 1993), 32.

11. Thomas Merton, "October 4, 1939, the Feast of Saint Francis," in *Run to the Mountain: The Story of a Vocation*, ed. Patrick Hart, Journals of Thomas Merton 1, 1939–1941 (San Francisco: HarperSanFrancisco, 1995), 40: "I work hard reading when I am not correcting papers—Augustine, Anselm, Grosseteste."

12. Kilcourse, *Ace of Freedoms*, 28.

13. Christopher Pramuk, *Sophia: The Hidden Christ of Thomas Merton* (Collegeville, MN: Liturgical Press, 2009), 179.

14. Thomas Merton, *New Seeds of Contemplation* (New York: New Directions, 1961), 290.

15. George Kilcourse has also highlighted this distinction. See Kilcourse, *Ace of Freedoms*, 31–32.

16. Merton, *New Seeds of Contemplation*, 291.

17. Ibid., 292.

18. Ibid.

19. Thomas Merton, "March 25, 1960," in *A Search for Solitude: Pursuing the Monk's True Life*, ed. Lawrence S. Cunningham, Journals of Thomas Merton 3, 1952–1960 (San Francisco: HarperSanFrancisco, 1996), 381.

20. Thomas Merton, "June 26, 1965," in *Dancing in the Water of Life: Seeking Peace in the Hermitage*, ed. Robert Daggy, Journals of Thomas Merton 5, 1963–1965 (San Francisco: HarperSanFrancisco, 1997), 259.

21. Bonaventure, *Collationes in Hexaemeron* 1.10, ed. Jose de Vinck (Paterson, NJ: St. Anthony Guild Press, 1970), 5–6.

22. Bonaventure, *Itinerarium Mentis in Deum* 6.7, trans. Zachary Hayes in *Bonaventure: Mystical Writings* (Phoenix: Tau Publishing, 1999), 112.

23. Thomas Merton, "August 13, 1965," in *Dancing in the Water of Life: Seeking Peace in the Hermitage*, ed. Robert Daggy, Journals of Thomas Merton 5, 1963–1965 (San Francisco: HarperSanFrancisco, 1997), 279.

24. Kilcourse, *Ace of Freedoms*, 5.

25. Merton, *New Seeds of Contemplation*, 296.

26. Thomas Merton, *The New Man* (New York: Farrar, Straus & Cudahy, 1961), 131.

27. Ibid., 131–32.

28. Ibid., 136–37.

29. Ilia Delio, *Christ in Evolution* (Maryknoll, NY: Orbis Books, 2008), 110.

30. Merton, *New Man*, 137–38.

31. This dimension of Franciscan spirituality finds its origin in Francis of Assisi's own writings and prayers. For more on this theme and its presence in the work of later Franciscan thinkers, see Ilia Delio, *The Humility of God: A Franciscan Perspective* (Cincinnati: St. Anthony Messenger Press, 2005).

32. Merton, *New Man*, 148.

33. Ibid., 148–49.

7. Paradise Consciousness: Modern Spirituality of Creation in a Franciscan Key

1. Kathleen Deignan, "Introduction: 'The Forest Is My Bride,'" in *When the Trees Say Nothing: Writings on Nature*, by Thomas Merton, ed. Kathleen Deignan (Notre Dame, IN: Sorin Books, 2003), 27.

2. Thomas Merton, "Letter to Mario Falsina [March 25, 1967]," in *The Road to Joy: Letters to New and Old Friends*, ed. Robert Daggy (New York: Harcourt Brace, 1989), 347–48.

3. For example, see Daniel Horan, *Francis of Assisi and the Future of Faith: Exploring Franciscan Spirituality and Theology in the Modern World* (Phoenix: Tau Publishing, 2012), 101–14.

4. For more on the phrase "paradise consciousness," see Patrick O'Connell, "Paradise," in *The Thomas Merton Encyclopedia*, ed. William H. Shannon, Christine M. Bochen, and Patrick F. O'Connell (Maryknoll, NY: Orbis Books, 2002), 349–51.

5. For further discussion of these two texts, see Monica Weis, *The Environmental Vision of Thomas Merton* (Lexington, KY: University Press of Kentucky, 2011), 9–21, 126–56.

6. Patrick O'Connell, "The Traditional Sources of Thomas Merton's Environmental Spirituality," *Spiritual Life* 56 (2010): 155.

7. Thomas Merton, "September 26, 1939," in *Run to the Mountain: The Story of a Vocation*, ed. Patrick Hart, Journals of Thomas Merton 1, 1939–1941 (San Francisco: HarperSanFrancisco, 1995), 24.

8. Deignan, "Introduction," 25.

9. See Weis, *Environmental Vision*, 22–47.

10. Ibid., 29. Also, see Ruth Jenkins Merton, *Tom's Book*, ed. Sheila Milton (Monterey, CA: Larkspur Press, 2005).

11. Thomas Merton, "January 2, 1941," in *Run to the Mountain*, 282.

12. Weis, *Environmental Vision*, 25.

13. Ibid., 26.

14. Bonaventure, *Itinerarium Mentis in Deum* 1.7, ed. Zachary Hayes (St. Bonaventure, NY: Franciscan Institute Publications, 2002), 62.

15. Thomas Merton, "April 5, 1958," in *A Search for Solitude: Pursuing the Monk's True Life*, ed. Lawrence S. Cunningham, Journals of Thomas Merton 3, 1952–1960 (San Francisco: HarperSanFrancisco, 1996), 190.

16. Weis, *Environmental Vision*, 64–65.

17. Thomas Merton, "October 5, 1957," in *Search for Solitude*, 123–24.

18. Merton, "September 26, 1939," 27.

19. Thomas Merton, "December 4, 1940," in *Run to the Mountain*, 270 (italics in original).

20. Angela of Foligno, "*The Memorial*: The Stages of Angela's Inner Journey," in *Angela of Foligno: Complete Works*, ed. Paul Lachance (New York: Paulist Press, 1993), 169–70.

21. Thomas Merton, "April 13, 1965," in *Dancing in the Water of Life: Seeking Peace in the Hermitage*, ed. Robert Daggy, Journals of Thomas Merton 5, 1963–1965 (San Francisco: HarperSanFrancisco, 1997), 227.

22. Thomas Merton, "Conference on Angela of Foligno [April 1965]" (unpublished transcription by Daniel Horan from audio recording, Thomas Merton Center, Bellarmine University).

23. See Horan, *Francis of Assisi*, 109–13.

24. Ilia Delio, *A Franciscan View of Creation: Learning to Live in a Sacramental World* (St. Bonaventure, NY: Franciscan Institute Publications, 2003), 7.

25. Francis of Assisi, "The Canticle of the Creatures," in *FAED*, 1:113–14.

26. Eric Doyle, "'The Canticle of Brother Sun' and the Value of Creation," in *Franciscan Theology of the Environment: An Introductory Reader*, ed. Dawn Nothwehr (Quincy, IL: Franciscan Press, 2002), 157–58.

27. I have written on this subject elsewhere with regard to *The Canticle*'s treatment of death; see Daniel Horan, "Embracing Sister Death: The Fraternal Worldview of Francis of Assisi as a Source for Christian Eschatological Hope," *Other Journal* 14 (January 2009), http://theotherjournal.com.

28. Doyle, "The Canticle," 158–59.

29. Ibid., 159.

30. For more, see Daniel Horan, "Light and Love: Robert Grosseteste and John Duns Scotus on the How and Why of Creation," *Cord* 57 (2007): 243–57.

31. Keith Douglas Warner, "Get Him Out of the Birdbath! What Does It Mean to Have a Patron Saint of Ecology?" in Nothwehr, *Franciscan Theology of the Environment*, 370. See also Keith Douglas Warner, "Franciscan Environmental Ethics: Imagining Creation as a Community of Care," *Journal of the Society of Christian Ethics* 31 (2011): 143–60.

32. Warner, "Get Him Out," 371.

33. Leonardo Boff, *Cry of the Earth, Cry of the Poor*, trans. Phillip Berryman (Maryknoll, NY: Orbis Books, 1997), 203–4.

34. Ibid., 205.

35. Ibid., 211.

36. Thomas Merton, "November 4, 1964," in *Dancing in the Water of Life*, 162.

37. Thomas Merton, "April 13, 1963," in *Turning toward the World: The Pivotal Years*, ed. Victor A. Kramer, Journals of Thomas Merton 4, 1960–1963 (San Francisco: HarperSanFrancisco, 1996), 312 (italics in original).

38. Thomas Merton, *The Sign of Jonas* (New York: Harcourt Brace, 1953), 292.

39. Merton, *Sign of Jonas*, 340.

40. Thomas Merton, "July 22, 1956," in *Search for Solitude*, 51.

41. For more on this, see Weis, *Environmental Vision*, esp. 9–92.

42. Thomas Merton, "The Wild Places," in *Thomas Merton: Selected Essays*, ed. Patrick O'Connell (Maryknoll, NY: Orbis Books, 2013), 450.

43. Some early work in this area can be found in O'Connell, "Traditional Sources," and Weis, *Environmental Vision*. Nevertheless, further study of the Franciscan influence and resemblance in Merton's work is still needed.

8. Seeing the World as It Really Is: Prophecy at the Heart of the Christian Vocation

1. Thomas Merton, *The Springs of Contemplation: A Retreat at the Abbey of Gethsemani*, ed. Jane Marie Richardson (New York: Farrar, Straus & Giroux, 1992), 49.

2. Ibid.

3. Thomas Merton, *Raids on the Unspeakable* (New York: New Directions, 1966), 159.

4. Merton, *Springs of Contemplation*, 157–58.

5. See, for example, Kathleen Deignan, "Road to Rapture: Thomas Merton's *Itinerarium Mentis in Deum*," *Franciscan Studies* 55 (1998): 281–97; and Daniel Horan, "Thomas Merton's Vernacular Franciscan Theology," *Merton Journal* 16 (2009): 26–36.

6. Merton, *Springs of Contemplation*, 133.

7. Niels Christian Hvidt, "Prophecy and Revelation: A Theological Survey on the Problem of Christian Prophecy," *Studia Theologica* 52 (1998): 150–51.

8. Daniel Horan, "Profit or Prophet? A Franciscan Challenge to Millennials in Higher Education," *AFCU Journal* 8 (2011): 69.

9. Merton, *Springs of Contemplation*, 81.

10. Ibid., 157.

11. Gerald Twomey, ed., *Thomas Merton: Prophet in the Belly of a Paradox* (New York: Paulist Press, 1978); Paul Dekar, *Thomas Merton: Twentieth-Century Wisdom for Twenty-First-Century Living* (Eugene, OR: Cascade Books, 2011); Mario Aguilar, *Thomas Merton: Contemplation and Political Action* (London: SPCK Publishing, 2011).

12. Second Vatican Council, *Gaudium et Spes* ("Pastoral Constitution on the Church in the Modern World"), no. 1.

13. For an excellent article that convincingly makes this point, see David Golemboski, "Life of a Stranger: How Thomas Merton Pitched In by Dropping Out," *Merton Journal* 15 (2008): 19–24.

14. Thomas Merton, *Seeds of Contemplation* (New York: New Directions, 1949); Thomas Merton, *The Sign of Jonas* (New York: Harcourt Brace, 1953).

15. Thomas Merton, *Conjectures of a Guilty Bystander* (Garden City, NY: Image, 1968); Thomas Merton, *The Cold War Letters*, ed. Christine M. Bochen and William H. Shannon (Maryknoll, NY: Orbis Books, 2006).

16. Thomas Merton, *The Asian Journal of Thomas Merton*, ed. Naomi Burton Stone, Patrick Hart, and James Laughlin (New York: New Directions, 1973), 308.

17. Merton, *Asian Journal*, 307–8.

9. No Longer Strangers: Thomas Merton and Franciscan Interreligious Dialogue

1. Thomas Merton, *Conjectures of a Guilty Bystander* (Garden City, NY: Image, 1968), 143. The translation of the quotation from Eulogius is mine from the original French: "Des hommes comme Saint Seraphim, Saint François d'Assise et bien d'autres, ont accompli dans leur vie l'union des Églises."

2. Most notably, Patrick O'Connell, "Franciscanism," in *The Thomas Merton Encyclopedia*, ed. William H. Shannon, Christine M. Bochen, and Patrick F. O'Connell (Maryknoll, NY: Orbis Books, 2002), 161–63.

3. Thomas Merton, "The Christian in World Crisis: Reflections on the Moral Climate of the 1960s," in *Seeds of Destruction* (New York: Farrar, Straus & Giroux, 1964), 181.

4. Ibid., 181–82.

5. Kathleen Warren, *Daring to Cross the Threshold: Francis of Assisi Encounters Sultan Malek al-Kamil* (Rochester, MN: Sisters of St. Francis, 2003), 22–23.

6. J. Hoeberichts, *Francis and Islam* (Quincy, IL: Franciscan Press, 1997), 10.

7. Ibid.

8. Ibid., 11.

9. Francis de Beer, "St. Francis and Islam," *Concilium* 149 (November 1981): 11–12.

10. Chapter 1 of the *Regula non bullata* begins as follows: "The rule and life of these brothers is this, namely: 'to live in obedience, in chastity, and without anything of their own,' and to follow the teaching and footprints of our Lord Jesus Christ." Francis of Assisi, "The Earlier Rule," in *FAED*, 1:63–64.

11. Ibid., 1:74.

12. There is some debate concerning the dating of Francis's encounter with Malik al-Kamil. Raoul Manselli places the entire trip within the time between May 9, 1218, and August 29, 1219; see Manselli, *St. Francis of Assisi*, trans. Paul Duggan (Chicago: Franciscan Herald Press, 1988), 222–23. Walbert Bühlmann, developing his theory based on the creation of chapter 16 of the *Regula non bullata*, suggests that Francis and his companions stayed in Egypt between July 1219 and spring 1220. See Bühlmann as quoted in Hoeberichts, *Francis and Islam*, 45. Warren supports the dating between September 1 and 16 of 1219. See Warren, *Daring to Cross*, 46.

13. De Beer, "St. Francis and Islam," 16–17.

14. While there is still some debate over whether Francis's mission to Egypt was in fact a peaceful opposition to the crusade, I

concur with those scholars who believe this to be Francis's primary motive. For a list of those writers who agree with this theory, see Warren, *Daring to Cross*, 36–37n18.

15. Ibid., 33.

16. Hoeberichts, *Francis and Islam*, 5.

17. De Beer, "St. Francis and Islam," 15.

18. Warren, *Daring to Cross*, 42.

19. Ibid., 44–45.

20. Jacques de Vitry, *Historia Occidentalis*, in *FAED*, 1:584.

21. Warren, *Daring to Cross*, 49.

22. Francis de Beer, *We Saw Brother Francis*, trans. Despot and LaChance (Chicago: Franciscan Herald Press, 1983), 88.

23. Ibid.

24. See Francis of Assisi, "The Canticle of the Creatures," in *FAED*, 1:113–14.

25. Hoeberichts, *Francis and Islam*, 61.

26. Francis of Assisi, "The Earlier Rule," chap. 16, v. 6, in *FAED*, 1:74.

27. Laurent Gallant, "Francis of Assisi Forerunner of Interreligious Dialogue: Chapter 16 of the Earlier Rule Revisited," *Franciscan Studies* 64 (2006): 58–59.

28. Francis of Assisi, "The Earlier Rule," chap. 16, v. 7, in *FAED*, 1:74. See also Gallant, "Francis of Assisi," 63n15 (italics added).

29. Gallant, "Francis of Assisi," 59–60.

30. See David Flood and Thadee Matura, *The Birth of a Movement*, trans. Paul LaChance and Paul Schwartz (Chicago: Franciscan Herald Press, 1975), originally published David Flood and Thadee Matura, *La Naissance d'un Charisme* (Paris: Editions Franciscaines, 1973).

31. Diagram as presented by the author in Gallant, "Francis of Assisi," 61.

32. Ibid., 73.

33. Francis of Assisi, "The Earlier Rule," chap. 7, vv. 3–4, in *FAED*, 1:68.

34. Thomas of Celano, *"The Life of Saint Francis,"* bk. 1, 7:16, in *FAED*, 1:194.

35. Kenneth Himes, "The Inaugural Keynote Address on the Occasion of Inauguration of Fr. Kevin Mullen, O.F.M., Tenth President of Siena College" (unpublished text), October 1, 2007, 7–8.

36. Thomas Merton, "A Letter to Pablo Antonio Cuadra concerning Giants," in *The Collected Poems of Thomas Merton* (New York: New Directions, 1977), 372–91.

37. Ibid., 387.

38. William H. Shannon, *Thomas Merton: An Introduction* (Cincinnati: St. Anthony Messenger Press, 2005), 95.

39. Thomas Merton, *New Seeds of Contemplation* (New York: New Directions, 1961), 47–48.

40. William Apel, *Signs of Peace: The Interfaith Letters of Thomas Merton* (Maryknoll, NY: Orbis Books, 2006), 105.

41. Allan McMillan, "Seven Lessons for Inter-faith Dialogue and Thomas Merton," *Merton Annual* 15 (2002): 194.

42. Ibid., 198 (italics added).

43. Merton, *New Seeds of Contemplation*, 51.

44. Merton, *Conjectures of a Guilty Bystander*, 144 (italics in original).

45. Thomas Merton, "April 11, 1959," in *A Search for Solitude: Pursuing the Monk's True Life*, ed. Lawrence S. Cunningham, Journals of Thomas Merton 3, 1952–1960 (San Francisco: HarperSanFrancisco, 1996), 273.

46. Thomas Merton, *Mystics and Zen Masters* (New York: Farrar, Straus & Giroux, 1967), as quoted in Apel, *Signs of Peace*, xiv–xv.

47. Merton, *Mystics and Zen Masters*, 10.

48. Ibid., 17.

49. Ibid., 39.

50. Ibid., 65.

51. Ibid., 70.

52. Ibid., 79.

53. Ibid., 112.

54. Lawrence Cunningham, *Thomas Merton and the Monastic Vision* (Grand Rapids, MI: Eerdmans, 1999), 51–52.

55. Merton, *New Seeds of Contemplation*, 45.

56. Ibid., 2–3.

57. Ibid., 40.

58. Thomas Merton, "Day of a Stranger," in *Thomas Merton: Selected Essays*, ed. Patrick O'Connell (Maryknoll, NY: Orbis Books, 2013), 232–39.

59. Patrick O'Connell, "Day of a Stranger," in *Thomas Merton Encyclopedia*, 104.

60. Scott Thomas, "Franciscan Guide to Dialogue," *Tablet* 260 (October 2006): 8–9.

61. Thomas Merton, *Contemplation in a World of Action* (Notre Dame, IN: University of Notre Dame Press, 1999), 182–83.

10. Becoming Instruments of Peace: How Francis and Merton Challenge Us to Live Today

1. Thomas Merton, "The Christian in World Crisis: Reflections on the Moral Climate of the 1960s," in *Seeds of Destruction* (New York: Farrar, Straus & Giroux, 1964), 181.

2. Michael Robson, "Introduction," in *The Cambridge Companion to Francis of Assisi*, ed. Michael Robson (New York: Cambridge University Press, 2012), 4.

3. For a text of particular relevance, see Jacques Dalarun, *The Misadventure of Francis of Assisi: Toward a Historical Use of the Franciscan Legends*, trans. Edward Hagman (St. Bonaventure, NY: Franciscan Institute Publications, 2002). The original Italian edition is *La Malaventura di Franceso d'Assisi: per un uso storico delle leggende francescane* (Milan: Edizioni Biblioteca Francescana, 1996).

4. Francis of Assisi, "The Testament," v. 14, in *FAED*, 1:125 (396): "sed ipse Altissimus revelavit michi quod deberem vivere secundum formam sancti Evangelii." The most recent critical edition of Francis's writings is Carlo Paolazzi, ed., *Francesco D'Assisi: Scritti* (Rome: Collegio San Bonaventura, 2009).

5. Jacques Dalarun, *Francis of Assisi and Power* (St. Bonaventure, NY: St. Bonaventure University, 2007), 17.

6. Francis of Assisi, "The Earlier Rule," chap. 5, vv. 9–12, translation from Dalarun, *Francis of Assisi and Power*, 21. See also *FAED*, 1:67 (250).

7. Francis of Assisi, "The Earlier Rule," chap. 6, vv. 3–4, in *FAED*, 1:68 (252): "Et nullus covetur *prior*, sed generaliter omnes vocentur *fratres minors*. Et alter alterius lavet pedes" (italics added).

8. Dalarun, *Francis of Assisi and Power*, 29 (italics added).

9. For more on this kenotic theme, see Ilia Delio, *The Humility of God: A Franciscan Perspective* (Cincinnati: St. Anthony Messenger Press, 2005).

10. Francis of Assisi, "The Earlier Rule," chap. 16, v. 6, in *FAED*, 1:74.

11. William H. Shannon, *Thomas Merton: An Introduction* (Cincinnati: St. Anthony Messenger Press, 2005), 106–7.

12. Thomas Merton, *Passion for Peace: The Social Essays of Thomas Merton* (New York: Crossroad, 1995), 12. For more on the difference in editions between the version published in *The Catholic Worker* and what eventually appeared in *New Seeds of Contemplation*, see William Shannon's introductory note in *Passion for Peace*, 23–24 (in the abridged version, 2006).

13. Shannon, *Thomas Merton*, 111.

14. Merton, *Passion for Peace*, 249.

15. James Forest, "Thomas Merton's Struggle with Peacemaking," in *Thomas Merton: Prophet in the Belly of a Paradox*, ed. Gerald Twomey (New York: Paulist Press, 1978), 15–16.

16. Thomas Merton, *No Man Is an Island* (New York: Harcourt Brace, 1955), 131.

17. See Daniel Horan, "Digital Natives and the Digital Self: The Wisdom of Thomas Merton for Millennial Spirituality and Self-Understanding," *Merton Annual* (2011): 109.

18. Thomas Merton, *New Seeds of Contemplation* (New York: New Directions, 1961), 33.

19. Merton, *New Seeds of Contemplation*, 35–36.

20. The primary source for his Christian anthropology is the theological and philosophical work of John Duns Scotus (d. 1308). For more on this, see Daniel Horan, "Thomas Merton the 'Dunce': Identity, Incarnation and the Not So Subtle Influence of John Duns Scotus," *Cistercian Studies Quarterly* 47 (May 2012): 149–75.

21. Robert Imperato, *Merton and Walsh on the Person* (Brookfield, WI: Liturgical Publications, 1987), 125. Furthermore, Christine Bochen, in her introduction to Merton's published "Cold War letters," explains that Merton's worldview in the midst of the Cold War is best described as a form of "Christian humanism" that is founded on his theological anthropology and understanding of the Incarnation. See Christine Bochen, "Introduction," in *The Cold War Letters*, by Thomas Merton, ed. Christine M. Bochen and William H. Shannon (Maryknoll, NY: Orbis Books, 2006), xxvii–xxx.

22. See Merton, *New Seeds of Contemplation*, 37–46; and Thomas Merton, *The Monastic Journey*, ed. Patrick Hart (Kalamazoo, MI: Cistercian Publications, 1992), 39–43.

23. Merton, "Christian in World Crisis," 118.

24. For example, "But of course it is a special obligation of the Christian who, as a follower of Christ, must be a peacemaker" (ibid.).

25. Ibid., 123.

26. Ibid., 165.

27. Ibid., 126–28.

28. Ibid., 126.

29. Patrick O'Connell, "Nonviolence," in *The Thomas Merton Encyclopedia*, ed. William H. Shannon, Christine M. Bochen, and Patrick F. O'Connell (Maryknoll, NY: Orbis Books, 2002), 332.

30. See Thomas Merton, *Ishi Means Man: Essays on Native Americans* (Greensboro, NC: Unicorn Press, 1976), 26–27.

31. Thomas Merton, "Gandhi and the One-Eyed Giant," in *Gandhi on Nonviolence*, ed. Thomas Merton (New York: New Directions, 1964), 10.

32. Ibid., 8.

33. Thomas Merton, "In Acceptance of the Pax Medal, 1963," in *The Nonviolent Alternative*, ed. Gordan Zahn (New York: Farrar, Straus & Giroux, 1971), 258.

Conclusion: Finding Francis in Unlikely Places

1. Thomas Merton, "Terror and the Absurd: Violence and Non-violence in Albert Camus," in *The Literary Essays of Thomas Merton*, ed. Patrick Hart (New York: New Directions, 1981), 240.

Appendix: Merton's Prayer to St. Francis of Assisi

1. Thomas Merton, "September 6, 1941, Our Lady of the Valley," in *Run to the Mountain: The Story of a Vocation*, ed. Patrick Hart, Journals of Thomas Merton 1, 1939–1941 (San Francisco: HarperSanFrancisco, 1995), 405–7.

INDEX